MILL VALLEY, CALIFORNIA

Presented by

DR. W. MORGAN PATTERSON

Baptist Relations with Other Christians

Edited by James Leo Garrett

JUDSON PRESS, VALLEY FORGE

BAPTIST RELATIONS WITH OTHER CHRISTIANS

Copyright © 1974
Judson Press, Valley Forge, PA 19481

Library of Congress Cataloging in Publication Data

Garrett, James Leo.
    Baptist relations with other Christians.

    Includes bibliographical references.
    1. Baptists—Relations. I. Title.
BX6329.A1G37   286   73-16788
ISBN 0-8170-0602-8

Printed in the U.S.A.

Contributors

Alexei Bichkov is general secretary, All-Union Council of Evangelical Christians-Baptists, Moscow, U.S.S.R.

Gerald L. Borchert is dean and professor of New Testament, North American Baptist Theological Seminary, Sioux Falls, South Dakota, U.S.A.

Sergio Corda is former instructor in church history, Baptist Theological Seminary, Rüschlikon-Zürich, Switzerland.

Emanuel A. Dahunsi is professor of New Testament, Nigerian Baptist Theological Seminary, Ogbomoso, Nigeria.

William R. Estep, Jr., is professor of church history, Southwestern Baptist Theological Seminary, Fort Worth, Texas, U.S.A.

Edward A. Freeman is pastor of the First Baptist Church, Kansas City, Kansas, U.S.A., and president of the National Sunday School and Baptist Training Union Congress, auxiliary to the National Baptist Convention, U.S.A., Inc.

James Leo Garrett, Jr., formerly professor of Christian theology, Southern Baptist Theological Seminary, Louisville, Kentucky, is now director of the J. M. Dawson Studies in Church and State and professor of religion, Baylor University, Waco, Texas, U.S.A.

D. Mervyn Himbury is principal and lecturer in church history, Whitley College, University of Melbourne, Parkville, Victoria, Australia.

Princeton S. Hsu is general secretary of Baptist Press, pastor of Tsim Sha Tsui Baptist Church, and professor in Hong Kong Baptist Theological Seminary, Hong Kong.

John David Hughey, Jr., is secretary for Europe and the Middle East. Foreign Mission Board of the Southern Baptist Convention, Richmond, Virginia, U.S.A.

Ilia Ivanov is co-pastor of the Moscow Baptist Church and president of the All-Union Council of Evangelical Christians-Baptists, U.S.S.R.

Denton Lotz is ecumenical representative of the American Baptist Foreign Mission Society for central and eastern Europe, now residing in Rüschlikon-Zürich, Switzerland.

Azariah McKenzie is general secretary, Jamaica Baptist Union, Kingston, Jamaica.

Mrs. Louise Paw is overseas program associate, American Baptist Churches in the U.S.A., Valley Forge, Pennsylvania, U.S.A.

Ernest A. Payne, former general secretary, Baptist Union of Great Britain and Ireland, now serves as one of the presidents of the World Council of Churches and resides in Pitsford, Northamptonshire, England.

Raymond O. Ryland is associate professor of religious studies, University of San Diego, and deacon, Immaculata (Roman Catholic) Church, San Diego, California, U.S.A.

Rudolf Thaut is president of the Theological Seminary of the Bund Evangelisch-Freikirchlicher Gemeinden in Deutschland, Hamburg, Federal Republic of Germany.

Robert G. Torbet is ecumenical officer, American Baptist Churches in the U.S.A., Valley Forge, Pennsylvania, U.S.A.

Jarold K. Zeman is professor of church history, Acadia Divinity College, Acadia University, Wolfville, Nova Scotia, Canada.

Table of Contents

Dedicated to the memory of

DR. JOSEF NORDENHAUG

(1903-1969)

General Secretary, Baptist World Alliance,

1960-1969,

one of whose last responsibilities

was the appointment of members to

the Commission on Cooperative

Christianity

Preface

Baptist Christians tend to be known for their sectarian separatism more than for their cooperation with other Christians and their devotion to Christian unity. Yet in their ranks have been John Bunyan, who insisted that the lack of believer's baptism be no bar to church membership among Baptists; William Carey, who first proposed a worldwide interconfessional missionary conference; T. T. Eaton, who called for the serious study of the Holy Scriptures as the basis for the quest for Christian unity; and Walter Rauschenbusch, who aroused the social conscience of lethargic Protestantism. In more recent years Martin Luther King, Jr., crossed denominational lines in a crusade to remove racial barriers, and Billy Graham has drawn together Christians of numerous denominations for the common task of evangelism.

On the one hand, the reasons for the existence of Baptists as a distinct Christian fellowship have included a protest against decadent and crippling ecclesiasticism. On the other hand, Baptists have often participated in and even given leadership to expressions of Christian togetherness, cooperation, and unity that transcend denominational lines. At the same time that some Baptists have been and are noncooperating separatists in isolation from other Christians, sometimes on account of persecution or ostracism and sometimes because of their own persuasion, and often also in isolation from their fellow Baptists, other Baptists have joined in new organic Protestant church unions wherein their distinctive Baptist identity has ceased to exist.

The actual story of Baptist attitudes toward and relations with other Christians throughout the world is one that has not been sufficiently told or understood, even by those who are reasonably well informed about Baptists.

One of the primary tasks of the Commission on Cooperative Christianity of the Baptist World Alliance from its establishment in 1968 has been the authorization, preparation, presentation, and circulation of study papers on various segments of this story. Every geographical region of the world in which there are Baptists today has been investigated, and all the major Baptist bodies in the United States have been considered. Such papers, presented in the Commission's annual sessions in Baden, Austria (1969); Tokyo,

Japan (1970); Wolfville, Nova Scotia, Canada (1971); Kingston, Jamaica (1972); and Einsiedeln, Switzerland (1973), now with some modification and updating appear in this present volume. Both the diversity and the common patterns existing among Baptists in reference to non-Baptist Christians and Christian communions can become more evident.

The editor wishes to express his gratitude to the contributing authors, both those who are members of the Commission on Cooperative Christianity—Borchert, Corda, Dahunsi, Estep, Freeman, Himbury, Hsu, Thaut, and Torbet—and those who have not been—Bichkov, Hughey, Ivanov, Lotz, McKenzie, Mrs. Paw, Payne, Ryland, and Zeman. It is doubtless a sign of the extent of present-day Christian cooperation that the chapter on the Southern Baptist Convention has been written by a Roman Catholic lay theologian, Raymond O. Ryland. Special thanks are due to the cochairman and to the secretary of the Commission on Cooperative Christianity, Rudolf Thaut and Gerald L. Borchert, and to the two associate secretaries of the Baptist World Alliance who have had responsibility for coordinating the work of its five commissions, Frank H. Woyke and Carl W. Tiller, all of whose cooperation and counsel have contributed greatly to this volume. The editor is also indebted to the following persons for specific instances of assistance: Theodore F. Adams, Richmond, Virginia; Olin T. Binkley, Wake Forest, North Carolina; C. E. Bryant, Washington, D.C.; Ronald F. Deering, Louisville, Kentucky; C. Ronald Goulding, London, England; John F. Havlik, Atlanta, Georgia; Leon McBeth, Fort Worth, Texas; Louis E. McCall, Louisville, Kentucky; B. D. Rumbold, Parkville, Victoria, Australia; C. Allyn Russell, Concord, Massachusetts; C. Penrose St. Amant, Rüschlikon-Zürich, Switzerland; Robert G. Torbet, Valley Forge, Pennsylvania; and Albert W. Wardin, Nashville, Tennessee.

To President Duke K. McCall and to the Board of Trustees of Southern Baptist Theological Seminary, Louisville, Kentucky, the editor wishes to express his abiding gratitude for the support which has made possible his service as chairman of the Commission on Cooperative Christianity. Miss Mary Jean Aiken, Miss Alicia Gardner, and their office services staff have ably prepared much of the typescript, and Mrs. Sylvia B. Odenwald of Baylor University has generously assisted in proofreading.

James Leo Garrett, Jr.

CHAPTER 1

Great Britain

Ernest A. Payne

BAPTISTS AND MENNONITES

The first Baptist church in modern times was formed in Holland in the seventeenth century by a group of religious exiles, of whom John Smyth and Thomas Helwys were the leaders. They were in contact with and had been helped by Mennonites. Smyth came to doubt whether he had been right in baptizing himself before baptizing his companions, and after Helwys had led some of the group back to London to bear their testimony there, Smyth applied to join the Mennonite church in Amsterdam. A number of those who stayed in Holland followed his example. The London church and those which sprang from it in the early decades of the seventeenth century (usually known as General Baptist churches, their doctrine of redemption being Arminian rather than Calvinist) kept in contact with the Dutch Mennonites by correspondence and occasional personal visits. They were clearly conscious of a basic kinship, but the direct links were soon broken. In the eighteenth and nineteenth centuries there were few contacts. When the Baptist World Alliance was formed in 1905, however, Mennonite statistics were included with Baptist ones. Mennonites have sent fraternal delegates to several of the Baptist World Congresses, and of recent years efforts have been made to renew acquaintance.[1]

13

BAPTISTS AND CONGREGATIONALISTS

The Particular (or Calvinistic) Baptist churches of the seventeenth century sprang from a London Separatist congregation. In Commonwealth times it was from Separatist Puritanism that the Independents or Congregationalists emerged. There was not always complete separation between Baptists and Independents. John Bunyan, for example, was an influential figure who taught that "differences of judgment about water baptism" should be "no bar to communion," that is, to fellowship together in a local gathered church. In Bedfordshire and neighboring counties Baptist and Congregational churches formed one "association" or "union" from the seventeenth to the twentieth century. Not all seventeenth-century Baptists approved of Bunyan's attitude. By the close of the century, Baptists, Congregationalists, and Presbyterians were generally recognizable as separate communities with their own distinctives. They had been granted limited rights under the Toleration Act of 1689. They became known, however, as "The Three Denominátions," frequently acted together, and secured the right of access to the throne. With the Protestant Dissenting Deputies (a lay group) as one of their main agencies, the three bodies campaigned with the Quakers for full civil rights. Toward the end of the eighteenth century a number of new local churches were established which allowed differences among their members on the question of baptism, and even where membership was not "open," the Communion table was. Following the Evangelical Revival and the Industrial Revolution, the Nonconformist churchesæexperienced rapid growth. National unions were formed (Baptist Union, 1812–1813, reorganized 1831; Congregational Union, 1808, reorganized 1832; Presbyterian Church of England, 1844). These denominations then started on separate, though still closely parallel and friendly, development. They thought of themselves as kin and as allies. In the closing decades of the nineteenth century, even before the Free Church Council movement, there were those who envisaged the uniting of the Baptist and the Congregational denominations. Two joint annual assemblies were held, and when the International Congregational Council was formed in 1891, some of its leaders hoped for a world organization which would include both bodies. A further group of "Union Churches" was established in England in the early years of the present century. In the last two or three decades, however, Congregationalists have moved officially toward the Presbyterians (as they did in the last decade of the seventeenth century) and away from the Baptists. In October, 1972, Presbyterians in England and Congregationalists in England and Wales formed together the United Reformed Church, which, though not large in size, is expected to play an important role in church relations in Britain.[2]

COOPERATION IN THEOLOGICAL EDUCATION

During the closing decades of the nineteenth century, Baptists and Congregationalists began to cooperate in the training of ministers. A joint examination board was set up. In London, Regent's Park College, New College, and Hackney College worked together. Mansfield College, from its opening in Oxford in 1886, received Baptist students, and close cooperation continues since Regent's Park College moved there in 1927.[3]

BRITISH FREE CHURCH COUNCILS

British Baptists played a leading part in the last decade of the nineteenth century in the establishment of local Free Church Councils and a National Free Church Council. Many regarded this movement as a step toward a United Free Church of England. That this did not follow was due in part to the political controversies which developed over national education and other issues from 1902 onward. The failure led Dr. J. H. Shakespeare, secretary of the Baptist Union from 1898 to 1924, to lead in the setting up of the Federal Council of the Evangelical Free Churches in 1919. Within a few years this body became the agency through which representative Free churchmen conferred with Anglicans following the "Appeal to All Christian People" issued by the Lambeth Conference of Anglican Bishops in 1920. In 1939 the National Free Church Council and the Federal Council were amalgamated. Closer union between the associated churches has been more than once discussed, so far without success. When church union discussions were resumed following the Archbishop of Canterbury's Cambridge Sermon of 1946, they were between individual churches (i.e., denominations) as such and not between the Free Church Federal Council and the Church of England.[4]

OVERSEAS COOPERATION AND UNION

The Baptist Missionary Society sent representatives to the Edinburgh World Missionary Conference of 1910. Its secretaries have shared in the development of the Conference of British Missionary

Societies and the International Missionary Council. The Baptist Missionary Society has engaged in a number of cooperative and united enterprises, e.g., Serampore College, schools in North India and Bengal, the Vellore Medical College; Shantung Christian University and the Christian Literature Society of Shanghai; the Theological Institute at Kimpese and the Congo Protestant Council; Calabar High School and the United Theological College, Kingston, Jamaica. During the last decades of the Baptist Missionary Society's work in China, the churches it had established joined the Church of Christ in China. The Christians connected with British Baptist work in Ceylon are involved in the current discussions of and schemes for church union, while in North India most have joined the United Church of North India, one of their number being a bishop of the new Church.[5]

WORLD COUNCIL OF CHURCHES

The Baptist Union sent representatives to the Stockholm Life and Work Conference (1925). It had been agreed to send delegates to the Lausanne Faith and Order Conference (1927), but when the Southern Baptist Convention drew back, the decision was rescinded. Two unofficial British Baptists attended. This was soon felt to be a mistake, and Dr. M. E. Aubrey, secretary of the British Union from 1925 to 1951, and one or two other British Baptists became members of the Faith and Order Continuation Committee. The Baptist Union was represented at the Oxford Conference on Church, Community, and State (1937) and the Edinburgh Faith and Order Conference (1937). Thereafter it was agreed to join the proposed World Council of Churches, and Dr. Aubrey became a member of the committee which drafted its constitution. The agreed quota of delegates and alternates was sent to the Amsterdam Assembly (1948), and this has been done at each subsequent assembly. Dr. Aubrey and the Right Honorable Ernest Brown served on the Central Committee from 1948 to 1954, and the present writer from 1954 to 1968, when he was elected to the Praesidium. Three British Baptists have served on the staff of the World Council in Geneva: Rev. Gwenyth Hubble, Rev. V. E. W. Hayward, and Dr. Glen Garfield Williams. The Baptist Union has been actively involved in all the Divisions and Departments.[6]

BRITISH COUNCIL OF CHURCHES

The British Council of Churches was formed in 1942, the initial meeting taking place in the Baptist Church House in London.

Baptists have shared fully in all the work of the Council and almost everywhere in the local Councils of Churches which have grown up in the last twenty-five years. Baptists, officially appointed from England, Wales and Scotland, were at the Faith and Order Conference in Nottingham (1964), which called the churches to consider covenanting together for union by 1980, and at the Church Leaders' Conference in Birmingham in 1972.[7]

WALES AND SCOTLAND

There have been separate unions of Welsh and Scottish Baptists since 1867 and 1869, respectively, but in many matters they act in association with the Baptist Union of Great Britain and Ireland. The Baptist Union of Wales and the Baptist Union of Scotland are both in direct membership with the British Council of Churches. Both Unions were initially members of the World Council of Churches. Neither has maintained its membership, the Welsh by voluntary default (content to be represented by the Baptist Union of Great Britain and Ireland), the Scottish Union because of sharp internal division on the matter. The Baptist Union of Wales has for some years been sharing in church union discussions, first with other Free churches, now with them and the Church in Wales (Anglican).[8]

IRELAND

The Baptist Union of Ireland consists of 78 churches and 9,761 members, almost all of them in Northern Ireland. It is linked historically with the Baptist Union of Great Britain and Ireland, but there have been few links since 1887. The Union is not in the Baptist World Alliance or the British Council of Churches and takes part in few joint church activities even in its own territory.[9]

CONSERVATIVE EVANGELICALS

Of recent years some British Baptists, chiefly those who describe themselves as "Conservative Evangelicals" and are members of the Baptist Revival Fellowship, an organization which has met annually in conference since 1954, have been critical of Baptist involvement in the Ecumenical Movement. Debate on the matter was stimulated by the Nottingham Conference. Since Vatican Council II, Roman Catholic "Consultant Observers" have been invited to both the British Council of Churches and the World Council of Churches. In some places Roman Catholics have sought membership of local Councils of Churches. This has led some (not all) of the members of the Baptist Revival Fellowship to urge the withdrawal of the Baptist Union from the British Council of Churches and the World Council of Churches. In 1967 the Baptist Union Council produced a substantial report directed mainly to the Nottingham Conference recommendations. It stated, *inter alia:*

> That for Baptists to weaken their links with either the British Council of Churches or the World Council of Churches would be a serious loss to themselves and would make it more difficult for Baptists to present their distinctive witness and heritage to others. . . . That so far no plan of church union or scheme for basically altered Church Relations has been put forward in Britain to which Baptists could unitedly or near unitedly give assent, but that their close study of current discussions and negotiations, whether as official "Observers" or not, is of great importance.

The report was sent to the churches and associations for their study, and, in the light of comments received, some critical in one direction, some in another, a further report was adopted in 1969 and taken to the Annual Assembly. The following resolution was there adopted by 1,125 votes to 356:

> In the light of the responses sent by churches and Associations relating to the Report, *Baptists and Unity,* this Assembly endorses the conclusions in the document *Baptists and Unity Reviewed,* thus giving support to the conclusions of the Report.
>
> Furthermore, recognizing that there are differences of conviction among Baptists regarding inter-Church relations and that members of the Union have the right to engage in or refrain from participation, it calls on all members to maintain, in their differences, a mutual trust and love that accords with their fellowship in Christ.[10]

OTHER INTERDENOMINATIONAL AGENCIES

In addition to all that has been set out above, it should not be forgotten that British Baptists have corporately as well as individually supported interdenominational bodies, such as the British and Foreign Bible Society (1804), the National Sunday School Union (1803), the Evangelical Alliance (1846), the Temperance Council of the Christian Churches, etc., playing a considerable part in their leadership, the shaping of their policies, and their financial support. They have also been active in joint evangelistic efforts of various kinds.

THE BAPTIST UNION AND THE
STRICT AND PARTICULAR BAPTISTS

The Strict and Particular Baptists form a group of churches which rejected the moderate, evangelical Calvinism of Andrew Fuller (1754–1815), clinging to what is often described as High Calvinism and to membership and participation in the Lord's Supper being confined to those only who have been immersed as believers. These churches have been somewhat chary even of associating with one another on a regional basis, but there are now in existence the Metropolitan Strict Baptist Association (62 churches), the Suffolk and Norfolk Strict Baptist Association (39 churches), the Cambridgeshire and East Midland Union (22 churches), the National Strict Baptist Federation, and the Strict Baptist Missionary Society. Local relationships between Strict Baptist churches and those in membership with the Baptist Union vary from the nonexistent to the friendly. The chief official contact is through the Particular Baptist Fund (1717), from which Strict Baptists can still receive help. The Federation asked the Baptist Union to represent it in War Damage negotiations, and this has continued in the Churches' Main Committee, a body which deals with legislation affecting the churches and which includes representatives of the Church of Scotland, the Roman Catholic Church, and the Anglican and Free churches.

BAPTISTS AND THE CHURCHES OF CHRIST

From 1941 to 1952 representatives of the Baptist Union held what were described as "unofficial conversations" with members of the Churches of Christ (Disciples). In spite of many similarities of outlook and procedure, the conversations revealed considerable differences in theological emphasis. After the Nottingham Conference, correspondence took place to see whether a new series of conversations might be initiated. It would appear, however, that the Churches of Christ, who have now a membership of only 5,619, are inclined to look in other directions than the Baptist Union for future developments. They have asked for conversations with the United Reformed Church.[11]

CHAPTER 2

Northern Europe

Rudolf Thaut

HISTORICAL DEVELOPMENT

Although Northern Europe consists of very different countries, Baptist attitudes and relations to others in this area are similarly defined because of the following three factors:

1. Baptists in Northern Europe constitute a small minority and have a history of only a little more than a century. Before the middle of the nineteenth century there were no Baptists in any of these countries. The origin of the Baptist churches must be seen in connection with the period of revival which spread throughout this area during the nineteenth century. The Baptist churches are the result of one stream of this movement. They were usually started by newly converted Christians who discovered the order and meaning of baptism in their study of the New Testament. Although ties with the much older Anglo-Saxon Baptist movement were quickly established, they were not there in the beginning. Therefore, one should look for the center of Baptist beginnings on the continent in Hamburg and the ministry of Johann Gerhard Oncken (1800-1884).[1] From Hamburg, contacts were soon made with groups of believers in other countries who had also been gripped by the true meaning of baptism and who were searching for a church composed of believers only.

2. When considering the relationship of Baptists to other Christian groups, we must remember that Europe is the continent that was the first to be Christianized. This happened within the first centuries after Christ. The union of Church and State had

21

already taken place during the time of the Roman Empire. Not even the Reformation and the work of Luther and Calvin broke this Church-State union. The Protestant churches became State churches just as the Catholic church had been up to that time. From a legal and institutional point of view, today they are no longer State churches in some of these countries. However, if we look at it practically, they have assumed a very similar position as *Volkskirchen*. This means that more than 90 percent of the population belongs to either the Protestant or Catholic churches and that these State or former State churches continue to have a privileged position above all other churches. On the other hand, within these churches there are few practicing Christians to be found in Northern Europe, that is, people who attend church regularly or at all.

The Baptists in the first decades of their existence were persecuted harshly by these churches as sectarians and heretics. As State churches they cooperated with the state government in this persecution. In later years Baptists were more or less tolerated as sects. In most cases this situation did not change really decisively until the time during and after 1945.

3. The Northern European countries are overwhelmingly Protestant (Sweden, Finland, Norway, and Denmark). This report, however, also includes the Netherlands as well as the two countries which were the home of the Reformation, Germany and Switzerland, even though there are strong Catholic populations in these countries. (The two German states will not be dealt with separately, because the relations between the various churches in both areas are the same.) In the whole of Northern Europe, including the Netherlands, Germany, and Switzerland, inter-church relations are defined by the historical fact that the Protestant State churches and *Volkskirchen* of these countries are the cofounders and decisive supporters of the Ecumenical Movement. As a result, there prevails in this area an ecumenical and open climate, to be sure in the manner as it has developed in the World Council of Churches, whose headquarters are in Geneva, Switzerland.

FROM ANTAGONISM TO UNDERSTANDING

Certain historical developments, as well as the definite minority status of Baptists, have substantially determined the relationship of Baptists to other churches in Northern Europe.

Offensive as well as defensive attitudes developed on both sides. The Baptists never really considered the State churches as true churches. This view was due mainly to the fact that the majority of church members did not profess Christ as Lord and did not take part in the life of the church. In the German language a distinction is made between these two types of churches. The religious institution is known as *Kirche* (The Church), while the Baptists and other Free churches use the term *Gemeinde* (congregation, or fellowship) for themselves. It is also important to remember that, due to their origin during the period of revival in Europe, Baptists have advocated a conservative biblical theology. On the other hand, theological liberalism and rationalism have at various times been widespread in the Lutheran and Reformed churches. As already mentioned, these churches persecuted the Baptists as heretics and sectarians. Since they lay a claim on the whole population, or at least on those baptized as infants, they see every conversion and baptism as proselytism, if the person involved is not a child from a Baptist family. This is still a live issue.

In contrast to this antagonism, the Free churches and small groups within the State churches which came into being through the awakening in the nineteenth century have had a close fellowship across the boundaries of their denominations right from the beginning. It is because of this historical fact that the Baptists in Northern Europe seldom had "exclusive" thoughts with regard to their own denomination. They always had some sort of ties with the other Free churches and even with believing individuals from the State churches. J. G. Oncken, the founder of the German Baptist movement who greatly influenced the Baptist beginnings in many European countries, was one of the founders in 1845 of the Evangelical Alliance, meeting in London. To this day the Baptists are active members of the Alliance and closely cooperate with the other Free churches, mostly Methodists and Congregationalists, in all of these countries. Therefore, even if in a limited way, they realized ecumenical fellowship at a time when between all other churches in Northern Europe there were still high and almost insurmountable barriers which prevented almost any communication or cooperation.

In recent times there have been several factors which are beginning to change the attitude of Baptists to the State churches and the attitude of the State churches to the Baptists and other Free churches. Among these the most important are *(a)* the growing estrangement of the greater part of the membership of the State churches due to the secularization taking place today; (b) the fact that Lutheran and Reformed bishops, theologians, and pastors have been confronted on the international level through the Ecumenical Movement with Baptists and Methodists and thus discovered them as churches of importance in the world; and (c) the changing structure of society which makes it more important than ever before that all Christians and churches support one another in their mission work.

Even though many individual Baptists and often leading personalities of the Baptist unions are very active in different ecumenical groups and activities, on the whole it must be said that today the attitude of Northern European Baptists to the Ecumenical Movement as expressed in the World Council of Churches is quite varied. At this time in Northern Europe only the Baptist Union of Denmark is a member of the World Council of Churches. All the other unions are more or less reserved in their attitude toward this organization. The feeling is emphasized that unity *within* the Baptist union is much more important than membership in the World Council of Churches, if this affiliation leads to separation among Baptists. However, there are still noteworthy groups that not only look favorably on the Ecumenical Movement but are also very active in ecumenical activities (foreign missions, relief work, etc.). The strength of these groups varies from country to country. For the most part they cooperate in many ways with other churches on the local level. Recently this cooperation has included Roman Catholics, because especially in Northern Europe groups in that church which are turning to a Bible-oriented theology are gaining strength.

MANNER AND EXTENT OF COOPERATION WITH OTHER CHRISTIAN BODIES TODAY

Baptists in Northern Europe are involved in several kinds of relationships with other Christians. The following are some of the organizations with which Baptists are affiliated.

1. The Evangelical Alliance: All Baptist unions participate in and share responsibilities in the Alliance.

2. World Council of Churches: Only the Baptist Union of Denmark belongs. Baptists in the Netherlands belonged until 1963, when the Union left the World Council of Churches at the insistence of a number of local churches.

3. Conference of European Churches: Baptists Unions in Denmark, Sweden, East and West Germany, and Switzerland are members.

4. National Councils of Churches: Baptist Unions in Denmark, Sweden, and West and East Germany belong to their national ecumenical councils. Although the national councils in both East and West Germany are not very effective, there are a number of very effective ecumenical organizations in which Baptists are involved, often in leading roles.

The report from Denmark seems to be typical for the development in Northern Europe:

In the period 1954-1968 the Ecumenical Council has strengthened its work. During this time a more practical and unbiased relationship has evolved. The effect of this has been more respect for our Baptist Work. Also, the fear of cooperation with us is disappearing. An ecumenical study group in which two Baptists participate has been working on the question of baptism for three years and will publish a book on its findings. In 1968 a group of young people started a new ecumenical group. They are "activists" insofar as they are not content with discussions which are merely inside the "walls of the church" and merely concerned with doctrinal questions. They are concerned with the Church-World relationship.[2]

The Baptists in the Netherlands held membership in the ecumenical council of the Netherlands during the same time that they were members of the World Council of Churches, i.e., from 1948 to 1963. Until 1968 they sent an official observer to the council meetings. However, a new organization was then formed in which now even the Roman Catholics are fully involved. Although the Baptist Union leadership suggested to the Union that it should apply for guest membership in the new council, the General Assembly of the Baptist Union recently defeated the proposal. This means that now the Dutch Union does not have any official ecumenical contacts. However, there are ecumenical contacts in theological education, e.g., Dutch Baptist students do their studies at the Reformed Faculty of Theology at the University of Utrecht.

The Baptist Union in Norway is a member of the official contact group between the Protestant churches in that country. Attempts to convert this group into a more formal council of churches did not succeed, although Baptists had been in favor of this new development. The Baptist Union has held membership in the Missionary Council since 1915.

5. Free Church Councils: Among the Free churches there is close cooperation in all countries. Especially in Germany and Sweden

there are Free Church Councils in which the Baptists are actively engaged. The recent situation in Sweden has been reported by Dr. David Lagergren, general secretary of the Swedish Baptist Union, as follows:

> The talks about integration and later on about closer cooperation between Free Churches in Sweden ended up in 1971 without any tangible result. The work of the Free Church Council of Sweden continues, however, and has even been strengthened and enlarged during the last few years, mainly due to the fact that the State authorities have invited all Free Churches and denominations to share in the distribution of some State grants of a new kind. This has led to the formation of a cooperative committee of Swedish Free Churches in which no less than thirteen denominations—from "low church" movements to Pentecostalists—take part. All these denominations have recently agreed to a common statement on a proposal from a State Committee about a changed relationship between the Church of Sweden and the State.[3]

6. Cooperation between different Baptist groups within the same country: Unfortunately, in several countries of Europe, there are, besides the Baptist Union, which belongs to the Baptist World Alliance, also groups of Baptists which not only refuse membership in the world body but also refuse to join with other Baptists in their own country. In Northern Europe, this is true only of several independent congregations in the Netherlands. There are also two Baptist groups in Sweden, the Baptist Union and Orebro Mission. The latter does not belong to the Baptist World Alliance. However, in the last few years a new fellowship has developed between these two groups. The former general secretary of the Baptist Union of Sweden, Dr. Erik Rudin, reported in 1970:

> The reason for the split was partly theological and partly a question of policy and organization. Most of the contradictory opinions, however, have been eliminated during the last years, and the two groups work in a spirit of good fellowship with each other. At various times through the years the Baptist Union has suggested that the two denominations should consider the possibility of reunion. In 1965 a delegation discussed matters of common interest, joint missionary projects, etc. The Orebro Mission representatives have declared that they are not prepared to recommend a reunion since their churches would not accept it.

SUMMARY

In summary it can be said, in spite of all the sectional and individual differences, that the Baptists in Northern Europe do not think or live with an "exclusive" mentality. There is a basic openness toward other Christians and churches, especially toward those which require decision for Christ as the basis of membership.

However, since this region has been conditioned by the history of the State churches and since the Free churches are a small minority group, there are still today some special problems which prevent further cooperation. Nevertheless, Baptists today with their pattern of the church feel that they have a special mission among the Christians of Northern Europe. Within recent years new possibilities and challenges have appeared which are beginning to change the attitudes and relationships of Baptists to other Christian groups. These are, in summary:

1. the Ecumenical Movement, through which we have again discovered each other as brothers;

2. the process of secularization, which leads us from our battle against each other to "striving together for the faith of the Gospel";

3. the second industrial revolution with the development toward a mass society, in which the different Christians and churches fulfill their mission only as they work together;

4. new theological and ideological developments, which are erasing the theological fronts between confessions and leading to new groupings which cut through all denominations.

In a world of turmoil, we Baptists of Northern Europe are searching for *the* way which the Lord will show us to fulfill his commission, for ourselves and together with other Christians.

CHAPTER 3

The Union of Soviet Socialist Republics

Alexei Bichkov and Ilia Ivanov

ORIGIN AND DEVELOPMENT OF THE EVANGELICAL MOVEMENT IN RUSSIA

In 1867 Nikita Voronin, a Molokan, was baptized as a believer in the turbulent Kura River in the city of Tbilisi in the Caucasus, and this event is considered to be the beginning of the Baptist movement in Russia.[1] The sixteenth-century Reformation had given to the people in Western Europe the Bible in the vernacular and made it accessible to all. A little later there also appeared in Russia the first translations of some separate books of the Bible in Russian, Ukrainian, and Byelorussian. By the beginning of the nineteenth century, people living in Russia had the opportunity to read the Gospels in their own language. The Bible Society published some books of the Bible in Polish, Georgian, Armenian, and Lithuanian, besides those in Russian. In 1823 for the first time the whole New Testament was published in the Russian language, and in 1876 the Russian Synodal Bible was published. Now the inhabitants of Russia could read the Bible in translations that compared favorably with the best in Western Europe.

God sent great workers, wise men filled with the Holy Spirit, to preach the gospel in Russia. These servants of God came from the various strata of society, from the aristocracy (M. M. Korf, V. A. Pashkov, A. P. Bobrinsky, and others) and from the common people (I. Ryaboshapka, M. Ratushny, D. I. Mazaev, I. S. Prokhanov, V. G. Pavlov, and others). Their selfless service under different circumstances and amid various difficulties deserves the respect and gratitude of Evangelical Christians and Baptists.

The Russian Orthodox Church, which did much for the benefit of the Russian people, specifically in translating the Bible into Russian, still remained conservative and irreconcilable with different-minded Christians. But despite the pressure and difficulties, the Evangelical movement was spreading. By the movement's fiftieth anniversary in 1917 there were nearly one hundred thousand in the membership of the Baptists, who had arisen in the Caucasus and the Ukraine, and the Evangelical Christians, who had originated among the aristocracy in St. Petersburg.

After the October Revolution one of the first decrees of the Soviet government was the Decree on Separation of the Church from the State. It established the equality of all religions before the law. The first decade following the Revolution was a time of considerable growth among the Baptist and Evangelical Christian churches. At the same time the Pentecostal movement, headed by I. Voronaev, came into existence.

New historical conditions called forth new tasks for the leaders of the Baptists and the Evangelical Christians, principally witnessing to Christ and proclaiming the gospel in an atheistic state. It was necessary to work out precise criteria for defining the words of Christ, "Render to Caesar the things that are Caesar's, and to God the things that are God's" (Mark 12:17, RSV). Significant personal contributions to such definition were made by leaders such as Alexander Karev and Jakov Zhidkov. One cannot say that the process of stabilization is over and that relations among Evangelical Christians-Baptists and legislation are in full harmony. But the great majority of Evangelical Christians-Baptists observe the legislation on religion and successfully practice their service for Christ and for fellowmen.

CHRISTIAN UNITY

In 1944 the Baptists and the Evangelical Christians united to form the All-Union Council of Evangelical Christians-Baptists (AUCECB), with Jakov Zhidkov as president. In 1945 the majority of Pentecostals joined the AUCECB on the basis of the August Agreement, which, to some extent, restricts the practice of distinctive Pentecostal features, namely, speaking in tongues, prophecy, healing, etc., at their worship services. In 1963 the

Mennonite Brethren also united with the AUCECB. They recognize personal salvation and believer's baptism by immersion, as Baptists do.[2] Today the AUCECB unites nearly half a million believers. The gospel is being preached in all the languages of the people within the Soviet Union. During the last fifteen years the AUCECB has published both a Bible and a hymnal. Its magazine, *Bratskii Vestnik* ("Fraternal Herald"), enjoys wide popularity, fosters unity among the brotherhood, and educates believers in a deeper knowledge of eternal truth.

The spirit of separatism and isolation peculiar to the early history of Baptists and Evangelical Christians is being gradually replaced by the spirit of tolerance, respect, and fellowship in respect to Christians of a different persuasion. Ecumenical relations with many Christians of different beliefs are being developed and strengthened both inside and outside the Soviet Union. Friendly relations are now established between the AUCECB and the Russian Orthodox Church. Brotherly contacts are developing; exchanges of religious literature are taking place; and reciprocal visits and talks are occurring. Many foreign guests of the AUCECB receive a friendly reception at the Russian Orthodox Religious Center at Zagorsk, and the guests of the Orthodox Church, in their turn, meet a hearty welcome in the AUCECB.

Great common responsibility for the destinies of nations, for world peace, and for help to suffering peoples has contributed to Christian unity. Constantly keeping in mind the high priestly prayer of Jesus, Evangelical Christians-Baptists of the U.S.S.R. stretch out their hands of brotherly fellowship to all Christians, proclaiming Jesus Christ as Reconciler of the whole man to God and of people to each other.

THEOLOGICAL BASES OF THE AUCECB

On the whole, the theology of Evangelical Christians-Baptists in the U.S.S.R. rests on the acknowledgment of the Holy Scriptures as the foundation. Modern liberal doctrinal teachings do not have a noticeable influence among them. Faith in Jesus Christ as personal Savior, complete devotion to the service of Christ, joy and thirst for prayerful fellowship in the church, readiness to render assistance to one's fellowman, and the doing of everything out of love for Christ are the most characteristic features of the movement.

Bible study is the main subject in the two-year Bible correspondence course conducted since 1967. Nearly a hundred have been trained in these courses, and Bible reading is the foundation of the spiritual life and the source of power for service.

The spirit of pietism is typical of the Evangelical Christians-Baptists, but at the same time they do not keep away from reasonable acquaintance with the world of art, literature, and music. Church members love to sing, and there are numerous choirs and talented composers, conductors, and singers in their ranks. Hymns and songs used by the churches number more than two thousand.

Restrictions as to missionary work in the U.S.S.R. do not limit the rights of parents to bring up their children in the spirit of the gospel and to take them to worship services.

OVERSEAS RELATIONSHIPS OF THE AUCECB

The Evangelical Christians and Baptists have held membership in the Baptist World Alliance since its founding in 1905. I. S. Prokhanov and Jakov I. Zhidkov were elected as vice-presidents of the Baptist World Alliance. In 1954, due to the initiative of V. Carney Hargroves, now president of the Baptist World Alliance, contacts with Baptists in the United States and with the Baptist World Alliance were reestablished. During succeeding years the AUCECB was visited by such overseas Baptist leaders as Hargroves, Theodore F. Adams, Porter W. Routh, Harold E. Stassen, Robert S. Denny, Josef Nordenhaug, William R. Tolbert, David S. Russell, Erik Ruden, Andrew D. MacRae, T. B. McDormand, and Janos Laczkovszki and such Protestant leaders as Eugene Carson Blake and Philip Potter. Representatives of the AUCECB have also visited many countries and have taken part in many Baptist world congresses and regional conferences.

Besides its relationships with its fellow Baptists, the AUCECB is a member of the World Council of Churches and of the Conference of European Churches (Nyborg Conference) and participates in the Christian Peace Conference movement, which promotes dialogues and contacts so as to help find ways of cooperation in defense of peace among Christians of the East and the West. Evangelical Christians-Baptists enthusiastically support peace movements throughout the world and the reconciliation of people to God and to each other.

Responding to the call of the Tokyo congress of the Baptist

World Alliance to render material aid to the underdeveloped nations, believers related to the AUCECB have contributed voluntarily for these purposes through the Peace Fund in the U.S.S.R. During 1972 they contributed 150,000 rubles.

Evangelical Christians-Baptists believe that the Lord Jesus Christ will in the power of the Holy Spirit bring his people to the unity of the Spirit and the bond of peace.

CHAPTER 4

Eastern Europe

Denton Lotz

Prior to World War II the Baptists in Eastern Europe suffered greatly from the State churches, be it Catholicism in Poland, or Orthodoxy in Romania, or Reformed and Lutheran churches in Hungary. The Baptists were considered as sectarians by the larger Christian communions and suffered not only psychological persecution but in some cases actual physical persecution at the hands of so-called Christians.

Almost thirty years after the end of World War II the situation is entirely different. Baptist preachers in Poland exchange pulpits with Catholic priests on the World Day of Prayer. A Reformed bishop gives an opening address to the 125th anniversary of the Hungarian Baptists. Orthodox priests write to Baptist radio preachers for materials on the Bible.

What has happened? Significantly, under the Communist governments of Eastern Europe, the former State churches lost their once privileged status, and smaller church groups were placed on an equal status with them before the law. Thus it is that Baptists in Eastern Europe look to the days after the end of World War II as really an end to the religious persecution they experienced from the other larger churches. These larger churches have become more humble, have seen their error, and are gradually making their rapprochement with the Baptists.

To generalize, however, misses the point. It is necessary to judge the Baptist view toward ecumenicity in each particular country. We will give a cursory view of some examples and instances of how Baptists in Czechoslovakia, German Democratic Republic, Hungary, Poland, Romania, and Yugoslavia express their ecumenical hospitality in the framework of Baptist beliefs.

CZECHOSLOVAKIA

All Baptist students of theology must study at the Comenius Faculty, the faculty of theology of the Czech Brethren. As a result Baptist pastors right from the start of their studies have an ecumenical experience. Friendships which last even after graduation are made with students of other Protestant denominations. Thus it is not surprising that at special times there is pulpit exchange between Baptists and other churches. The Baptists in Czechoslovakia by their very name distinguish themselves "ecumenically" from other Baptists in Eastern Europe. The official name of the Baptists is the Union of Baptist Brethren. The use of the world "brethren" here is related historically to the movement of reform within Czechoslovakia started by the great martyr John Huss, who was condemned by the Council of Constance and burned at the stake in 1415.[1] Although Baptists cannot trace their history in Czechoslovakia back to Huss, by choosing the name "Baptist Brethren" they have desired to identify themselves with the larger historical movement for the reform of the Church and the return of the gospel. Also, the symbol used in all Baptist churches is that of the Czech Brethren, namely, a Communion chalice over the opened Bible. Cooperation with and membership in the Ecumenical Council of Czechoslovakia is a natural thing for these Baptists with this history. Contact and cooperation with the other Free churches is excellent. The Baptist hymnal is often used by other groups. Contact with the Catholics is only on a person-to-person level.

GERMAN DEMOCRATIC REPUBLIC

The Baptists in the German Democratic Republic share the same history and concern for relations with other Christians as their brethren in West Germany. Although in the nineteenth century they were persecuted by the State church, be it Lutheranism or Catholicism, this day has passed, and Baptists have been accepted into the wider fellowship of churches. In fact the editor of the

German Baptist newspaper, Günter Lorenz, is also the editor of the Press Service of the Ecumenical Council of the GDR. As in West Germany, the Baptists are called the Evangelical Free Churches. Although the great majority of this movement is made up of Baptists, also included are Plymouth Brethren (Darbyites) and some Pentecostals (Elim). The cooperation that the various congregations have among themselves is a great witness to the biblical notion of unity. Brethren and Pentecostals are allotted their rightful positions on the Executive Committee of the Union's council and also share in publishing the newspaper.

HUNGARY

The Baptists in Hungary celebrated in 1971 their 125th anniversary. Their history is one written under persecution, not only from Catholics but also from other Protestants. It was a peasant movement. In fact one of the heroes of the Baptists in Hungary was a peasant who had no more than two years of schooling and yet became a great evangelist. His name was Kornya, "Apostle to the Peasants." More than ten thousand were baptized by him. His generation of Baptists suffered burnings of their homes and churches.

According to the religious laws of the 1930s there were three categories: the "accepted," the "acknowledged," and the "tolerated" denominations. Total rights were enjoyed only by the "accepted" churches, but to this group belonged not one single denomination of the Free churches. On the other hand, the two Protestant churches—so-called historical churches—of this group, the Reformed and Lutheran churches, represented a common front against the autocratic and state church claims of the Roman Catholic Church.

Thus, historically speaking, the ecumenical churches of today were often the persecuting churches of yesterday. Yet remarkable changes have taken place. At the celebrations in November, 1971, in Budapest, Bishop Bartha of the Reformed Church spoke of the past sins of his church and movingly told how after World War II they asked for forgiveness. Then he said, "Only as we draw nearer to Christ, will we draw nearer to one another." [2]

Hungarian Baptists show specifically their active participation in cooperative Christianity by two specific actions: (a) They are members of the World Council of Churches. (b) They are members of the Free Church Council of Churches. Their most active participation is naturally in that movement closest to home. In the Free Church Council, Baptists have served in the offices of president and secretary. Pulpit exchanges are frequently organized, particularly during the Week of Prayer for Christian Unity. Now it is a common thing for Baptists to preach in Reformed churches and even to have a Lutheran professor teach at their seminary.

Presently the most significant of the common tasks is the new Bible translation, being undertaken in the framework of the Hungarian Bible Council and now nearly finished and ready for the press. These things would have been unheard of in another day.

POLAND

It is commonly said, "To be Polish is to be Catholic." In a country of thirty million, probably 95 percent of the population is Roman Catholic. Among so many, 2,500 Baptists are indeed few. This, however, has not prevented Baptists in recent years from contacts with Catholics and with the other small Protestant communities. There is a very active Ecumenical Council of Churches in Poland, composed of Lutherans, Methodists, Pentecostals, Orthodox, Polish Catholics, Mariavite Catholics, Reformed, and Baptists. The general secretary of the Council is a Baptist, Rev. Z. Pawlik, also secretary of the Baptist Union. Baptists are enthusiastic members of this Council.

Baptist students for the ministry study at the Theological Academy with all other Protestant students. Their own seminary offers special courses on Baptist history and distinctives, but generally the Baptist students complete their education in this ecumenical framework. Other Christian groups are eager to use the Baptist material, often translated by Polish Baptists. In this way Baptist ideas are shared with a much larger constituency than would otherwise be possible.

The Polish Baptists, as all Baptists in Europe, must witness in a secular society. Thus the "competition" of former years has disappeared between the churches, and the more searching question of how to proclaim the gospel today unites them. In one city the dean of a Catholic seminary preached in a Baptist church. In another town Catholic youth groups were invited to come to evangelistic meetings in a Baptist church, and they came. Since Vatican Council II, Polish Catholicism has instituted reforms which have been taken seriously in regard to relations with other churches. This has made for a much better atmosphere in which Baptist ministers now feel more free to communicate with Catholic priests. This is not to say that all differences have been eliminated, but the fact that discussions are taking place is a good sign of an ever-widening dialogue. Again, it is the Bible that brings Christians of various traditions together. Catholics eagerly buy the new Protestant translations, and Protestants buy the new Catholic translations.

ROMANIA

Historically, Baptist contact with Orthodoxy has been very limited, and when there was contact, it was often in the form of persecution. There is no denying the fact that prior to World War II Baptists were severely persecuted by the Orthodox government of Romania. Baptist World Alliance officials were helpless, even though continual protests were made. As in other countries, when communism came, it brought a certain judgment upon the old State churches. They lost their former privileges and prestige. Minority groups, such as Baptists, were guaranteed equality with these other groups. Thus, following World War II, Baptist work in Romania flourished and continues to do so. Baptists and Orthodox are suspicious and in some cases hostile to one another. Many Baptists feel that the Orthodox Church unjustly accuses them of "proselytism" and uses its influence to prevent Baptist expressions of faith, as shown in believer's baptism.[3] Thus, the ecumenical attitude of Baptists and Orthodox is at a standoff in Romania. But, compared to former years, there are signs of opening dialogues and respect for one another greater than at any other period of Baptist history in Romania. Through the good offices of the European Baptist Federation, as well as the Conference of European Churches, Baptist contact in Romania with the Orthodox has been increased. There has been no official contact or conversation between the churches, but on an individual basis there are instances of sharing and brotherly concern.

Romania has large national minorities of Hungarians and Germans. Protestants among these groups are largely Reformed or Lutherans. Baptist contact with Lutheran and Reformed minorities is minimal but good. Some of the teachers at the Baptist seminary in Bucharest have completed their studies at the Reformed seminary.

The largest Protestant group of Romanians is the Baptist group, followed by the Pentecostals. Initiatives for closer cooperation and better contact have been made by the leaders of the Baptist and Pentecostal groups. The question of "speaking in tongues" is as divisive in Romania as in other parts of the world. Romanian Baptists were observers at the last meeting of the Conference of European Churches. Through these contacts both Baptists and other groups have learned to see more of what they have in common than what divides them. The Baptists do not belong to any ecumenical council, national or international.

YUGOSLAVIA

Yugoslavia is unique in that it is composed of many national and cultural groups, very often each having its own religious history. The two basic majority groups are the Catholic Croatians in the North and the Orthodox Serbians in the South. Baptists exist in both areas and are thus confronted by different histories and religious traditions.

Relations with the Orthodox have always been more difficult. However, some Baptists have studied at the Orthodox seminary in Belgrade. Graduate study, however, is prohibited by the Patriarch. Basically, contact with the Serbian Orthodox is limited to informal and private contact between individuals.

In Croatia the Baptists have had better contact with the Catholics. This has come about largely through the meetings of Dr. Billy Graham. The Archbishop of Zagreb gave the open space near the Boys' Seminary in Zagreb for Billy Graham's meetings. The Orthodox paper *Vestnik* ("Messenger"), August 15, 1967, described the meetings: "[There were] several thousand listeners, out of whom only two thousand had seats. At the wish of Dr. Graham, an Orthodox priest read a text from the Bible first, and then a Protestant senior said the prayer. This successful evangelical meeting is also the first public manifestation of the ecumenical spirit and Christian love. The Christians of Zagreb will never forget it. It has definitely opened a new chapter in inter-religious relations. . . ." The eminent Catholic theologian and Council expert, Dr. Sagi-Bunic, said of these meetings, "Dr. Graham is also going to teach us ecumenism!"

In 1968 a Union of Protestant Churches was formed in Novi Sad, i.e., between Lutherans and Reformed. The Free Evangelical churches, including Baptists, did not join, because they were in favor of a Council of Churches rather than a Union. However,

Baptists and Lutherans and Reformed have gotten along quite well, and generally this has been marked by what Dr. Josef Horak, president of the Yugoslavian Baptist Union, calls "practical" ecumenism—reciprocal assistance in divine service, in church activity and common use of church buildings and accommodations.[4]

CONCLUSION AND SUMMARY

Two things should be emphasized: first, this is only a cursory preview of the Baptist relationship to other churches in Eastern Europe; and secondly, it is written by an outsider, and thus the personal touch and involvement are missing. For example, just as Baptist evangelism is very often from person to person, so, too, is the Baptist practice of ecumenism in Eastern Europe. This has not been particularly emphasized, and perhaps it should be mentioned here. Many Baptist laymen and preachers in Eastern Europe develop and encourage Christian fellowship, study, and prayer with their Christian brethren in other denominations.

Baptist cooperation with Christians of other persuasions in Eastern Europe is a dynamic and living relationship. Where the Bible is central to the relationship, Baptists will often be the first to join and encourage fellowship. Where evangelism is the concern, Baptists join hands with their brethren. Where prayer for unity is the occasion for meeting, Baptist churches and chapels are welcome meeting places. Where physical burdens necessitate sharing buildings, etc., Baptists enjoy the hospitality of others and gladly extend it to those without. Union of churches is a secondary concern, but unity in proclaiming Christ is an overruling guideline. It is an interesting phenomenon that Baptists and other Christian churches in Eastern Europe cooperate most when concerned with Bible study and proclamation. Division and separation and isolation of Baptists from cooperation are most evident where the primary reason for getting together is merely ecclesiastical politics or organizational machinations.

Baptists in Eastern Europe represent a minority ecclesiology but are indeed a dominant force for Christian witness that cuts across denominational, cultural, and historical lines. The inheritors of the State church tradition are to a certain extent bound by their previous history but are trying to get out of their old mold and meet the demands of the gospel in the new situation. The greatest contribution of Baptists to other traditions and to ecumenism in

Eastern Europe is the open display of a viable and dynamic church model which reaches men and women in this day with the joyful news of Christ.

CHAPTER 5

Southern Europe

Sergio Corda

This study represents only a provisional attempt to analyze the kind of relationship that Baptists have established with other Christians in Southern Europe, with particular emphasis on the recent past. Included in the study are France, Italy, Spain, and Portugal.

The sources which have been used may be grouped into three categories: general works on Baptist history and life; national Baptist periodicals of the countries concerned;[1] and interviews with representative individual Baptists of the countries under examination.[2]

THE RELIGIOUS SCENE

The most "Latin" form of Christianity, Roman Catholicism, is in all four countries the religion of the overwhelming majority. Protestants (with France as a relative exception) are only negligible minorities. The religious situation may be sketched as follows (the figures are rounded up and based on 1960 information):[3]

Country	Population	Roman Catholics (In percentages)	Protestants (Number of)
France	45,000,000	89.7	900,000
Italy	49,000,000	99.5	150,000
Spain	30,000,000	99.6	30,000
Portugal	8,000,000	96.5	45,000

43

FRANCE

Protestants: The vast majority of French Protestants are either Reformed (480,000) or Lutheran (300,000). The Free churches number only a few thousand members.

Baptists: Organized Baptist work in France started around 1835.[4] By the turn of the century there were approximately 2,500 Baptists in the country.[5] Since the middle of the nineteenth century two main groups of Baptists have emerged out of administrative, doctrinal, and personal differences. This division has continued into the present. The "Association Evangeliques des Eglises Baptistes" had a dozen churches or groups in 1955.[6] The "Fédération des Eglises Baptistes de France" was the stronger body and had about twenty churches at the time of the dissension. After World War II the membership shrank to only about one thousand.[7] In 1965 there were slightly over two thousand members, forty churches, a monthly paper, two children's homes, a home for the aged, and a school for pastors.[8] Women and young people have their own national association. There are also a few Baptist churches which are independent of both the Association and the Federation.

ITALY

Protestants: The oldest Italian Protestants are the Waldensians, a reformed church with about 30,000 members. The Methodists are about 3,000 in number, while the Adventists and the Brethren number slightly less. Italian Lutherans are less than 1,000 strong. The Pentecostals, who have over 100,000 members, are more numerous than all of the other Protestants put together.

Baptists: Baptist work in Italy started as a private missionary enterprise of a few British Baptists in 1863. Baptist missionary societies, both American and English, entered the field in the early 1870s.[9] In 1923 the work was unified under the sponsorship of the Southern Baptist Convention. In 1956 the Italian Baptists took over full responsibility for the work, though with the financial help of the Southern Baptist Convention. Today, Italian Baptists are about five thousand in number in about sixty churches or groups. The young people and the Baptist women have their own national organizations.

SPAIN

Protestants: The Brethren, with 6,000 members, are the most numerous group of Spanish Protestants. The Reformed group is called Iglesia Evangélica Española and has about 3,800 members. The Iglesia Española Reformada Episcopal represents the Anglican type and has about 1,000 members. The last two are the only Spanish churches affiliated with the World Council of Churches. Adventists number slightly more than 5,000 and the Pentecostals about 3,500. Other Free churches, independent or joined in local associations, have approximately 5,000 members.[10]

Baptists: Baptist work in this country may be dated from the year 1870.[11] In 1920 the Southern Baptist Convention agreed to take over full responsibility for missionary work in Spain. There were five Baptist missionary agencies working in the country at that time. There was no cooperation among them and even some antagonism. The Baptist Union was formed in 1929.[12] Small Baptist groups have dropped out of the Union and are related to an Interdenominational Mission in Canada.[13]

During the last decades the growth of Baptists in Spain was relatively rapid. In 1922 there were 667 members,[14] but in 1952 about 1,600,[15] and in 1965 over 4,000.[16] Young people and Baptist women have been organized into national unions.

PORTUGAL

Protestants: Today the community of Evangelical churches numbers about 45,000,[17] while around the year 1930 it was estimated to have approximately 10,000 members.[18] At that date, the percentage of the larger groups was as follows: Anglican type (Lusitanian church) 20 percent; Congregationalists 15 percent; Brethren 14 percent; Methodists 14 percent; Baptists 11 percent. Smaller groups followed.[19]

Baptists: The first Baptist church was organized in 1908.[20] Brazilian Baptists supported the work for several years, and in the 1950s the Southern Baptist Convention joined them. After World War II the Conservative Baptist Foreign Mission Society, U.S.A., entered the field. In 1959, beside two independent Baptist congregations, there were two Portuguese Baptist associations with a grand total of almost 2,000 members.[21]

BAPTISTS AND THE EVANGELICAL CHURCHES

As small minorities in a hostile Catholic environment, Baptists in Southern Europe have developed sharply different types of relationships with and attitudes toward the Roman Catholic

Church on the one side, and the Evangelical churches on the other. This section is devoted to their relations with and attitudes toward the latter group.

RELATIONS

To give, as far as possible, a general picture, it seems best to group Baptist relationships with other Evangelical churches according to several topics, comparing the national differences within each section.

Worship

French, Italian, and Spanish Baptists share with other Protestants a common version of the Bible instead of the various Catholic versions in the same language.

In France the Baptist hymnal is used also by some other Free churches, while Reformed and Lutheran churches have their own hymnbooks. Italian Baptists have shared the same hymnal with Waldensians and Methodists since 1922. Spanish Baptists have their own hymnal, which is also adopted by a few other independent churches.

Cultural Life

Baptists have their own seminaries, though occasionally some pastors receive part of their training in seminaries of other denominations.

Each national Baptist union has its own periodical. Italian Baptists have also a weekly paper, *Nuovi Tempi,* in common with Waldensians and Methodists, as well as a bimonthly periodical for young people, *Gioventú Evangelica,* a common magazine since 1962.

Associations of Protestant students exist in France and Italy, but Baptists participate in them only as private individuals, and not as representatives of Baptist groups.

Committees

The Protestant Federation of France, organized in 1905, includes Baptists. They are also officially related to the Evangelical Mission of Paris and to the French Alliance for the Bible.

Italian Baptists have been members of the Federal Council of the Italian Evangelical Churches since its foundation (1946), together with the Waldensians and the Methodists. In 1967 the Federal Council merged into a Federation of Evangelical Churches in Italy, which includes Waldensians, Methodists, Baptists, and Lutherans. A Federation of Evangelical Youth Groups has also been formed. The Baptist Sunday school work is closely related to that of the Waldensians and Methodists.

A Spanish Evangelical Council is the only committee which relates Spanish Protestants and Baptists on a national level, and it is only consultative in nature. A Council for Evangelical Defense deals with matters of relations between the State and Evangelical minorities. Baptists withdrew from it in 1968. Pastoral associations or councils exist locally or regionally for practical purposes, and Baptists in general participate in them.

In Portugal a Council for Cooperation among the Evangelical Churches has been organized, but "its activity is very limited."[22]

Congresses

In France the Protestant Federation organizes periodic national congresses to which Baptists also send their representatives. At the 12th General Assembly of French Protestants in 1966 the idea of transforming the Federation into the United Evangelical Church of France was discussed, but Baptists are against such a project.[23]

In Italy the first National Congress of Evangelical Churches was held in 1920.[24] Waldensians, Methodists, Free Evangelicals, and Baptists were represented. The idea of a Federation was discussed, but no action was taken.

The second National Congress met in 1965. Besides Waldensians, Methodists, and Baptists, the Brethren and the Pentecostals were also represented. The main resolution concerning the foundation of a Federation was enacted two years later.

Evangelical congresses were held in Spain in 1919 and 1929. Their resolutions concerned mainly the defense of religious freedom and the observance of joint prayer services among Evangelicals.[25]

ATTITUDES

France

Although Baptists participate with Lutherans and Reformed in the same Federation, they seem to be more open for cooperation with the churches of revivalistic type. This impression is confirmed by the report given at the Baptist convention of 1964 on the subject of Baptist relationships with the other Evangelical churches.[26] Baptist relationships with the churches of professing believers were reported to be very good, but relations within the Protestant Federation were minimal. Baptists are the smallest group, the only one which is not pedobaptist, the only believers' church, the only congregationalists, and the only church which is not a member of the World Council of Churches.

On the other hand, the attitude of French Baptists toward the churches of revivalistic type, particularly in regard to evangelistic activity, is much more cordial.[27]

Italy

In Italy, Baptists appear to have a closer relationship with pedobaptist churches like the Waldensians and the Methodists than with believer's baptism churches. With the Pentecostals or the Brethren, for instance, the Baptists have very little connection. As early as 1951 the first national Congress of Evangelical Youth was stressing ecumenical relations among Protestants. The Baptist Youth Congress of 1962 resolved "to cooperate more closely with Waldensian and Methodist young people, particularly in the fields of publications and summer camps."[28] The churches in general moved more slowly but steadily in the same direction. At the convention of 1967 the resolution to become members of the Protestant Federation was accepted without real opposition, although stress was laid on full respect of Baptist autonomy.[29]

Spain and Portugal

In general it seems correct to say that every denomination in these two countries works in its own field without caring much for the others. From the limited connections established with other Protestants and the scanty references to them in their periodical literature, it appears that Baptists just respect them as good neighbors. The awareness of "spiritual unity" helps to overcome the "scandal of divisions."[30]

BAPTISTS AND ROMAN CATHOLICISM

No kind of stable connection has been established between Baptists and Roman Catholics in any of the four countries. Occasional encounters, however, are becoming less rare in some places. In Italy, for instance, Baptists were represented for the first time at the Week for Ecumenical Studies of Camaldoli, organized by the Catholic Secretariat for Promoting Christian Unity.[31] In Spain, Baptist Pastor José Cardona was invited to speak at the Universities of Salamanca and Valladolid in 1966.[32]

In all four countries, the traditional attitude of Baptists toward the Roman Catholic Church has been one of stern opposition and condemnation. Roman Catholics, on the other side, have opposed, reviled, and sometimes persecuted Baptists, together with the other Protestants, in each of the four countries which are under consideration here.

But a different attitude seems to have emerged, at least in some circles, during the last decade. The language has become less offensive, the anti-Catholic polemics less ironical and bellicose. But the most striking development is the increasing attention given by Baptists to the problem of Christian unity. Beginning with the 1960s—after Vatican II had been announced—this topic rapidly grew in importance in all four national magazines.[33] This renewed interest developed in two main directions: the attempt to elaborate a correct concept of Christian unity and the effort to evaluate correctly the ecumenism of the Roman Catholic Church. Let us examine each of these separately even though they are related.[34]

CHRISTIAN UNITY

Baptists of Southern Europe seem to agree on the idea that Christian unity should not be thought of in terms of structural or institutional unity, which is inconceivable for them not only in regard to the Roman Church, but also among Protestants themselves. The main reason given for this is Baptist congregationalism. Over against the institutional unity, however, the value of spiritual unity is emphasized. This unity is a gift of God, they say, and it exists already between the Evangelical churches. Reciprocal love and cooperation among them should be increased, particularly in the area of evangelism and social service. In regard to the Church of Rome, however, even spiritual unity is very difficult to realize. The main obstacle is Catholic ecclesiology, or rather Rome's claim to be the only true church of Jesus Christ. Such an exclusive claim, wherever it exists and whenever it is raised, makes spiritual unity impossible.

CATHOLIC ECUMENISM

As for Baptist evaluations of Roman Catholic ecumenism, three main attitudes seem to be typical of the 1960s.

1. There are some who think that what is happening within the Roman Catholic Church does not concern Baptists at all. Thus the election of the new pope, for instance, was ignored or reported simply as a matter of chronicle, and Vatican II was considered not an ecumenical Council, but an internal meeting of the Church of Rome.

2. Many think that Catholic ecumenism is simply a new tactic to make painless the return to Rome of the other Christians. Thus, to invite non-Catholic observers to Vatican II was only a matter of courtesy (and Baptists were right in refusing to send their official representative). No change is seen as possible in the area of Catholic doctrines; therefore the reasons that called for the Reformation are valid today as they were four centuries ago.

3. Some think that substantial changes are taking place within Catholicism, making closer cooperation possible. Admittedly it is too early to evaluate how deep these changes go, but Baptists acknowledge that the Spirit can blow where he wills and accomplish things that were unthinkable a few years ago. This requires readiness on their side to abandon old prejudices and to adjust to radical new situations.

CHANGES AND TRENDS

The traditional attitude of Baptists has been one of respectful or friendly neighborliness toward other Protestants, with different emphasis according to the national situation, and of stern opposition against Roman Catholicism.

After World War II, the relationship with Protestants improved in various degrees in the different countries, particularly in regard to religious freedom, evangelism, and social service. Everywhere the attitude toward Roman Catholicism remained one of distance and distrust.

During the last fifteen years renewed attention has been given to the problem of Christian unity. As a result, Baptists developed new forms of fellowship and cooperation with other Evangelical churches in some areas, while toward Catholicism a new attitude of cautious interest and sometimes of confident hope is timidly emerging alongside the old antagonism. Alongside the old distrust, there is a new tendency "to wait and see." Among these Baptists, who are sometimes attacked but more often tolerated by the majority, there exists what might be called the attitude of Gamaliel: [35] wait and see what happens before we judge, lest we be found fighting against God.

CHAPTER 6

American Baptist Churches in the U.S.A.

Robert G. Torbet

The relationships under consideration in this presentation are of the greatest importance to American Baptists as they are to all other Christians in our world today. We live in a time when mankind is increasingly impatient with the building of Berlin walls and the erection of barriers to mutual understanding and fellowship which will eliminate the threat of war and ensure some degree of peace that is more certain than we have known in our troubled century.

But even more impressive as a reason for the importance of the topic is the very nature of the Christian gospel which we proclaim: that God is reconciling the world to himself through the ministry of Jesus Christ and his church in the world. But how can the world believe that this Good News is dependable unless we who bear the name of Christ become God's showpiece of what the love of Christ can do to create a new humanity bound together in mutual concern by the transforming power of divine love at work in our hearts? Therefore, we must take seriously the prayer of our Lord for the unity of the church as he expressed it on the night of his betrayal in the long ago (John 17:20-21).

We may begin this presentation by summarizing briefly the position of American Baptists in the movement toward Christian unity which has characterized the history of the church in the twentieth century.

53

AMERICAN BAPTISTS AND CHRISTIAN UNITY

From the inception of the Northern Baptist Convention in 1907, American Baptists have been involved officially as participants in various national expressions of Christian Protestant unity in the United States. They were participants in the Foreign Missions Conference of North America organized in 1893, and in the Home Missions Council organized in 1908. Also, in 1908, the Convention became a charter member of the Federal Council of Churches of Christ in America. Later, American Baptists became members of the International Missionary Council (1921) and the International Council of Religious Education (1922). In 1950 the Convention participated in the formation of the National Council of Churches of Christ in the U.S.A.

To the present time, American Baptists have participated overseas in national Christian councils established in Asia and Africa in the 1920s. They also were represented in the World Conference on Faith and Order and the Universal Christian Council for Life and Work which arose out of the World Missionary Conference of 1910. When the World Council of Churches was provisionally constituted in 1938 at Utrecht, the Northern Baptist Convention was a participant.

The Northern Baptist Convention entered into a merger with the Free Will Baptists in 1911. When, however, the Convention was invited in March, 1919, to participate in a council to consider organic union of several denominations in an Evangelical Church of the U.S.A., the Executive Committee declined on the grounds that organic union with other denominations was impossible. The reasons given included such explanations as the following: (1) The Convention is a collection of independent democratic churches and so cannot enter into plans of union. (2) The Baptists' rejection of sacerdotalism and sacramentalism and their view of local church ordination would be unacceptable to some other communions.[1] Between 1930 and 1947, the Convention engaged without success in merger talks with the Disciples of Christ. Since 1961, conversations have been authorized by the General Council with the Church of the Brethren, the Disciples of Christ, and Seventh Day Baptists, all of which denominations share with American Baptists a commitment to believer's baptism. But beyond this familiar context there has not been widespread enthusiasm for church union, as became evident from the Baptist response to the Consultation on Church Union.

The Consultation had come into existence in response to a call issued by Dr. Eugene Carson Blake, then Stated Clerk of the United Presbyterian Church, U.S.A., to denominations that had emerged out of divisions created by efforts to reform the Church of England in the seventeenth and eighteenth centuries. In time nine major denominations with a common heritage of Reformed theology and an Anglican church background—Presbyterians, Disciples, Methodists, and Episcopalians—appointed commissions to engage in the quest of a new Church of Christ Uniting that would be truly catholic, truly evangelical, and truly reformed. This bold venture had a strong appeal for many American Baptists who felt a closer tie with these churches in ecumenical relationships than with some other Baptist bodies with whom they had little contact.

It is not surprising, therefore, that the General Council responded favorably in 1963 to an invitation from the Consultation on Church Union to appoint observer-consultants to attend its annual plenary sessions. Then, when the Consultation in 1965 invited all denominations represented by observer-consultants to become full participants, the General Council undertook a study of the invitation. After several months of earnest discussion and exposure to widespread debate within the Convention, the Council members voted in February, 1966, not to seek full participation at that time, but to maintain the observer-consultant relationship.

To avoid giving the impression that this decision was a retreat from the movement toward greater Christian unity, the Council also voted to increase American Baptist participation in councils of churches and in efforts to strengthen unity among Baptists. Behind this decision was a feeling that the churches were not yet ready to engage in church union across a wide spectrum of denominations. Certainly there was no basis for widespread support of participation in the Consultation. Some argued that the talks had advanced beyond a point where the Baptist position regarding infant baptism, the bishop's office, and creeds could be influential. Others were convinced that the achievement of unity among Baptist bodies was a goal to be preferred over seeking union with other denominations. Those who wanted to be involved in the search for a new and more inclusive church were keenly disappointed with the decision.

The decision, in fact, reflected a divided house on the issue. There were almost as many who favored participation as there were those who opposed it. To offset the effects of polarization, the

General Council created a Commission on Christian Unity with Convention approval in May, 1966. The Commission was to engage in a study of the issues surrounding Baptist involvement in Christian unity and to participate in such conversations with other church bodies as should be authorized by the General Council.

The action was timely, for the issues were numerous and complex. For some, there seemed to be the likelihood of American Baptists being left on the sidelines of progressive American Protestantism if they were to have no part in the union talks of the main-line denominations with whom they were involved in so many cooperative relationships in councils of churches and in the cooperation of local congregations in many communities. For others, there was a pressing need for American Baptists to heal divisions among Baptist bodies and so to strengthen the Free church position in the ecumenical movement. For still others, it did not seem necessary that the issues should polarize Baptists in either direction. For them, the option was to engage in a deepening of ecumenical responsibility through councils of churches, while at the same time seeking to unite the Baptist fellowship interracially as well as ecclesiastically. It became increasingly clear that Baptists, like other Christians, would need to be drawn more and more in the days ahead into contacts with people of other faiths and with people of no faith. The issues demanding attention were not restricted to ecclesiastical concerns, but included survival concerns arising out of overpopulation, worldwide hunger, and the threat of nuclear destruction.

These varied concerns were caught up in a Statement on Christian Unity prepared by the Commission and adopted as a Standing Resolution by the Convention in May, 1967. It was intended to be a basis of general agreement from which American Baptists might pursue together an honest quest for the leading of the Holy Spirit in determining their role in the Christian world mission needed in the present day. Aware of the truth that the followers of Christ are already one in him, the Statement affirmed an obligation of Baptists to discover in what sense they are one and to manifest this oneness more fully. Grateful to the commitment of their Baptist forebears "to such principles as religious freedom, the priesthood of all believers, and believer's baptism," and for the enrichment received from the witness of other Christians to an understanding of the fullness of the gospel, they saw Christian unity, not as "an end in itself, but a means whereby the ultimate mission of God's redemption of the world may be accomplished."[2] During the next two years, the Commission on Christian Unity formulated, with assistance of the Advisory Board for Theological Studies, "An American Baptist Reaction to the Principles of Church Union and Guidelines for Structure of the Consultation on Church Union." Through subcommittees, it was also involved in dialogue with the Roman Catholics, in merger talks with the Church of the Brethren, and in conversations with the Progressive National Baptist Convention to explore closer working relationships with the American Baptist Convention. In addition, members of the Commission encouraged the initial planning of a National Baptist Leaders' Consultation held in Washington, D.C., November 18-20, 1967, under the auspices of the North American Baptist Fellowship. They also participated in three regional Pastors' Conversations Concerning Christian Unity conducted in New York (November 6, 1967), Los Angeles (February 26, 1968), and Chicago (March 18, 1968).

Four major ecumenical emphases, developed by the Commission and the Division of Cooperative Christianity, received approval of the General Council in February, 1968. They called for intensifying and enlarging the ecumenical witness of American Baptists through the conciliar movement, for engaging American Baptists in a denominational program of ecumenical education looking toward an effective ecumenical strategy at all levels, for continued engagement in and evaluation of conversations and consultative relationships authorized by the General Council, and for engagement in conversations and cooperative efforts with other Baptists especially through the North American Baptist Fellowship.

These ecumenical emphases not only have given scope to the task of the Commission but have served to challenge American Baptists to give priority to the fuller dimensions of their life and mission.

For example, American Baptists, who are fairly well involved in councils of churches at the national and world levels, have allowed cooperative activities at this higher level to progress beyond the real understanding and commitment of local churches to the basic purposes of the ecumenical movement. Many American Baptists have enjoyed occasional celebrations in cooperation with other Christians nationally in the World Day of Prayer, in the Week of Prayer for Christian Unity, and in joint Thanksgiving services or

Good Friday observances. Some have joined in supporting relief projects through Church World Service or UNICEF. But they have neglected the task of bringing about the unity of the church where disunity is most evident and costly, that is, in local communities. The task of developing a local ecumenical witness is, to be sure, the hardest of all, for it threatens most immediately parochially vested interests and touches most painfully prejudices and pride of self-identity.

This local witness to Christian unity is essential for at least two reasons. One is that it can produce the atmosphere and understanding out of which national and world ecumenical bodies can move forward in their attempts to remove the barriers between Christians. The other reason is that it can provide in the community a continuing evidence of genuine love and harmony among Christians and of their united efforts to apply the gospel to the conditions and needs of men and women.

DEVELOPING NEW ATTITUDES AND RELATIONSHIPS

Since 1968, a number of ways have been developed to relate American Baptists more fully to the ecumenical dimensions of witness and mission in the days ahead.

1. One way has been to keep pastors and laity informed through a quarterly newsletter, *Christian Unity,* regarding the widespread and varied kinds of involvement of American Baptists in the conciliar movement, in the hope that an increasing number of churches will see the importance of participating in local and regional councils as well as in less formal modes of cooperation.

2. Another was to conduct in 1968–1969 a number of regional conferences of laity and clergy in areas where interest was strong for participation in the Consultation on Church Union. The purpose was to engage them in exploring ways of maintaining a close working relationship with Consultation churches short of participation in a plan of union. This proved useful in formulating recommendations to the General Council on the one hand and to the Executive Committee of the Consultation on the other hand. It also served as a useful educational process for American Baptists in finding creative ecumenical alternatives to church union for the crucial days ahead.

3. When it became evident that the proposed Plan of Union of the Consultation on Church Union was to include a provision whereby any local congregation of another denomination might

apply for membership in the new church, American Baptists requested that provision be made to permit such churches, if they wished, to remain in alignment with the parent body as well as to be a member of the new church. This was important also for a number of American Baptist congregations already in alignment with a denomination in the Consultation. The request was granted, and a provision was included in the proposed Plan of Union that would meet both of these needs.

4. "Guidelines for Interchurch Relations" were formulated in response to needs expressed in the regional conferences referred to above. They were designed to enable American Baptist congregations to participate in various patterns of cooperation across denominational lines while still maintaining a responsible relationship to the American Baptist Convention. Those who have, at the present time, no interest in such relationships are under no coercion to utilize them. But, if and when they do feel a need for such guidance, options are available for which there will be a background of experience of other American Baptist congregations.

5. In the fall of 1970, the Commission on Christian Unity completed the formulation of ecumenical objectives and strategies which were to be part of the denomination's "Mission in Reconciling Action for the Seventies." These pointed in the direction not only of a deepened commitment to cooperation with other Baptist bodies and with other Christian communions but also of a serious consideration of what should be the role of American Baptists in relation to the developing ecumenical trends among other Christian churches both locally and nationally. Local congregations and regional groups were encouraged to select specific goals and tactics which would be most appropriate to their respective situation and needs at a given time. Over a period of three to five years, it seemed to be possible for a congregation or area unit to emphasize most of the tactics suggested and so be involved in a well-rounded ecumenical strategy.

6. Because there was within the American Baptist Convention a variety of views concerning the degree of inclusiveness of the Christian fellowship, the Commission on Christian Unity prepared in 1971 "A Guide to Assist Churches in Examining the Nature, Extent, and Implications of Christian Fellowship." It was intended to provide a way by which American Baptists could

examine assumptions which they had about themselves with a view to enlarging their understanding of God's will for their relationships with other Christians. Indeed, it was believed that such a study could enrich the life of congregations by deepening their appreciation of the biblical meaning of fellowship at a time when there was need for the unifying power of a community fused together by the Holy Spirit despite many diversities within it.

7. The Division of Cooperative Christianity and the Commission on Christian Unity continued their responsibilities in specific relationships authorized by the General Council. These included in the seventies: (a) culmination of talks that led in 1970 to an "associated relationship" of the American Baptist Convention with the Progressive National Baptist Convention which encouraged a free flow of fellowship and cooperation between the two national bodies; (b) the achievement in 1973 of the same kind of relationship with the Church of the Brethren; (c) continued dialogue with Roman Catholics on issues which involved a sharing of insights concerning the church, its polity, and its mission, with joint publication of a progress report of the dialogue entitled *Growing in Understanding; (d)* a continued observer-consultant role in the Consultation on Church Union.

AMERICAN BAPTIST ECUMENICAL INVOLVEMENTS

How involved are American Baptists in ecumenical witness and mission? To get at the facts, the Commission on Christian Unity authorized an approach in 1969 to executive ministers of city societies, state and regional conventions, and national program agencies to determine ways in which their administrative unit was involved in ecumenical participation. Replies came from thirty-one regional and city units and from all of the national boards and agencies. They varied in details, but in general they indicated that every executive was able to report some degree of cooperation by his group in the wider Christian fellowship. In numerous instances, the extensiveness of involvement revealed a growing readiness of American Baptists across the Convention for joint action in mission, and here and there for some kind of ecclesiastical unification.

The regional and local picture revealed substantial participation in councils of churches. Eighteen of the twenty-five state conventions reporting were members of a state council; and seven of eight city societies belonged to a city council. Two state conventions which were not members of a council participated unofficially in some phase of joint ministry conducted by the respective councils.

Joint action in mission was the predominant form of ecumenical involvement of American Baptists in regional areas, as it was nationally. In this respect, a variety of projects claimed their attention and support. They included involvement of the city societies and at least two state conventions in ecumenical ministries to meet concerns of the inner city; numerous cooperative campus ministries across the country; and a variety of cooperative projects, such as work among migrants in Arizona, ecumenical camp planning and joint sponsorship of laboratory and mission-training conferences in a half dozen states, joint planning for parish development in at least nine states, and joint staff development on the principle of one mission of all churches in an area, as in Massachusetts, Cleveland (Ohio), and to some extent in Idaho.

A notable example of cooperation was in Puerto Rico, where for many years American Baptists had been cooperating in an Evangelical Union Seminary (to educate ministers for five denominations) and in a Protestant Council of Churches which conducted cooperative ministries in state institutions, on campuses, and in the use of radio. A more recently developed ecumenical project was a training program for pastors in slum areas shared by Protestants (including Baptists) and Roman Catholics. Puerto Rican pastors were being sent to the Urban Training Center in Chicago for this new ministry to destitute people.

The most advanced move of American Baptists to some form of ecclesiastical unification was reported by Rhode Island Baptists. The state convention's Committee on Ecumenical Relations was exploring cooperation with a similar committee in the United Church of Christ. The Convention received in November, 1968, a recommendation from its Board of Managers to "respond affirmatively to the invitation of the Rhode Island State Council of Churches to engage in conversation and consultation regarding closer ecumenical associations and work and witness with other Christian bodies in Rhode Island and that a committee of six be appointed to represent our Convention." To facilitate closer relations and a mutual recognition of memberships of the various churches in the state, a policy of open membership was recommended to American Baptist churches by the Board of Managers.

A further notable instance of encouragement by American Baptists of ecclesiastical unification was evident in the growing conversations and increasing development of joint projects with congregations of the Church of the Brethren. In nearly all states where the two communions shared a witness, executive secretaries of both groups were furthering these contacts.

An appreciable number of American Baptist churches were engaged in ecumenical conversation with Roman Catholics, principally through "living-room dialogues." This development was reported particularly by the District of Columbia Baptist Convention, the Arizona Baptist Convention, and the Vermont Baptist Convention. Local correspondents report that this activity was typical of what was going on in many areas of the denomination.

The national picture was even more impressive, for national program agencies had long been involved in interdenominational cooperation. Indeed, many of their efforts in witness and mission had been effective to the degree in which they had been performed ecumenically. These efforts had not in any way compromised the unique witness of American Baptists. Instead, they enabled Baptists to share their insights and contributions with other communions and to be benefited, in turn, by the insights and contributions of other Christians.

The chief avenue for this ecumenical participation was conciliar, that is, through the National Council of Churches of Christ in the U.S.A. and the World Council of Churches. Within each of these councils were cognate units which roughly paralleled the units of mission within the Convention. These are described in the following paragraphs, using the new names of units in the restructured American Baptist Churches in the U.S.A. (as the American Baptist Convention was renamed when restructure proposals were adopted in May, 1972) and in the National Council of Churches (as it was restructured by vote of its Ninth Assembly in December, 1972).

The Board of International Ministries cooperates fully in the National Council of Churches through the Division of Overseas Ministries and through representation on the Governing Board of the Council. The Board of International Ministries also has representation in the World Council of Churches and the executive committee of the Baptist World Alliance. In virtually every geographical area of the Board's involvement, the indigenous Baptist conventions to which it is related are members of their respective national Christian councils. Several of these have joined the World Council of Churches. Most of the Baptist conventions in Asia belong to the East Asia Christian Conference. The Baptist Convention in Zaire is in the All-Africa Conference of Churches.

The Board of International Ministries cooperates in many interdenominational institutions and projects, such as Union Christian College (Assam), Serampore College (India), Andhra Christian Theological College (South India), Japan International Christian University, Chung Chi College (Hong Kong), Thailand Theological Seminary, Evangelical Theological School of Kinshasa (Zaire), and Christian Medical College and Hospital (Vellore, India). This list is far from comprehensive of the Board's numerous ecumenical involvements. In addition, a number of American Baptist missionaries are on loan to ecumenical projects in several places. Plans call for further deployment of missionaries in response to specific appeals.

The Board of National Ministries is heavily involved, through program relationships, in the Division of Church and Society of the National Council of Churches. It also is involved in the NCC's Division of Overseas Ministries because of participation in refugee resettlement and Servicemen's Centers.

The Board of National Ministries is also a participant in new forms of task-oriented cooperation, such as the Interreligious Foundation for Community Organization (IFCO) and the Joint Strategy and Action Committee (JSAC), which is composed of six denominations plus one unit of the National Council.

On many of the fields in which the Board has missionaries, there is substantial ecumenical involvement. This is evident in several Christian centers, some church extension work, town and country larger parishes, and the chaplaincies (military, penal, and health institutions). The Board is represented on the General Commission on Chaplains and Armed Forces Personnel and on similar groups which exist for chaplains in mental, hospital, and penal institutions.

The Board of Educational Ministries participates in the National Council of Churches through its representatives on the governing board, in program units, and in department committees. Indeed, its educational ministry and curriculum development have a long history of such cooperation. Like the Southern Baptists, it served on the International Uniform Lessons Committee and the Committee on the Graded Series long before the National Council was organized. The most notable recent example of the values of such cooperation in Christian education has been the Cooperative Curriculum Project, an interdenominational study in which American Baptists participated from 1960 to 1965 to develop a broader base for the church's mission that would be soundly biblical, theological, and educational. Since 1965, the then named Board of Education and Publication developed, in cooperation with five denominations, a new curriculum based upon the insights of that Cooperative Curriculum Project. It is now available to American Baptist churches as the Christian Faith and Work Plan.

In 1968 the Board gave full approval to relating the work of its Department of Campus Christian Life to the United Ministries in Higher Education. As a consequence, American Baptists became one of ten denominations in an ecumenical campus ministry.

On the world scene, the Board of Educational Ministries participates in the World Council of Churches' Division of World Mission and Evangelism.

The Division of Communications, which is related to the Board of Educational Ministries, does much of its work ecumenically. Its Department of Radio and Television participates in the Broadcasting and Film Commission of the National Council of Churches and belongs to the World Association of Christian Communication. The Division cooperates with councils of churches in broadcasting in local areas and in developing a series of communication seminars. It also uses and contributes to the Religious News Service, which is an interfaith channel.

The Ministers and Missionaries Benefit Board is a member of the widely ecumenical annual Church Pensions Conference, an organization over fifty years old which functions outside the National Council of Churches. All major denominations are involved, including the Southern Baptists. Indirectly, the M & M Board is further involved ecumenically through the relationships of the American Baptist Commission on the Ministry.

The Commission on Christian Unity, related to the General Board, is by its very nature ecumenical. Its basic task is to encourage a deeper understanding of the meaning of Christian unity and to pursue conversations with other bodies upon authorization of the General Board. Through the Office of Ecumenical Relations, the ecumenical representation of American Baptists is administered and the contacts of the denomination with other bodies are coordinated and developed. The Office of Ecumenical Relations is particularly related to the Commission on Regional and Local Ecumenism and the Faith and Order Commission in the National Council, to the Committee on Interpretation and Support of the World Council, to the Baptist World Alliance and North American Baptist Fellowship, to Religion in American Life, and to the American Bible Society. It also seeks to maintain close contact with committees on cooperative Christianity in regional and state conventions and in city societies of the denomination.

The unit known as *American Baptist Men,* related to the Board of Educational Ministries, has a staff relationship to the Department of United Church Men in the National Council of Churches and is also concerned with the Men's Department of the Baptist World Alliance.

American Baptist Women, also related to the Board of Educational Ministries, is involved in ecumenical participation in four principal ways: (1) cooperation in the North American Baptist Women's Union, which conducts a Baptist Day of Prayer and holds an assembly every five years for fellowship and inspiration; (2) cooperation in Church Women United of the National Council of Churches, which involves participation in such programs as racial integration, legislation on major issues, training of leadership, and Women in Community Service; (3) participation in a Commission on Coordination of Men and Women in Church and Society, and, (4) encouragement of cooperation with the Church of the Brethren and the Progressive National Baptist Convention, Inc., respectively.

The Division of World Mission Support is related to the Commission on Stewardship and Benevolence in the National Council of Churches. Through its Department of American Baptist Films, the Division of World Mission Support is related to the NCC's Broadcasting and Film Commission.

From this brief survey, it becomes clear that American Baptists are involved in ecumenical witness and mission in a variety of ways. This trend is in response to a growing awareness that, together with other Christians, they can be more effective in their ministry to human needs in these changing times.

CHAPTER 7

Southern Baptist Convention (U.S.A.)

Raymond O. Ryland

Throughout the United States there are Southern Baptist churches sharing with congregations of other traditions in a wide variety of community service programs. Many Southern Baptists (pastors, missionaries, college chaplains, denominational leaders, seminary professors) work closely with their counterparts in other denominations. Yet there is among Southern Baptists a consistent majority opinion sharply opposed to denominational involvement in the Ecumenical Movement. For over half a century this majority opinion has been expressed through actions of the Convention in its annual sessions and through its agencies.

Ironically, the story of Southern Baptist relations, as a denomination, with other Christian bodies properly begins with an account of ecumenical pioneering by a Southern Baptist leader and by the Convention itself. Under the prompting of that leader (and presumably of the Holy Spirit), the Southern Baptist Convention was the first denominational body to summon other traditions to what is now called Faith and Order discussions.

A SOUTHERN PROPOSAL IN THE 1890s

In 1910 an Episcopal bishop had a vision. This vision is significant because it is commonly regarded as marking the beginning of the modern Faith and Order Movement. While attending the Edinburgh Missionary Conference, Bishop Charles H. Brent, a missionary in the Philippines, had a vision of the churches coming together in a similar conference to discuss issues of doctrine.

Primarily at his instigation, the General Convention of the Protestant Episcopal Church issued a call in 1910 for a world conference to study matters of Faith and Order. After long delay, the first Faith and Order Conference was held in Lausanne, Switzerland, in 1927.

In 1889 a Southern Baptist pastor and denominational editor had caught a similar vision. Bishop Brent's vision has been well described and widely reported. Thomas Treadwell Eaton's vision has scarcely been noted even by Southern Baptists. His anticipation of key features of contemporary Faith and Order conferences has never been acknowledged.

In the twenty years prior to his death in 1907, Eaton was both pastor of the Walnut Street Baptist Church in Louisville and editor of the *Western Recorder*. He first outlined his vision of Christian unity in an editorial in the last issue of his paper for 1889. The only way to help bring Christians together, he insisted, is to study the Bible anew, to learn what it teaches on the points over which Christians are divided. He proposed that "representative men and competent scholars" from the denominations come together to "consider the differences of belief from the Bible standpoint." Even though scholars could not agree on all points, they could establish some agreement and clear the field of "much useless and cumbersome rubbish." He urged the denominations that had been talking about Christian union to consider this approach.[1]

At its meeting in Fort Worth in 1890, in line with resolutions submitted by Eaton, the Southern Baptist Convention suggested that other denominations appoint "representative scholars" to study together the biblical teaching on those points of doctrine and polity over which the denominations are divided. At least, said the Convention, this concerted study could help achieve "a better understanding of the issues involved." It was also proposed that the results of such a conference "be widely published in all denominational papers, so that the Christian public may be thoroughly informed" and that "progress may be made toward true Christian union."[2]

In an editorial in late 1890 Eaton explained that, while each denomination claims to base its peculiar doctrines in Scripture, Christians have not divided simply because they disagree on what the Bible teaches. Differences in doctrine first arise "from the depths" of men's "consciousness" and "from the influences around them. . . . " Then they run "to the Bible to hunt texts to support that doctrine." In other words, "The difference of doctrine precedes the difference of interpretation [of Scripture]."[3] Here Eaton foresaw problems with which the Faith and Order Movement would wrestle several decades later: the relation of Scripture and tradition and the role of "non-theological factors" in Christian disunity.

Almost as noteworthy as Eaton's pioneering proposal was the lack of response. At their annual convention in the fall of 1890, the Disciples of Christ took note of the Southern Baptist message. Otherwise the plea fell on deaf denominational ears. Eaton sent copies of the resolutions to a number of denominational papers, with a request for their reactions, but received no replies. In one of his many reminders to his readers about the 1890 "deliverance," he asked why there had been an "ominous and protracted silence" on the part of other denominations. The reason, he insisted slyly, could not be that other traditions thought Baptists' opinions were unimportant. After all, those who advocated Christian union never tired of declaring: "The 'narrow' and 'illiberal' views of Baptists are the great barrier to union." Therefore, Eaton concluded, "What Baptists think on the subject is thus admitted to be of supreme importance."[4]

The 1894 session of the Convention appointed a committee to reply to a fraternal letter received from the Disciples of Christ. In their response to the 1890 convention's proposal, the Disciples had begun analyzing issues which needed to be discussed. The Convention committee agreed that the time had come to move beyond generalities, but again insisted that these matters be handled by a conference of scholars. The committee assured the Disciples' convention that "our convention has committed itself to co-operation in the effort to bring about such a conference" as it had called for in 1890. If the Disciples would appoint a committee, the Southern Baptist Committee would ask the next convention to join in "trying to induce as many as possible of the other denominations to enter into the proposed conference."[5]

The Disciples evidently misunderstood the Convention's insistence on dealing in depth with basic theological issues. The Baptist concern for careful study seemed to some Disciples merely a lack of interest in Christian unity. Not long after the Disciples' convention received the Baptist reply to its fraternal letter, one of the Disciples' papers reported that the spirit of the report was "kind and cordial, but there seemed to be little enthusiasm upon the subject of union." The Baptists "are evidently not very anxious for union. Their fondness for denominational peculiarities stands in the way." [6]

At the 1895 Southern Baptist Convention the messengers were informed that the Disciples' convention had postponed action on the Baptist committee's response. There the story ends. Never again did any *Annual* refer either to this exchange or to the 1890 convention's proposal which had provoked the exchange.

In retrospect, one can see that Eaton probably expected too much from the work of scholars, even scholars guided by the Holy Spirit. Yet he clearly anticipated the direction which the Faith and Order Movement would later take. In his editorials he rejected two extremes in ecumenical outreach (the lowest-common-denominator approach, and the "ultimatum" approach), which have been tried and found wanting. He urged the kind of painstaking faith and order discussions to which many Christians were finally led a generation later. He called attention to the role of "non-theological factors" and divergent traditions in Christian disunity. He insisted on wide dissemination of the results of the proposed conference, as the later movement tried to do.

SOUTHERN BAPTIST RESPONSE TO OTHER ECUMENICAL PROPOSALS

At its session in 1911, the Southern Baptist Convention received the Episcopal church's call for a world conference to discuss matters of Faith and Order and voted to accept the invitation. The committee appointed to reply favorably reported to the 1912 convention that it had expressed its gratitude for the "increasing spiritual unity among all the true followers of our Lord." In behalf of the Convention, the committee had promised to use "all suitable means" to promote "this real, impressing and growing union among all Christians." While the Baptist committee could see no possibility of organic union, it believed the matter should be fully discussed. The Convention committee asserted that great progress would surely be made toward unity of belief and practice when Christians "sit together and on terms of loving and prayerful intercourse" seriously consider their varying points of view, at the same time submitting themselves "more and more fully to the guidance of their common Lord and Saviour." [7]

In 1913 the most influential of all Southern Baptist statements on Christian unity was issued by the Baptist General Convention of Texas, meeting in Dallas in November. This statement is the basis of the Southern Baptist Convention's pronouncements on Christian union in 1914, in 1919, and in 1938; it is also reechoed in the Baptist World Alliance's "Message" to the world in 1923. The Texas document was largely written by James B. Gambrell, then editor of the *Baptist Standard* and professor at Southwestern Baptist Theological Seminary in Fort Worth. No one in the twentieth century has left on Southern Baptist life an imprint whose magnitude greatly exceeds that of Gambrell. His influence is especially dominant in Southern Baptist attitudes toward ecumenical involvement.

The position paper of the Texas convention expressed deep interest in all efforts being made "to reunite the scattered and ofttime antagonistic forces of Christendom." The convention declared: "We long for Christian union. We pray for it and will labor for it," but only on a scriptural basis; "we insist that it cannot and should not be secured on any other basis."[8] In this statement, as always, Southern Baptists distinguished between spiritual union and organic union, stressing the necessity for the former and rejecting the latter.

Then followed a summary of other Baptist beliefs, coupled with the assertion that Christian unity can be accomplished only when Christians agree in the truth. The Texas convention vigorously protested current efforts by ecumenical leaders to destroy denominational loyalties in order to bring about Christian unity. At the same time it referred to plans then being made for a Faith and Order Conference, expressing its belief that "a frank and fraternal communication of views and sentiments, through the public press and otherwise, would be helpful." The statement ended with a stirring call to Baptists throughout the world to turn with renewed zeal to "the propagation of those principles we all believe to be divinely given. . . ."[9]

The high-water mark of Southern Baptist interest in the Ecumenical Movement, as focused in planning for the Faith and Order Conference, was set in 1914. The report of the Faith and Order committee that year was optimistic; progress was being made, even though the conference probably could not be held for a number of years. In 1914 also the Convention produced its "Pronouncement on Christian Union and Denominational Efficiency," in some respects the most irenic ecumenical statement in the Convention's history.

The pronouncement begins by acknowledging that many evils have arisen out of Christian divisions. Jesus' prayer in John 17 and the many exhortations to unity in the Epistles clearly reveal that Christian unity is a matter of deepest concern to Jesus and his apostles. Southern Baptists stand squarely behind "every movement and cause" in which Christians of divergent beliefs may share "without doing violence to the sacred mandates of conscience and without impairing their sense of loyalty to Christ."[10]

The committee which prepared the statement (Edgar Young Mullins wrote the doctrinal section) set forth its conception of Southern Baptist views on key theological issues: the individual's relation to God, the meaning of regeneration and of baptism, the nature of the church, the church's relation to the state and to the world. Compromise, the pronouncement declared, has no place in the furtherance of Christian unity. "Much good will come of fraternal conference and interchange of view." A deeper unity of belief will arise only out of a "deepening and enriching of the life in Christ among Christians of all names. . . ."[11] Meanwhile, all Christians should cooperate in efforts toward moral, social, and civic reform (commonly known as "secular ecumenism").

The section on "denominational efficiency," written by Gambrell, has a different tone. It outlines a seven-point program for girding up Baptist loins, including the following measures: complete denominational and local-church autonomy; no "entangling alliances" with other groups holding different views of church life and order; devotion of all Southern Baptist resources to denominational enterprises; greater emphasis on training all Southern Baptists and enlisting them in the work of the denomination; seeking greater denominational harmony.[12]

There can be no doubt that the pronouncement as a whole is the "most definitive of all pronouncements of the Southern Baptist Convention concerning the ecumenical movement. . . ."[13] It is also the most diversely interpreted pronouncement of the Convention. Here is an example of the range of interpretation. On the one hand, it has been asserted that in this statement the Convention said "no" to the Ecumenical Movement. Estep's reference to the pronouncement gives little hint of its irenic tone.[14] On the other hand, Roberts-Thomson says, "The [1914 Convention's] statement on Christian union breathes a fine spirit, and urges co-operation in every way possible between God's people, pending the realisation of union."[15]

Who is right? In a sense, both are. The Convention did say "yes" to the Ecumenical Movement in its statement on Christian unity; the Convention said "no" to the Ecumenical Movement in the statement on denominational efficiency. The former statement is irenic, the latter is strongly denominational in tone. This contrast springs not alone from differences in the attitudes of Mullins and of Gambrell, the respective authors of the two sections. Combining two statements of widely differing tones seems to reflect the ambivalence of the Southern Baptist Convention toward the Ecumenical Movement at that time. The evaluation one makes of the stand taken by the 1914 convention depends on which of the two sections one emphasizes. Most Southern Baptists who have written about the 1914 convention seem to have focused on what Gambrell wrote about denominational efficiency, rather than on what Mullins said about the good to be realized by "fraternal conference and interchange of view."

The 1915 session of the Convention gave permanent structural form to its commitment to the planning of a Faith and Order Conference, naming the president and the two secretaries as a standing committee. The Convention voted to "re-affirm its interest" in the movement to bring about "a larger, more intelligent and practical unity among the followers of Christ" in all parts of the world. It also stressed "its sympathy with all sincere and wise efforts to secure among all Christians ever nearer approaches to that unity of the Spirit" which issues from loyalty to Jesus Christ.[16]

MISGIVINGS AND ALARM ABOUT
THE ECUMENICAL MOVEMENT

The 1916 report of the Convention's standing committee for the proposed conference marks the turning point in the Convention's attitude. The report itself is tentative and cautious. The real question, said the committee, is not whether such a conference should be held, but whether divided Christians are willing to undertake that effort. Except for the involvement of the Episcopalians there is no sign that the "prelatical bodies" (the hierarchically structured traditions) are willing to enter discussion about a Faith and Order Conference.

In its recommendation that the Convention continue its commitment to the proposed conference, the standing committee listed three arguments. The fact that the committee felt the need to offer arguments itself indicates a shift in stance. That shift appears also in the arguments themselves, which imply a less open attitude to dialogue. Southern Baptists should continue to participate in the planning because they must bear their witness to the necessity of the separation of church and state, the superiority of Baptist polity to vast ecclesiastical establishments, and the meaning of unity in distinction to uniformity.[17]

In 1918 the Convention committee had a new chairman, James B. Gambrell. The committee told the Convention that Baptists should always be ready "to meet their brethren of other communions in open, frank and brotherly conference on the vital matters of Faith and Order." The committee urged support of the conference so that Baptists could explain to other Christians and to the world "the grounds on which our people feel justified in maintaining a separate existence. Also, the grounds upon which it seems to us all Christians should unite."[18] Both the order in which the reasons are given and the relative weight attached to each are significant.

Shortly after the convention Gambrell wrote an article on "The Union Movement and Baptist Fundamentals." The article reflects Gambrell's mixed feelings about closer relationships with other denominations; it also shows plainly which feeling dominated the mixture. Having been appointed by the Southern Baptist Convention, Gambrell said he eagerly looked forward to meeting representatives of other denominations and to "lay[ing] on the table the things most certainly believed by Baptists as the true Apostolic ground upon which the Christian world may be reunited."[19]

As Gambrell went on to discuss "Baptist fundamentals" and the "union movement," the warmth (not to say vehemence) of his feelings about the union movement emerged. He described the union movement in the context in which Southern Baptists have always opposed it—on foreign mission fields. There he saw what seemed to him a widespread effort, well-financed and ably led, to establish a lowest-common-denominator faith; an effort sharply to delimit and parcel out to denominations the areas in which they could carry on missions; an effort to establish union schools and literature to break down doctrinal barriers among denominations at work on foreign fields; an effort to build up "indigenous churches" free to adapt and interpret the Christian message as they saw fit. All this Gambrell believed he saw, and more. He spoke in strongest terms against it: "If Baptists believe their fundamentals worth anything; if they have any conscience toward God concerning them," then the only attitude they can take "toward the seducing, undoing apostasy fostered by this movement" is an attitude of "consistent and persistent opposition."[20]

The same issue of the *Journal* gave a sampling of opinions on this subject. The opinions came from executive secretaries of the state Baptist conventions aligned with the Southern Baptist Convention. The secretary from Arkansas expressed his feelings with great vigor:

> The colossal Union Movement is a colossal blunder, but it threatens us Baptists unmistakably. My word to all the Baptist preachers of the land would be:
> Smite, smite, hip and thigh, the "bastard" Union movement, dear preachers of God's Book, by calling every Baptist soul under the reach of your prophetic voice to toe the denominational line, and then show his faith by his fruits.[21]

With one exception, the other opinions are similar to this and Gambrell's.

The growing Southern Baptist opposition to the Ecumenical Movement was further deepened by events involving home missions. When Gambrell's Committee on the World Crisis made its report to the 1918 convention, it urged more freedom for the denominations for religious work among soldiers in army camps in this country. Early in 1918, when the committee looked at this problem, it was, like Elijah's cloud, very small, "like a man's hand." In a year's time, when the Convention met in 1919, that small cloud had grown to cover the sky. It blotted out the ecumenical sun for the Southern Baptist Convention and its most influential leader, James B. Gambrell.

REJECTION OF THE UNITY MOVEMENT

At the opening of the Southern Baptist Convention in 1919, Gambrell gave a presidential address. This was the first presidential address in the Convention's history; it was also the most important, so far as the Convention's relations with other Christian bodies are concerned.

Gambrell vigorously attacked War Department policies which, he said, were calculated to break down denominationalism and to give Catholics an enormous advantage over non-Catholics in ministering to their men in the armed forces. At first Baptists had been allowed to send "camp pastors," ministers with no military connection, into the camps to serve Baptists soldiers and to evangelize those not converted to Christ. Other denominations enjoyed a similar privilege. This permission was later withdrawn, and the denominations were forced to channel their efforts through such interdenominational agencies as the YMCA. Moreover, while Protestants labored under these restrictions, Roman Catholics enjoyed a relatively free hand in their work among the soldiers.

Toward the end of his address, Gambrell summoned Southern Baptists to put their denominational fences in good order. Baptists must go it alone; they "are bound . . . to preach the full truth . . . of the divine revelation and make Christ's program, given in the Great Commission, effective wherever men live. . . ." Finally, he urged the Convention "to send out to our fellow Baptists everywhere a rallying call" which will unite them in delivering in all lands "the unique message of Christ and His apostles which we hold in trust for our brothers" throughout the world.[22] The Convention resoundingly approved Gambrell's address and arranged to send a copy of it to every Southern Baptist pastor and to deliver a copy by committee to the president of the United States.

In his book, *Baptists and Their Business,* published the same year, Gambrell explained why the objectionable government policies led him to reject the Ecumenical Movement. He charged that the unionizing movement had taken over war work of the denominations during World War I. He indicted John R. Mott, well-known ecumenical figure and leader in the YMCA, as being primarily responsible for the War Department's policy. He claimed that as general secretary of the International Committee of YMCAs Mott had persuaded the War Department to adopt his plan for religious work among the soldiers. The plan allowed for three expressions of religion in the camps: "Judaism, Catholicism, and YMCA-ism." as Gambrell called them.[23]

Southern Baptists like Gambrell had seen for years what appeared to be clear-cut efforts by leaders of the union movement to erase denominational lines in foreign mission work. Now they had felt at home the effects of that same effort. This frustration of their evangelistic work was the catalyst which precipitated the (by then) vast amount of Southern Baptist misgivings about, and negative feelings toward, the Ecumenical Movement. Sternly and almost unanimously the Convention rejected further participation in the organized movement. For half a century the 1919 convention's declaration on Christian union has accurately expressed the convictions of the Convention and a strong majority of Southern Baptists.

The 1919 statement began by insisting that Jesus intended spiritual unity, not "external and organic unity," for his people. Any scheme for unity which involves leadership "which we cannot appoint or dismiss, but to which we must in some degree surrender our autonomy" is simply "impossible for Baptists." Baptists have a "distinct witness to bear," and it must not be "mutilated or enfeebled." "To syndicate our denomination with other denominations would impair, if it did not destroy, this message." Southern Baptists have their own methods for carrying on their work. Instead of wasting time and causing confusion with "fruitless discussions of impracticable proposals" for unity, Southern Baptists must organize for themselves a program "so large, so progressive, so constructive, that it shall challenge the faith and imagination of our people." They will continue to work and pray for "a Scriptural union," but will resist all attempts to bring about "union on any other basis."[24]

The final action taken by the 1919 convention with regard to the Ecumenical Movement was to appoint a committee to issue the "rallying call" to other Baptists, which Gambrell had asked for in his presidential address. Normally the committee would have reported to the next year's convention. So urgent was the need felt for the publication of this report that it was released to the denominational press early in 1920. The Fraternal Address of 1919, as it is known, was the most extensive statement of doctrine prepared by the Convention to that time. In its section on Christian union, it reiterated Baptist opposition to schemes for organic union which would create a totalitarian ecclesiastical organization embracing (and controlling) all Christians. All Baptists must concentrate on their missionary and educational programs, which can bring to the whole world the Christianity of the New Testament, "unmixed with errors brought over from earlier ages of autocratic and sacramental doctrines of the church."[25]

"THE QUESTION IS SETTLED FOR SOUTHERN BAPTISTS"

After reelection as president, Gambrell went from the 1919 convention to address a meeting of the Northern Baptist Convention (now the American Baptist Churches in the U.S.A.) in Denver. Shortly thereafter he wrote his impressions of both conventions.

The chief accomplishment of the Southern Baptist Convention of 1919, in his opinion, was its dispatch of the Ecumenical Movement. He felt that it was clear that Southern Baptists would join no federation, would follow no interdenominational leadership. "This ought to conclude the whole matter," putting an end to "irritations and confusions" created by leaders of the Ecumenical Movement, "men who are undoubtedly seeking leadership of all non-Catholic bodies in America." Whatever may come, "the question is settled for Southern Baptists."[26] Gambrell was right; the question was indeed settled for half a century or more.

Six years later the Convention briefly mentioned the subject of Christian unity in its "Statement of Baptist Faith and Message." Article 22 on "Co-operation" stressed the need for cooperative endeavor within and between congregations. The last two sentences spoke of Christian unity. In the New Testament, Christian unity is "spiritual harmony and voluntary co-operation for common ends by various groups of Christ's people." This kind of cooperation "is permissible and desirable" among the various denominations, provided that "the end to be attained is [it] self justified" and the cooperation "involves no violation of conscience or compromise of loyalty to Christ and his Word as revealed in the New Testament."[27] This article was repeated in the 1963 convention's statement of faith and message.

The one exception to Gambrell's dictum ("the question is settled") was the participation by the president of the Convention in the Edinburgh Conference on Faith and Order in 1937. At the insistence of W. O. Carver, the Convention in 1937 appointed George W. Truett of Texas to attend the Oxford Conference on Church, Community and State "as spokesman of this Convention."[28] Truett was unable to fill this role; consequently the Executive Committee appointed the Convention president, John R. Sampey, his wife, and two others as "representatives" of the Southern Baptist Convention at both the Oxford and Edinburgh conferences of 1937.

Three times in a decade, in 1938, 1940, and 1948, the Convention reaffirmed its policy of isolation from the Ecumenical Movement. The 1940 statement was the Convention's reply to a request by ecumenical leaders that the Convention send delegates to the World Council of Churches then being formed. The Convention expressed "the sincere desire of our hearts" for the unity of all Christ's followers, "not necessarily in name and in a world organization, but in spiritual fellowship with the Father and the Son." Several reasons were given for declining the invitation: the Convention had no "ecclesiological authority"; its constituent churches would not accept any attempt to exercise "ecclesiastical authority over them"; the Convention would not want to do anything which might "imperil the growing spirit of co-operation on the part of our churches" in "giving the gospel of Christ, as we understand it, to all men everywhere."[29]

Another invitation from the World Council of Churches came in 1948, this time to send delegates to the first general assembly of the Council at Amsterdam. Restating its position of 1940, the Convention asserted that its declining membership in the World Council "positively and definitely" reflected a policy which "continues to please our constituency with perhaps increased conviction. . . ."[30]

Between 1949 and 1953 the Convention adopted resolutions presented by its Committee on Common Problems with Northern Baptists, later called the Committee on Relations with Other Religious Bodies, against any "compact or agreement . . . with any organization, convention, or religious body that would" compromise Southern Baptists or "appear to be a step toward organic union,"[31] against Southern Baptist entry "into organic connection with the Federal Council of Churches of Christ in America"[32] or with the later National Council of Churches,[33] and against "the dangers of interdenominationalism and nondenominationalism."[34]

THE RETURN OF OPENNESS TO DIALOGUE?

In the mid-1960s the winds blowing across Southern Baptist country began to have noticeably less ecumenical chill. Something of a thaw may have set in at the 1965 convention. That year President Wayne Dehoney reaffirmed Southern Baptist opposition to "abolishing denominationalism" and to "abandoning our denominational distinctives." At the same time, he urged his fellow Baptists to remember that "our real enemies are the devil and the forces óf materialism, secularism, and atheism— not other Christians and Baptists in other national bodies." He challenged Southern Baptists to seek "broader channels of communication and cooperation that will not compromise our conscience, our doctrine or our autonomy."[35]

Acting on a motion made the previous year, the Convention's Executive Committee recommended to the 1968 convention that Southern Baptists engage in ecumenical activity in the field of evangelism. The recommendation also requested the Home Mission Board to consider calling a conference of evangelism leaders from various denominations to plan more effective ways of bringing people to God through Jesus Christ. One significant result of this interest was the Southern Baptist involvement in "Key '73." One of the most widely based ecumenical endeavors thus far in this country, Key '73 was a concerted effort by 130 Protestant traditions and by Roman Catholics to reach every person in North America with the gospel of Christ in 1973. Southern Baptists were represented in all planning stages of Key '73 and served on its executive committee. The Home Mission Board's Division of Evangelism provided the leadership for Southern Baptists participating in Key '73.

The first ecumenical conference sponsored by an agency of the Southern Baptist Convention was held at Southern Baptist Theological Seminary in Louisville, in June, 1967. The theme of this conference was "the believers' church." Participating were 150 representatives of over a dozen traditions which practice believer's baptism only, including eight families of Baptists and five of Mennonites. Also present by invitation were official observers from the National Council of Churches and the Roman Catholic Bishops' Committee for Ecumenical and Interreligious Affairs. The participants explored their common heritage from the "Radical Reformation" and resolved to multiply their contacts with one another.[36]

Near the end of his study in preecumenical relations between Baptists and Roman Catholics, James Leo Garrett noted that, unlike other Baptists, Southern Baptists have not had experience in dialogue with Protestants and Eastern Orthodox. In a prescient vein he observed it is possible, "though ironical, that Southern Baptists may learn by talking with Roman Catholics how to talk with Protestants!"[37] In recent years, Southern Baptist leaders and scholars have been more deeply involved in dialogue with Roman Catholics than with Christians of any other tradition.

During the 1966 convention in Detroit, C. Emanuel Carlson, executive director of the Baptist Joint Committee on Public Affairs, revealed that he had been contacted by the Most Reverend John S. Spence, auxiliary bishop of Washington, D.C., about dialogue between Baptists and Catholics. Among Southern Baptists this contact first bore fruit in a dialogue sponsored by the Ecumenical Institute of Wake Forest University, May 8-10, 1969. Representative Southern Baptist pastors, scholars, and denominational officials met with Catholic clergy and laity delegated by the Catholic Bishops' Committee for Ecumenical and Interreligious Affairs.

The second dialogue, sponsored jointly by the Ecumenical Institute and by the Bishops' Committee, took place February 4-6, 1970. The setting was St. Joseph's Abbey in St. Benedict, Louisiana. A few months later the third conference was convened, May 12-14, in Louisville. The fourth dialogue between Southern Baptist leaders and Roman Catholic delegates is significant in that it was sponsored by the Convention's Home Mission Board (through its Department of Interfaith Witness) as well as by the Bishops' Committee. The meeting occurred in Daytona Beach, Florida, February 1-3, 1971. A fifth gathering of Southern Baptist and Roman Catholic representatives met at Belmont Abbey, North Carolina, May 14-16, 1973. This conference was arranged by the Wake Forest Ecumenical Institute and the five bishops of the Atlanta Province of the Catholic Church in the United States.

Agencies of the Convention have also expanded in recent years the outreach of their dialogue to include the Jews.[38]

"THROUGH THE MAZE OF DIVIDED CHRISTENDOM . . . THE GOLDEN THREAD"

The thermometer for taking a denomination's ecumenical temperature has long been the membership roll of a council of churches (local or national or world). Using this thermometer on the Southern Baptist Convention and its churches, ecumenical doctors have pronounced Southern Baptists ecumenically dead. With no Christian funeral they have buried Southern Baptists in the ecumenical potter's field set aside for the "non-cooperating" (that is, dead) denominations. On the Southern Baptist gravestone, leaders of the ecumenical establishment have inscribed harsh epitaphs: "the problem child of American Protestantism," "perverse American Southern Baptists," "missionary imperialists."[39]

Now comes the shocking realization that the burial may have been premature. The establishment is no longer certain what constitutes ecumenical death. Even the thermometer itself is about to be discarded; not only its accuracy, but even its relevance is widely denied. In recent years ecumenists have proclaimed the end of the "conciliar era." Financial and moral support for the establishment is dwindling. From many sides comes the demand that councils of churches (on all levels) be replaced by new methods of working at Christian unity. Ecumenists confess that after two generations they are simply tired of "playing with ecumenical erector sets." [40]

Sixty to eighty-five years ago, Southern Baptists working through the Convention sought dialogue with other traditions. At the same time, and consistently down to the present, they have made a strong case against participating in the ecumenical organizations which have dominated the scene. They have affirmed their desire for true Christian unity, while insisting it cannot be achieved simply through membership in an ecclesiastical structure. They see little evidence that denominations committed to these structures are growing into unity of belief and practice. Judging by the usual outward criteria of vitality, they argue that those denominations committed to the ecumenical establishment seem to be handicapped, rather than helped, by their involvement. [41]

Consistently with their principles, Southern Baptists are now seriously conversing with other Christians and with Jews. Dialogue which is truly "sharing of treasures" must benefit all concerned. Where will it all lead? No one knows how divided Christians can be united in the faith without compromise. But everyone does know that Jesus Christ intends his people to be one. With that knowledge, said the Southern Baptist Convention in 1914, all Christians are obligated to press on in seeking unity:

> We firmly believe that a way may be found through the maze of divided Christendom out into the open spaces of Christian union only as the people of Christ follow the golden thread of an earnest desire to know and do His will. [42]

CHAPTER 8

Negro Conventions (U.S.A.)

Edward A. Freeman

To the discriminating reader of any chronicle of events in the history of the United States of America, the roots of organized religion among Negroes are clearly to be found in tracing the early history of the country. The first evangelical efforts in the United States or the colonies, as they were called then, were directed toward the Indians. For many years Christians in America had no particular thought in connection with the Negro, although he had been brought to the colonies along with the early settlers. As late as the latter part of the seventeenth century there existed among many of the colonists the sentiment that the Negro belonged outside "the pale of Christianity."[1]

HOW THE NEGRO GOT INTO THE EVANGELICAL PALE

However, a conversion of faith on the part of some few of the early settlers offset this belief to the extent that later it led to the conviction that, after all, the Negro had possibilities for salvation and that he was not the infidel that he was generally considered to be. It soon became apparent to the colonists and explorers, whose interests were chiefly in the commercial aspect of their American enterprise, that the Indian failed to show the capacity for the labor market as their undertakings demanded, so they were forced to resort to the Negro for this market. Now this failure of the Indians to fit into the economic picture presented a grave problem to the early missionaries. Because of the unwritten law that a Christian could not be held as a slave, the exploiting class found itself opposing the proselytizing efforts of the missionaries.

As the situation became more acute and the debate waxed hotter and hotter between the planters and the missionaries, the crux of the situation was whether the slaves should be liberated upon being converted to Christianity. This burning question found its way "to the sovereigns and council tables of Europe." It was later "provided in the royal decrees of Spain and France that Africans enslaved in America should be merely indoctrinated early in the principles of the Christian religion. This regulation produced a clash between the missionaries who were interested in human souls and the planters who were not interested in religion" but were very suspicious that "too much enlightenment might inspire" the blacks "with hope of attaining the status of free men." This situation eventually led to unfavorable repercussions and persecution for the missionaries.[2]

HELP AND SELF-HELP

With the organization of the Society for the Propagation of the Gospel in Foreign Parts, in 1701, in London, the pace of Protestant evangelism was greatly accelerated, and the picture, though dark for the Negro, began to brighten. From the very beginning this Society felt that the conversion of the Negro was as important as that of the whites and the Indians. Such "distinguished churchmen as Bishops Lowth, Fleetwood, Williams, Sanderson," and others "persistently urged" the missionaries in America to follow this policy. In "1784 Bishop Porteus published an extensive plan for the effectual conversion of the slaves, contending that 'despicable as they are in the eyes of man they are, nevertheless, the creatures of God.'"[3]

A new stage in the process of evangelism among Negroes was reached when a special school to train Negroes to share in missionary work themselves was established in Charleston, South Carolina, in 1743. From time to time, similar efforts and movements were encouraged and promoted by the bishops of the Church of England. Special sermons which aided them in their duties to the whites and Negroes in evangelism were published and distributed among the missionaries. Several leaders among Negroes were produced by these institutions. Toward the end of the first half of the eighteenth century the Great Awakening advanced the cause of all the socially disinherited in America, including the Negro. It may be safely concluded that the Great Awakening and the political philosophy of manhood rights which made the American Revolution so successful also produced a more favorable spirit toward the Negro by the Quakers and other religious groups. Resolutions were later passed by the Methodists, Presbyterians, and Baptists against the slave system.[1]

FRUITS OF THE GREAT AWAKENING

When the Baptists and Methodists began the revivals in the South during the latter part of the eighteenth century, large numbers of Negroes were attracted by their form of religious worship and were received into these churches. The appeal of the Baptists and Methodists to the Negroes has been ascribed by some scholars to the Negro's African background. The fact that the majority of the Negroes in the United States flocked into the Baptist churches seemed to Herskovits to be due to certain features in the Negro's African heritage. He declared:

> The importance of baptism in the ritualistic practices of Negro Christians has often been commented upon. It is not unreasonable to relate the strength of adherence to this practice to the great importance of the river-cults in West Africa, particularly in view of the fact that, as has been observed, river-cult priests were sold into slavery in great numbers.[5]

Even though the same methods and appeals were used by both the Methodist and Baptist churches, the largest number of Negroes "were attracted to the Baptists because their organization" and polity were attractive to them. "The form of self-government practiced by the Baptists was most favorable for the growth of Negro congregations. The Baptists permitted and encouraged Negroes to become preachers, who exercised their gifts" in the mixed congregations as well as in the predominantly white congregations.[6]

THE FIRST NEGRO BAPTIST CHURCHES

"Generally, the Negro slaves were not permitted to have their own churches," although a few "sprang up among the free Negroes prior to the Civil War." However, "the main source of what is today the Negro [or Black] church in America was found in the religious life of the slaves" who were granted these privileges by their owners. In some areas "it was unlawful for them to meet . . . unless some white persons were present and written permission granted by the owners."[7] Notwithstanding that, the membership of many churches, especially in the South, was from one-half to three-fourths Black.

The first Negro Baptist church of which there is any record was at Silver Bluff, in Aiken County, South Carolina. It was formed by eight slaves on the plantation of George Galphin near Augusta, Georgia, between 1773 and 1775. Two slaves who were members and became noted preachers were David George and Jesse Peters. David George was pastor until the capture of Savannah by the British in 1778, when he fled to Shelburne, Canada, and founded the First Baptist Church there. He later went to Freetown, Sierra Leone, West Africa, in 1788. Jesse Peters went to Savannah, Georgia, and assisted Abraham Marshall (white) to organize the First African Baptist Church in 1788. George Lisle, who was converted in 1773, went to Silver Bluff and preached in the early years of its existence, probably as its first pastor. He went to Savannah in 1779 with the British troops and resided there until 1782, when he went to Kingston, Jamaica, where he founded the First Baptist Church.[8]

Other churches among Negroes in America were organized in various parts of the country as follows: The Harrison Street Baptist Church of Petersburg, Virginia, in 1776; the First African Baptist of Lexington, Kentucky, in 1790; the First African Baptist in Philadelphia, Pennsylvania, in 1809; the Joy Baptist in Boston, Massachusetts, in 1805; the Abyssinian Baptist, New York City, in 1809; the First Baptist in St. Louis, Missouri, in 1827; the Nineteenth Street Baptist in Washington, D.C., in 1839.[9]

THE SAFETY VALVE

Churches such as these were avenues to unify the thinking of the Negroes along religious and social lines and were used also as a medium to give momentum to the Abolition Movement by the leaders. The biggest boon to the Abolition Movement came when the leaders and ministers of the Methodist, Baptist, Presbyterian, Quaker, and Episcopalian national and local bodies gave their endorsement to it and exerted a favorable influence in it. Later, several of these national bodies grew lukewarm on abolition and receded from their original stand. The Negro churches of various denominations united freely, forgot the doctrinal differences, and began working cooperatively for their independence.[10]

ORGANIZATIONS ABOVE THE LOCAL CHURCH LEVEL

Despite the many methods used to circumvent the moral responsibility involved in this great controversy over slavery, the split among the white national bodies came for the Methodists in 1844, the Baptists in 1845, and the Presbyterians in 1861. When the churches in the South shut their doors to the Negro, such action caused trouble for the free Negroes in the South as well as in the North. These free Negroes were forced to flee to the North and West along with the runaway slaves. This produced organizations above the local church level, such as state and national bodies to keep the movement unified and directed. In 1840 the American Baptist Missionary Convention, comprising churches in the New England and Middle Atlantic states, was organized. Missionaries from this body and other smaller bodies were sent to the South to help the churches and runaway slaves in that area. In 1863, at its twenty-third annual meeting in Washington, D.C., a committee called upon President Abraham Lincoln to discuss the protection of their missionaries on southern soil.

President Lincoln responded with the following order:

Executive Mansion
Washington, D.C.
August 31, 1863

TO WHOM IT MAY CONCERN:
Today I am called upon by a committee of colored ministers of the gospel who express a wish to go within our military lines and minister to their brethren there. The object is a worthy one, and I shall be glad for all facilities to be afforded them, which may not be inconsistent with or of a hindrance to our military operations.

A. Lincoln[11]

At their forty-sixth session in 1886, this body united with the Northwestern Convention, took the name Consolidated American Baptist Missionary Convention, and continued to carry on work in the South. In 1880 the Foreign Mission Convention was organized at Montgomery, Alabama, by W. W. Colley, who was a returned missionary from West Africa under the Southern Baptist Convention. The burden of his appeal was to begin work in Africa by the Negroes of America, since the Africans were not as favorably disposed to the white missionaries as the Negro missionaries.[12]

In 1886, William J. Simmons called a meeting at St. Louis, Missouri, to organize the American National Baptist Convention to "discuss questions pertaining especially to the religious, educational, industrial, and social interest" of Negroes and to give opportunities for the better "thinkers and writers to be heard." [13] In 1893 the Baptist National Educational Convention was organized at Washington, D.C. The chief purpose of this group was to work for an "educated ministry in the leadership of the churches." [14]

THE NATIONAL BAPTIST CONVENTION

In 1895, in Atlanta, Georgia, the National Foreign Mission Convention (organized 1880), the American National Baptist Convention (organized 1886), and the Baptist National Educational Convention (organized 1893) merged to form the National Baptist Convention. This new body was to promote the combined objectives of the three groups forming it. [15] The first president of the new convention was E. C. Morris. Most of the efforts for the next few years were spent in readjustments, realignment, and reorganization. During this time a controversy arose among the Negro Baptists concerning the publication of literature. To this time, the then American Baptist Publication Society was publishing most of the literature used by all these Baptist groups, including Southern Baptists as well. Negro Baptists contended that some of their writers should be used by the Northern Baptists. This was done, but the Southern Baptists objected strenuously and withdrew and intensified their own publication work. In order to placate the Southern Baptists, the Northern Baptists withdrew the Negro writers, but it was too late to save publication contracts for Southern Baptists. This was an insult to the National Baptists, who withdrew themselves and organized their own publishing house. [16]

THE LOTT-CAREY FOREIGN MISSION CONVENTION

The Lott-Carey Baptist Foreign Mission Convention was formed in 1897 in Washington, D.C. Its constituents were "men and women of the Atlantic States," who had been educated under "the American Baptist Home Mission Society of the Northern Baptist Convention." The Lott-Carey leaders joined the National Baptist Convention because there was thorough accord between the two groups on the work of foreign missions. The Lott-Carey group made foreign missions its slogan and its only reason for existing as a separate group. However, later the Lott-Carey group withdrew from the National Convention when the foreign mission headquarters was moved from Louisville to Philadelphia and when the

National Baptist Convention withdrew the publication of its literature from the American Baptist Publication Society.[17] The Lott-Carey group returned to the Convention in 1905, but withdrew later and never returned, although the president remained as a member of the board of the Convention until 1922. This group was later incorporated as a society and not as a convention.

THE CONTROVERSY AND ATTENDING STORM

The new publishing agent for the National Convention was organized under the Home Mission Board and under the title "The National Baptist Publishing Board" and not "of the National Baptist Convention," as were other boards. This seemingly small issue generated into a national controversy which led to a split of the Convention in 1915. However, the Publishing Board was amazingly successful and soon became the leading financial agency of the Convention. This development produced a storm when attempts were made to have this board come under the Convention. The great question was, "Who owned the publishing house, the Convention or the small group who operated it?" When an attempt was made to incorporate the National Convention and all its agencies under it in 1915 at Chicago, Illinois, there was a split which resulted in two national bodies—the National Baptist Convention of America and the National Baptist Convention, U.S.A., Inc.

In going their separate ways from 1915 to the present, the two conventions have had parallel interests and concerns for foreign missions, home missions, education, benevolences, stewardship, evangelism, doctrines, and denominational affiliations. In 1952 at Chicago, Illinois, the National Baptist Convention, U.S.A., Inc., attempted to give tenure to the presidency of the Convention. After some heated debate, a vote was taken which favored this move. However, it was revealed that, according to the constitution of the Convention, no matter which dealt with changing or amending the constitution could be voted on after the second day of the convention. The records reveal that this action took place on the third day, and thus it was rendered invalid. A long debate on the validity of this action ensued until 1957, when the president ruled that the issue of tenure was dead. This led to a series of litigations until 1960. The court then ruled that the matter of tenure was invalid according to the Convention's own constitution. This led to the second split in Kansas City, Missouri, in 1961. Resulting from this separation was the Progressive National Baptist Convention, Inc.[18]

All three of these national bodies are represented in the same ecumenical groups from the local scene to the world scene. The attitudes toward and participation in these groups are about the same, since there are no doctrinal differences or differences in polity.

NEGROES AND CATHOLICISM

The colony of Maryland on the Atlantic coast presented an opportunity for Catholics to work with Negroes during the eighteenth century. Despite some opposition to evangelizing Negroes, the early priests and missionaries in Maryland considered it their duty to enlighten the slaves. The instruction for the communicants of the Roman Catholic Church made it necessary that Negroes learn at least in a meager way the doctrines of the Church. However, the Catholic pioneers' rationale for evangelizing the Negro was not altogether encouraging, since the Negro fitted into the picture only as an economic factor and not as an object of Christianity. Due to the positive attitude of the Catholic priests and missionaries, the colonists developed a tolerant attitude, and Negroes were evangelized to a limited degree. It was generally felt that "the nearer the blacks were kept to the state of brutes . . . the more useful they would be as laborers."[19]

Although the Anglican and Catholic groups were the first church groups of Christianity to evangelize the Negro, the overwhelming majority did not embrace these groups but instead went into the Methodist, Baptist, and Presbyterian churches. The Quakers, with all of their simplicity, did not draw a large number to their persuasion either. The Latin liturgy of the Roman Catholic Church and the ritualistic conformity required by the Anglicans too often baffled the Negro's understanding and, even when he had made a profession of faith, left him in a position of being compelled to accept the spiritual blessings largely on the recommendation of the missionaries proferring them. The simplicity of the Quakers set forth as an attack on the forms and ceremonies of the more aristocratic churches equally taxed the undeveloped intellect of certain Negroes, who often wondered how matters so mysterious could be reduced to such ordinary formulae.[20]

BAPTIST RELATIONSHIPS

The three national Baptist conventions comprise a combined membership of about 10,000,000, with the National Baptist Convention, U.S.A., Inc., claiming 6,000,000. All of these conventions cooperate in the Baptist Joint Committee on Public Affairs, the North American Baptist Fellowship, and the Baptist World Alliance. Cooperation with the Alliance has extended from its beginning in 1905 until the present, with officers from these conventions having served, or now serving, as one of the vice-presidents of the Alliance. All three conventions worked with the Baptist Jubilee Advance Committee, which led in the celebration of the 150th anniversary of the organization of Baptist work on a national scale in North America. This celebration was held in 1964 at Atlantic City.

ECUMENICAL PARTICIPATION

All three conventions are active participants in the local councils of churches in the communities where these councils, or their counterparts, exist. They actively share, and in many cases hold offices, in state councils of churches and maintain the same relations with the National Council of the Churches of Christ in the U.S.A. Dr. John W. Williams of the National Baptist Convention of America served as one of the vice-presidents of the latter body. These conventions hold membership on the various divisions and commissions of the World Council of Churches. Negroes serve on the boards of all of the above-named groups and share in the business and budgets as well.

The National Baptist Convention, U.S.A., Inc., works through its Foreign Mission Board with the Overseas Ministries of the National Council of the Churches of Christ in the U.S.A. This relationship began in 1966. The Convention has participated through its Sunday School Publishing Board in and with the International Council of Religious Education since its inception and with the Division of Christian Education of the National Council of the Churches of Christ in the U.S.A. Members of the Sunday School Publishing Board have served on the Uniform Lesson Committee down through the years, and the present chairman of the Committee of the Uniform Series, or CUS, is Dr. Maynard P. Turner, Director of Publication of the Sunday School Publishing Board. One of the former board members, Dr. Marshall Talley, served on the Advisory Board of the International Council of Religious Education during the translation of the *Revised Standard Version* of the Bible.

THE NEGRO CONVENTIONS AND CHRISTIAN UNITY

It can be safely concluded that these bodies work with great hope and expectations in the movement for Christian unity. They furnish participants from the local and community level to the world level. Each year their churches, for the most part, join in the Week of Prayer for Christian Unity with other churches of the community. Although there is no particular effort toward organic union among these conventions as bodies and other Protestant groups, and it seems that all three conventions stand somewhat against organic union, there is a favorable sentiment among them to work together in principle with other religious bodies to ensure a united witness for Jesus Christ in our present society and to bring the full impact of his teachings and gospel message upon the nations of the world.

There is also quite a favorable sentiment prevailing among Baptists of both racial groups in the United States to work closer together and, where possible and feasible, engage in joint discussion activity at convention levels. This is a wholesome sign of the stirring of the Holy Spirit among us, leading us toward the fulfillment of our Lord's prayer "that they may be one."

CHAPTER 9

Other Conferences and Associations (U.S.A.)

Gerald Leo Borchert

The quest for freedom from European state-supported ecclesiastical institutions and from large church organizations has left an indelible mark upon Baptist polity and practice in the United States, especially upon the Baptist groups herein reviewed. The new world offered Baptists the long awaited opportunity to express this freedom, whether they were Calvinistic or Arminian in orientation. Some Baptists have been subjected to divisions in the context of freedom and, in an effort at preserving what they consider to be significant, have drifted either by design or chance into relatively isolationistic positions. Others have found the experience of religious liberty to be invigorating. They have approached other denominations not out of fear of diluting their stand or of joining some mythically conceived super-church, but from a sense of opportunity to contribute the strength of their Baptist witness to both a church and a world which are desperately in need of the healing power of Christ Jesus the Lord.

The term "ecumenism" is seldom used by these Baptists. They prefer the idea of cooperation, because many have experienced firsthand the cost of gaining religious liberty, and they desire that a clear sense of their religious freedom as Baptists be maintained.

A brief discussion of the cooperative attitudes and practices of each of these eleven selected groups of Baptists will follow. In the organization of this chapter, Baptist groups of similar background have been treated together; and because of the nature of this report and its implications for cooperative patterns, a specific division has been made between those groups which hold membership in the Baptist World Alliance and those which do not. The immense task of summarizing the attitudes and policies of these Baptists has been made possible because of the excellent cooperation received from denominational executives and historians. To them this writer is greatly indebted.[1]

I. MEMBERS OF THE BAPTIST WORLD ALLIANCE
BAPTIST GENERAL CONFERENCE

In 1852 Gustaf Palmquist started a Baptist Church for Swedish immigrants at Rock Island, Illinois. The Swedish General Conference, now known as the Baptist General Conference (BGC), was organized in 1879. Until recently, the BGC has had its closest fraternal relations with groups of similar ethnic origin, viz. the Mission Covenant Church and the Evangelical Free Church.

In 1943 the horizons of the BGC began slowly to broaden, and it joined the Baptist World Alliance (BWA). The Conference, however, did not participate in the Baptist Jubilee Advance, and it voted against becoming a member of the North American Baptist Fellowship in 1967, although a delegate is sent to the executive meetings. Because of a vocal minority opposing membership in the Alliance, a reaffirmation of relationship with the BWA was achieved in 1966 only by providing that churches wishing to be disassociated from the BWA would be listed in the annual reports. At that time twenty-eight churches were so listed and today the number is thirty-three. [2]

At the 1966 conference, the denomination voted to join the National Association of Evangelicals. Participation in the Evangelical Foreign Mission Association had begun in the early 1950s. Since that time, the BGC has actively participated in the work of various subsidiary evangelical organizations, including the Home Missions Association, the World Relief Program, and the Committee to Assist Missionary Education Overseas.

The BGC has participated in cooperative activities in Argentina, Brazil, Ethiopia, Japan, and the Philippines. The Osaka Biblical Seminary—a joint effort by the BGC, the Mennonite Brethren, and the North American Baptist General Conference—is in the process of dissolution because of withdrawal by the Mennonites. Cooperative discussions with the North American Baptist General Conference on the conference, Bible college, and seminary levels appear to have been rather unproductive. Although the BGC has not officially recognized the American Bible Society, it is represented on the advisory council. Representatives of the BGC have been active participants in the Baptist Joint Committee on Public Affairs.

The historian of the BGC, Virgil Olson, in reflecting upon the present somewhat hesitant mood of his conference, in spite of positive resolutions to the contrary, suggests that the difficulty with cooperative efforts today does not seem to be so much a matter of doctrine as a need for organizational "adjustments" to permit the possibility of greater interrelatedness with like-minded Christians. This scholar's perceptive dream undoubtedly has application far beyond the borders of his particular denomination.

GENERAL ASSOCIATION OF GENERAL BAPTISTS

The General Baptists (GB)[3] are so named because of their Arminian belief in a "general" atonement. They also affirm a conditional security over against strict Calvinist theology.

The GBs originated in England in the early seventeenth century and came to the American colonies in 1714. Although GBs nearly died out along the Atlantic seaboard, Benoni Stinson in 1823 raised the name again in a clash with extreme Calvinistic Baptists of southern Indiana and, accordingly, a GB church was formed at Evansville.

While Stinson was a firm believer in open communion, he shunned all appearance of organic interdenominational relationship. Thus, a pattern of aloofness in organizational relations became part of GB psychology. Nevertheless, even without Stinson's approval, closer fellowship with other Baptists was attempted, and in the 1860s membership was gained in the Free Baptist Convention. The Civil War and inadequacies in the relationship, however, led to a subsequent disassociation from the Convention.

When the General Association was formed in 1870, its avowed purpose was to bring together all Baptist bodies which shared in Arminianism; but the Association did not win local support until, five years later, it made a commitment to promote GB work. Between 1890 and 1900 the leadership made a serious effort to develop closer relations with other Baptists, but this led to the only rupture the General Association has experienced. This rupture effectively terminated further relationships with other denominations until the 1950s, when unproductive discussions were held with the Churches of God of North America.

In the second half of the 1960s, the General Association became members of the Baptist World Alliance and subsequently of the North American Baptist Fellowship. Effecting membership in these organizations did not occur without stormy debate. The issue was settled by means of a trial membership which seems to have proven to be nonthreatening to the Association's self-determining character. In correspondence, Ollie Latch suggests two other factors which have enabled the GBs to withdraw from their aloof stand and join the Alliance: the threat that smaller denominations would be engulfed by the Ecumenical Movement; and the fact that, while open communion has been affirmed, refusal to work for common fellowship, at least with other Baptists, seems to belie this affirmation.

NORTH AMERICAN BAPTIST GENERAL CONFERENCE

The North American Baptist General Conference (NABGC)[4] owes its beginning not so much to a single individual as to a mass immigration of Teutonic people, some of whom were Baptists in Germany and others of whom experienced conversion in their new land but sought to worship in their native language. While the church at Philadelphia founded by Konrad A. Fleischmann in 1843 is regarded as the first German Baptist church, others were springing up during this period in cities as far west as Missouri and Wisconsin and as far north as Ontario. Representatives of these churches assembled at Philadelphia in 1851 in order to encourage the work among German Baptists and for the purpose of developing a publication *(Der Sendbote)* and providing for ministerial education. The NAB Seminary was begun under August Rauschenbusch. His son, Walter, its most famous teacher, is well known for calling American churches to a social consciousness.

The extension of German Baptist work, however, apart from the encouragement and financial support of the American Baptist Home Mission Society, would have been greatly truncated. Many of the first ministers were employed as colporteurs. Churches were assisted by supporting gifts and an initial subsidy of two dollars for every dollar raised by German Baptists (later dollar for dollar) was paid to assist the *Bundeskonferenz* (General Conference) in ministering to the large influx of German immigrants during the last decades of the nineteenth century. This warm support has left an indelible impression on the NABGC in its relationships with other Baptists.

The fact that German Baptists were a recognizable minority group, not only in terms of language but in some sectors also in terms of dress, likewise contributed to developing perspectives. When living close to Mennonites, Baptists in the plains of the United States and Canada sought to develop cooperative meetings, but they were rebuffed by the Mennonites in a "prayer" controversy when Mennonites held that prayer was illegitimate in worship. Relations with Hutterites, Mennonite Brethren, and German Methodists, however, proved to be much more cordial and provided a balance to some of the unhappy relationships encountered with German Lutherans and Catholics.

Another factor which has led to the development of a cooperative stance among German Baptists is that German immigrants have been drawn not only from Germany but also from Holland, Poland, Russia, and various border nations. While the German Baptists have rather slowly given up their language due to the constant influx of new German-speaking immigrants, they can look to no single nation for their European heritage. This diversity has led to a sense of openness even in the approach to theological issues. Although they are generally conservative in orientation, these Baptists have adopted only a brief working statement concerning their faith. They have resisted comprehensive creedal statements as being divisive.

This conservatively oriented stance of openness has resulted in a general pattern of cooperation. In mission and relief work in Europe after the Second World War, the then 35,000 member NABGC was extremely active and by itself raised a million dollars for the Baptist World Alliance Relief Committee. In the Cameroon, higher education, such as at Bali College, is jointly staffed by Swiss Presbyterian and NAB teachers. In Brazil several cooperative relationships are in effect. The Seminary in Japan at Osaka, until the withdrawal of the Mennonite Brethren, was a cooperative work of three denominations, including the Baptist General Conference (BGC) and the NABGC.

As far as interdenominational cooperation is concerned, although comprehensive studies with the BGC have been undertaken, little has been effected up to the present, with the exception of some joint camping programs.

In the wider sphere the NABGC has participated actively in the Baptist World Alliance, the North American Baptist Fellowship, the Baptist Joint Committee on Public Affairs, the Baptist Jubilee Advance, and the American Bible Society. The services of the International Missionary Council were used prior to its merger within the World Council of Churches. The Conference has since joined the Evangelical Foreign Mission Association and participates in various other evangelical cooperative programs.

SEVENTH DAY BAPTIST GENERAL CONFERENCE

Consistent with their current affirmation "that the Church of God is the whole company of redeemed people gathered by the Holy Spirit into one body of which Christ is the head" (Statement of Belief, 1938), Seventh Day Baptists (SDB) have developed a significant stance of openness and cooperation both with other Baptists and with other denominations, while yet maintaining their historical convictions.

The history of SDBs[5] in the United States dates back to the visit of the English Sabbatarian, Stephen Mumford, in 1671 to Newport, Rhode Island. The withdrawal of seven members from the First Baptist Church there led to the formation of a SDB Church in 1672 and a statement being issued by the first minister, William Hiscox, and author Samuel Hubbard that, "We desire to be in love with all the saints of God, and as far as we can go on with them, and wherein we can't with all tenderness to wait on the God of light to show that to others he hath to us." Robert Torbet holds that the early SDBs were composed largely of "disappointed Fifth Monarchy men."[6] By 1744, as they grew in strength, they began to develop fraternal relations with the German SDBs at Ephrata, Pennsylvania. Twenty years later nine Sabbatarians joined in founding Rhode Island College (Brown University) and seven became trustees.

The SDB General Conference in the United States was organized in 1801–1802, and in 1820 interest was engendered in an English college fund-raising effort supported by Robert Burnside, a SDB pastor in London. Although some initial problems with the English Davis Charity funds were encountered, a warm friendship later developed between the English SDBs and the Baptist Union of Great Britain. This friendly relationship in England together with a sustained friendship with Baptists of Germany led American SDBs in 1936 to join the Baptist World Alliance. They have since been involved in the Baptist Jubilee Advance, the North American Baptist Fellowship, and the Baptist Joint Committee on Public Affairs. In 1963 a committee was named to work for increased understanding and cooperation with the American Baptist Convention.

Another relationship of SDBs was developed in 1844 through Rachel Preston's interest in Millennialism. This SDB laywoman was influential in introducing Joseph Bates and James and Ellen G. White to Sabbatarian literature. As a result the Sabbath became an important aspect of the Seventh-Day Adventist movement. While there are differences in the views of Scripture and doctrines of the church, fraternal delegates have from time to time been exchanged at conferences.

George H. Babcock, president of the Sabbath School Board, was a participant in the International Sunday School Association. He also developed Youth Excel Bands in 1881. The organization of Christian Endeavor, however, was not favorably received by the SDBs because of the emphasis upon the Sunday observance program. In the same vein SDBs have understandably been unresponsive to proposals respecting the Lord's Day Alliance, not simply, they aver, because of their Sabbath doctrine but also because of a conviction that the state should not legislate on such matters.

In the twentieth century SDBs have been very active in broad cooperative activities. They sent delegates to the Ecumenical Missionary Conference in New York City in 1900 and to the preliminary and organizational meetings of the Federal Council of the Churches of Christ in America in 1905 and 1908. Despite a vocal minority which has periodically expressed opposition, the SDBs by sustaining vote of their General Conference are constituent members of the National Council of the Churches of Christ in the U.S.A. and are represented on the General Board. Beginning in 1917, the SDBs were represented in both the Faith and Order and the Life and Work meetings held at Stockholm (1925) and Lausanne (1927). They were members of the United States provisional committee and joined the World Council of Churches at its inception in 1948. They have been represented at all meetings since that time, and their general secretary is a member of the Central Committee. Concerning the areas of foreign missions and Christian education, the SDBs have cooperated with and relied upon the services of the interdenominational agencies related to the structures of both the National and World Councils.

In 1917 a small group of churches in Michigan withdrew from the Church of God, Stanberry, Michigan, and became a group of SDB churches. In 1923 a conference of representatives met with these new churches to discuss cooperation, but theological divergencies have made close relationship impossible. These churches should not be confused with SDB churches discussed here.

II. NON-MEMBERS OF THE BAPTIST WORLD ALLIANCE
AMERICAN BAPTIST ASSOCIATION AND BAPTIST MISSIONARY ASSOCIATION OF AMERICA

The roots[7] of the American Baptist Association (ABA) and the Baptist Missionary Association of America (BMAA) lie in the Landmark controversy which developed largely in the Southern Baptist Convention during the last half of the nineteenth century. The Landmarkers placed stress upon the primacy of the local church and a recognition of pedobaptist fellowships only as "religious societies" and not as churches. Missionary societies were likewise frowned upon because missionary activity was viewed as originating in and supported by local congregations. An historical succession of Baptist churches from the New Testament era was usually affirmed.

The Baptist General Association was founded in 1905 at Texarkana, Arkansas, and renamed the ABA in 1924. Coordinated mission, literature, and educational programs have since been developed. The BMAA, first known as the North American Baptist Association, was formed by messengers from churches that had withdrawn from the ABA in 1950 because of a controversy related to the seating of messengers or delegates who were not members of the churches electing them. Theologically today, both the ABA and the BMAA continue the Landmark patterns of opposition to open communion. Because of the historical *raison d'être* of these associations, it is understandable that they have been slow in relating to interdenominational cooperative enterprises. Even today, as I. K. Cross indicates, "we have no affiliations, or active participation with other denominational groups—or Baptist groups either." They do not wish to be considered antagonistic in this matter, but consider that their stance is developed out of conviction.

CONSERVATIVE BAPTIST ASSOCIATION OF AMERICA; AND GENERAL ASSOCIATION OF REGULAR BAPTIST CHURCHES

The General Association of Regular Baptists (GARB) and the Conservative Baptist Association (CBA) are loosely allied families of Baptist churches which developed out of the Fundamental Fellowship of the Northern Baptist Convention because of a concern for the theological views of missionary appointees.[8] At preconvention meetings of the NBC in 1919–1921 a statement of faith known as the Goodchild Declaration, said to be a reaffirmation of historic Baptist Confessions, was adopted. In 1922 the Baptist Bible Union was formed, and T. T. Shields of Toronto became the first president, but it was short-lived. In 1933 the General Association of Regular Baptist Churches was formed when a large block of churches withdrew from the Northern Baptist Convention.[9] The less militant fundamentalist churches continued in the NBC, but differences in theology over missionaries remained unresolved, and in 1943 the Conservative Baptist Foreign Mission Society was formed. The CBA followed four years later and, as Bruce Shelley states, sought to steer a more moderate course than those whom they viewed as reactionary fundamentalists, like the GARB churches which had become linked with the American Council of Christian Churches, a group of reaction to the National Council of Churches.

The general attitude of the GARB toward cooperation is not said by them to be one of "ultra independence" but one of "definite separatist convictions" and "limited fellowship" based on the thesis that "it is the Baptist who lays aside the most!" In comparison, the perspective on cooperation of the CBA has been similar to that expressed by the National Association of Evangelicals, which, meeting in October, 1941, approximately a month after the formation of the American Council, stated that it was "determined to break with apostasy but . . . wanted no dog-in-the-manger, reactionary, negative, or destructive type of organization." Besides this evangelical association, churches of the CBA have cooperated in the work of Youth for Christ, Campus Crusade for Christ, Inter-Varsity Christian Fellowship, the Billy Graham Association, and other similar evangelical ministries on the local level.

NATIONAL ASSOCIATION OF FREE WILL BAPTISTS

Although Free Will Baptists (FWB)[10] link their history with the Arminian English General Baptists, their beginnings are probably more clearly found in the peripatetic evangelistic work of men like Paul Palmer in North Carolina during the 1720s. The movement was early beset both by Particular, or Regular, Baptist acquisition and restructuring of the poorly organized churches and by later Campbellite proselytizing.

The Freewill Baptist movement in New England and the northern states,[11] which was founded by Benjamin Randall in 1780 on Arminian and open communion beliefs, had an essentially separate existence from the Free Will Baptist churches of the South prior to its merger with the Northern Baptist Convention in 1911. The General Conference of Freewill Baptists had been in cooperative discussions with Northern Baptists and Disciples of Christ since 1880, and, although the Disciples withdrew, the discussions led to resolutions of merger and transference of home and foreign mission work to the Northern Baptist Convention. Those Freewill churches in the Plains states that did not enter into the merger in 1911 formed in 1916 the Cooperative General Association of Free Will Baptists. This latter body and the General Conference of Free Will Baptists, organized in 1921 and composed chiefly of churches in the Southeast, united in 1935 to form the National Association of Free Will Baptists.

Presently the FWBs are members of the Evangelical Foreign Mission Association. Although they held denominational membership in the National Association of Evangelicals from its inception, they have since withdrawn in favor of allowing each church the final decision of cooperation. As a denomination they have avoided most cooperative organizations and have with groups like the General Association of Regular Baptist Churches taken a stand against Key '73 as being compromise evangelism.

PRIMITIVE BAPTISTS AND PROGRESSIVE PRIMITIVE BAPTISTS

The Old School or Primitive Baptist (PB) Movement[12] in America developed in opposition to the formation in 1814 of the General Missionary Convention of the Baptist Denomination in the U.S.A. for Foreign Missions and the activities of Luther Rice. However, not until the influential anti-missionism decision of the Kehukee

Association of North Carolina in 1827 did significant divisions begin to occur from what this group termed as the Mission or New School Baptists (the forebears of the Northern [American] and Southern Baptist Conventions). Their basic objection was that revision of New Testament principles had been introduced into Baptist churches, especially in respect to the preaching of a general atonement, the theologically educated and salaried ministry, and the centralization of church government.

In the words of W. H. Cayce, the movement recognizes "no convention nor earthly head." Each church is independent, but for purposes of fellowship and encouragement annual associational meetings are held. These associations have no continuous existence and no power to act except when in session and are only advisory in relationship to churches. Because of the loose association and stress upon independence the movement has been subjected to fragmentation. On the one hand, some churches have withdrawn their association because of a hyper-predestinarian stance; whereas, on the other hand, revisionist groups have periodically developed which recognize revival meetings, structured church organizations, Sunday schools, the use of instrumental music in worship, and the toleration of secret societies. Most of these revisionist groups have slowly withered and died.

The Progressive Primitive Baptists, however, who were condemned for their use of instrumental music in 1919, have gradually gained strength and have developed various organizations, including women's and ministerial associations, homes for the aged, a pension foundation, and even educational institutions.

The Primitive Baptists have seen little value in cooperating with other groups, except that they maintain a corresponding fellowship with similar groups in Canada, England, and Australia. Their strong Calvinistic emphasis has led them to maintain an aloofness from most cooperative evangelical efforts.

CONCLUSION

From the decentralized aloofness of the Primitive Baptists to the highly cooperative involvements of the Seventh Day Baptists, the eleven groups selected for inclusion in this study represent almost every gradation of cooperation exhibited by Baptists in the world community of Christians. Even the procedures and the results of merger have been experienced by one of these groups—the Freewill

Baptists. Each group has sought to remain faithful to Jesus Christ in the pursuit of what it conceived to be God's purpose for the denomination in the world. Each group, likewise, reflects in its cooperation a conditioning based upon its experiences of the trustworthiness of fellow Christians. The conclusion of such a study, wherein one has come to respect each group's convictions in terms of its conditioning, cannot help but convince the student that historian Kenneth Scott Latourette's theme of "the exceeding greatness of the power . . . in earthen vessels" (cf. 2 Corinthians 4:7) well typifies the cooperative patterns of Baptists.

CHAPTER 10

Canada

Jarold K. Zeman

BAPTISTS ON THE CANADIAN SCENE *

In order to understand Canadian Baptist attitudes toward and relations with other Christians and churches we must remind ourselves, at the outset, of the main stages in the historical development of the organized Baptist movement in Canada and its relative strength in comparison with other Christian bodies in that country.[1]

There are three regional Baptist conventions. The United Baptist Convention of the Atlantic (formerly Maritime) Provinces was formed in 1906 through the merger of Regular (Calvinistic) Baptist and Free Will Baptist bodies in the provinces of Nova Scotia, New Brunswick, and Prince Edward Island. Baptist work in Newfoundland began only two decades ago. The Baptist Convention of Ontario and Quebec was organized in 1888. The dates of organization are somewhat misleading in view of the fact that the oldest Baptist churches in the Atlantic Provinces and Central Canada were founded in the late eighteenth century. Associations and other units of cooperation were established early in the nineteenth century. Baptist work in Western Canada began a century ago (1873). The Baptist Convention of Western Canada was organized in 1907 and reorganized as the Baptist Union of Western Canada in 1909, and it embraces the provinces of Manitoba, Saskatchewan, Alberta, and British Columbia.

The arrival of a small group of French-speaking Protestants

from Switzerland in 1837 led to the rise of French Baptist work in Quebec, later organized under the name, the Grande Ligne Mission. The ten French-speaking Baptist churches related to it joined together in the Union of French Baptist Churches in Canada in 1969.

The Fundamentalist-Modernist controversy in the mid-1920s resulted in a major division within the Convention of Ontario and Quebec. About one-seventh of the churches (70 out of 490) and approximately the same proportion of membership (8,500 out of 60,000) left the Convention. A similar disruption occurred in Western Canada. Several rival organizations were formed by the dissident churches. Most of these have since united in the Fellowship of Evangelical Baptist Churches (organized in 1953).

Aspirations toward a national (federal) organization can be traced as far back as the 1840s. They did not produce a workable organization until 1944. The Baptist Federation of Canada (BFC) embraces member churches of the three regional conventions (Atlantic, Ontario-Quebec, and Western) and of the French Union. Up to the present time, the regional conventions have not relinquished any of their major constitutional and executive powers in favor of the Federation. It exists primarily for fellowship, consultation, and as a national agency through which the majority of Canadian Baptists speak with a common voice on national issues and participate in international projects and agencies such as the Baptist World Alliance.

The picture of the Canadian Baptist mosaic would not be complete without reference to other Baptist groups which were originally organized into separate conferences on the basis of their ethnic origin. Nearly all ethnic Baptist churches have dual affiliation, with their ethnic conference and with the regional Baptist convention. The two major exceptions to this rule are the German Baptist churches, affiliated exclusively with the North American Baptist General Conference, and the formerly Swedish-speaking churches, which are now affiliated with the Baptist General Conference.

About thirty Negro Baptist churches are organized in two separate associations but are fully related to the conventions. There is also an undetermined number of independent Baptist churches which are unrelated to any convention or conference. A few churches in Western Canada are affiliated with the Oregon-Washington Convention of the Southern Baptist Convention.

Baptist Membership Statistics (1971)

	Churches	Members
I BAPTIST FEDERATION OF CANADA:		
Atlantic Baptist Convention	596	68,100
Ontario-Quebec Convention	380	46,700
Union of Western Canada	134	17,150
Union of French Churches	10	400
BFC Total	1120	132,350
II Baptist General Conference (Canada)	65	4,200
III North American Baptist General Conference	95	13,000
IV Fellowship of Evangelical Baptist Churches	330	33,000
V Other Groups and Churches (Fundamental, Independent, Primitive, Southern Baptist Churches)	150	12,000
TOTAL FOR CANADA	1760	194,550

Statistics for "Other Groups" (V) are only estimates based on their literature. Churches in groups I-III cooperate with the Baptist World Alliance; the others do not. The 1961 census of Canada reported a total of 593,553 persons (including children and adherents) who indicated Baptist affiliation or preference. The following census data indicate the changing Baptist strength, or weakness, in relation to other major religious groups in Canada.

Religious Affiliation: Percentage of Population

Census of Canada	1901	1921	1941	1961	1971
Anglican	12.8	16.1	15.2	13.2	11.8
Baptist	5.9	4.8	4.2	3.3	3.1
Greek Orth. & Catholic	0.3	1.9	2.8	2.3	2.6
Jewish	0.3	1.4	1.5	1.4	1.3
Lutheran	1.8	3.3	3.5	3.6	3.3
Mennonite	0.6	0.7	1.0	0.8	0.8
Methodist	17.2	13.2	see United Church		
Presbyterian	15.8	16.1	7.2	4.5	4.0
Roman Catholic	41.7	38.7	41.8	45.7	46.2
United Church	—	—	19.2	20.1	17.5
All Others	3.6	3.8	3.6	5.1	9.4
	100.0	100.0	100.0	100.0	100.0

The total population of Canada increased from 5,371,315 in 1901 to 18,238,247 in 1961, and to approximately 22 million in 1973. While the number of persons reporting Baptist affiliation (for census purposes) doubled from 1901 (319,234) to 1971 (667,245), the relative numerical strength of Baptists declined from 5.9 percent to 3.1 percent. The decline must be attributed to several factors, among them the mass immigration programs of the government (very few Baptist immigrants), the failure to reach French-speaking Canadians, and an increasing lack in spiritual vitality, clarity of convictions, and evangelistic outreach.

For almost half a century, Baptists have found it difficult to develop an unequivocal attitude to "the great ecumenical fact" on the Canadian ecclesiastical scene, the United Church of Canada. Formed in 1925, only two years before the Baptist schism, through the union of the large Methodist Church, the small Congregational Church and about one-half of the Presbyterian Church (the other half continues as a separate denomination), the United Church has grown in popularity as the distinctive Canadian church, an unofficial *Landeskirche*. From its beginning it claimed to be not only a united but also a uniting church which other denominations should join sooner or later. This expectation may now be fullfilled in a significant way as the Anglican and United communions, joined by the small Christian Church (Disciples of Christ), enter the final stage of negotiations for union. Opposition by vocal minorities in the Anglican and United churches and a notable lack of enthusiasm for the merger at the grass-roots level may defer the union for a few years. It is not likely to prevent it. The implications for Baptists and for other Protestants not involved in the merger of these large denominations are serious.

The combined strength of the Anglican and United churches represents nearly a third of the country's population, and more specifically, one-half of English-speaking Canada. The Roman Catholic constituency, predominantly French-speaking, has increased to one-half of the total population. In view of the rapid secularization of Canadian life and an increasing proportion of nominal church members, the significance of large numbers might be questioned. Nevertheless, Baptists constitute only a small segment within the remaining one-sixth of the population to be divided among the many "dissenting" Protestant denominations and other churches and religious groups.

As a result of these circumstances and trends, Baptists of Canada find themselves today in a peculiar situation, quite different from the position of their brethren both in the United States and in Great Britain, with whom they have had meaningful links for two centuries. In Great Britain, there has prevailed a great sense of unity among Free churches which for generations had suffered severe limitations at the hands of the established church. In the United States, churches with congregational polity constituted roughly half of American Protestantism in mid-twentieth century.[2] In Canada the small Baptist denomination remains the only sizeable group with congregational order. It is also the only denomination in Canada to plead consistently the case for believer's baptism.

One way to describe the ecumenical dilemma of Canadian Baptists in recent years might be to understand their existence as a tension between the "sect" and "church" types of Christianity. A polarization between the more "churchy" and the more "sectarian" types existed in the English Baptist movement from the beginning and can perhaps be explained, in part, by its two cradles, English Puritan Separatism and Continental Anabaptism (Dutch Mennonites). Examples of the two-fold heritage can still be found among Canadian Baptists in the diverse attitudes to the Bible, to higher education, to forms of worship, and to the role of the church in society.

The true historical significance of the planned Anglican-United merger in Canada may not be its ecumenical success but rather the fact that through it the Congregational and Methodist churches will have completed their "sect to church cycle" (the process of *Verkirchlichung)* and rejoined the mother church.[3]

The paradox of Baptist history in general, and of Canadian Baptist history in particular, seems to be the evidence that Baptists have seldom if ever succumbed to the pull toward "establishmentarian" Christianity. The tension between the church and sect patterns of Christianity has sometimes contributed to denominational divisions. When properly understood and held in creative tension, this paradox may yet prove to be the most important Baptist contribution to the life of the whole church of Jesus Christ in an ecumenical age. The realization of this underlying tension will aid us in our understanding of the ambivalent attitudes of Canadian Baptists toward cooperative Christianity.

COOPERATION WITH OTHER PROTESTANTS AND PROTESTANT CHURCHES

One may draw a legitimate distinction between involvement in nondenominational agencies and projects on the one side and interchurch cooperation on the other.

As individual Christians, as local churches and denominational bodies, Canadian Baptists wholeheartedly supported, and still do support, such nondenominational enterprises as the Bible Society, the Gideons, the Temperance Movement, the Lord's Day Alliance, and campus ministries.

In matters of interchurch cooperation on the local level, Baptists related to the Baptist Federation of Canada have been involved in cooperation with the Presbyterian and United churches, and usually also with the Anglican Church. Most Baptists outside the BFC have refused to work together with the pedobaptist churches except in such projects as city-wide evangelistic crusades. Many Baptist churches hold union services with the neighboring United and/or Presbyterian churches during the summer months. Joint weekday groups in children's and youth programs exist in many places. Most Baptist pastors participate in the Week of Prayer and Holy Week services and are active in the local ministerial associations. Joint-action projects in services to the aging, immigrants, and other persons in need are numerous.

Surprisingly enough, the concept of federated churches, larger parishes, and community churches has received very little support among Baptists and other Canadian Protestants. The lack of enthusiasm for wider cooperation at this level is probably related to the type of membership practiced by Baptists in Canada. While no statistics are available, it is estimated that only a few of the BFC churches have open membership. An increasing minority is experimenting with different types of associate membership, with varying degrees of limitations imposed on unimmersed members. The majority of the BFC churches and nearly all non-BFC churches practice closed membership.

Close links between Baptists and the United Church existed at the national level for three decades, particularly in Christian education and in the production of hymnbooks. Sunday school materials were produced jointly from 1937 to 1964. Cooperation was terminated only after a crisis which threatened to lead to another schism in the Convention of Ontario and Quebec. The official Canadian Baptist Hymnary produced by the three conventions in 1936 was identical with the 1930 hymnal of the United Church except for a few minor revisions. In 1971 the United Church published a new hymnal jointly with the Anglican Church. A distinctive Baptist Hymnal was produced by the BFC in 1973 to be used in their churches.

The termination of close cooperation with the United Church in two crucial areas of work is indicative of the gradual but highly significant changes in the ecclesiastical climate of Canada. As the United Church prepares for union with the Anglican Church and slowly moves away from its Free-church heritage, many Canadian Baptist leaders are undergoing a painful process of reassessment of Baptist destiny and role in Canada. The rising pressures of ecumenicity have further contributed to the resurgence of denominational consciousness. It remains to be seen whether it is merely a superficial defense mechanism, a panic of anxiety for denominational survival vis-à-vis the emerging ecclesiastical giants, or whether it will lead to creative leadership among the new generation of Canadian Baptists. Both options are in evidence at the present time.

ECUMENICAL DIALOGUE

Like their brethren in other lands, Canadian Baptists are divided on issues arising from the modern Ecumenical Movement.[4] By and large, the leadership in the Ontario-Quebec Convention has been involved in ecumenical contacts more actively than Baptists in the other parts of Canada. The proximity of the headquarters of Protestant denominations and of the Canadian Council of Churches (CCC) in Toronto made it convenient. Because of their regular involvement in ecumenical structures, Baptist leaders of Ontario have sometimes been accused by their brethren elsewhere of betraying Baptist witness. Yet some of the clearest statements of Baptist position have emanated from that Convention in recent years. It issued three documents on Baptist distinctives (1947, 1958, and 1965).[5]

The Atlantic Baptists published several booklets which confirm the resurgence of Baptist consciousness.[6] A writer representing the viewpoint of the Fellowship of Evangelical Baptists expressed a rejection of the Ecumenical Movement *per se*.[7]

In spite of repeated pleas for greater involvement in ecumenical dialogue, Canadian Baptists have been rather slow to seize the many emerging opportunities for Baptist witness through ecumenical conversations and joint action, whether at the local scene, regionally, or nationally.

THE CANADIAN COUNCIL OF CHURCHES

Baptists affiliated with the BFC became charter members of the Council, organized in 1944. Its membership includes all the major and several smaller Protestant denominations and some related organizations (YMCA, YWCA, SCM). Baptists outside the BFC were opposed to the CCC from the beginning. During the first two decades of its existence, the CCC enjoyed Baptist (BFC) support and cooperation. Baptists provided more than their proportionate share of funds, voluntary services, and full-time secretaries. In recent years, however, a rising tide of criticism directed against the CCC has spread in many sections of the BFC constituency. In 1962, the BFC Council declined to provide financial support for an Ecumenical Institute in Toronto which became affiliated with the CCC. The Convention of Ontario and Quebec undertook to support the Institute unilaterally. The BFC refused to endorse other CCC projects, especially after the CCC reorganization in 1968. Most Baptist leaders view with critical dismay the one-sided preoccupation with economic and political issues by the CCC leadership. In 1971, the Atlantic Convention voted to withdraw its representatives from and to terminate its financial support of the CCC.[8] The Union of French Baptist Churches withdrew in 1973.

THE WORLD COUNCIL OF CHURCHES

Canadian Baptists affiliated with the BFC gave full considera-tion to membership in the World Council of Churches at the time of its formation in 1948. Only the Convention of Ontario and Quebec voted (1949) in favor of joining the WCC. The Union of Western Canada did not approve of it, and the Atlantic (then called Maritime) Convention voted formally against it (1951).[9] The lack of agreement prevented the BFC as the national body from applying for membership. Attempts were made several times to reopen the question but did not result in action.

When it became obvious that the BFC as the national body would not seek membership in the WCC, the Convention of Ontario and Quebec decided in 1965 to explore the possibility of joining the WCC unilaterally. Apparently there was no objection on the part of the WCC. However, the Convention assembly in 1969 rejected the proposal to apply for membership. Additional information on the WCC was distributed to the churches, but no further action was taken.[10] It appears, therefore, that Canadian Baptists, like the majority of Baptist bodies related to the BWA, will remain outside the WCC. The rejection of membership in the WCC has not prevented individuals from taking part in conferences and study commissions sponsored by the WCC. Canadian Baptists not affiliated with the BFC are vehemently opposed to the WCC.

OTHER CHANNELS FOR COOPERATIVE CHRISTIANITY

Following the example set in other countries, evangelical and fundamentalist Protestants in Canada have organized councils and societies, some of which work in direct opposition to the CCC.

The Canadian Council of Evangelical Protestant Churches is a dwarfed branch of the American Council of Christian Churches, formerly led by Dr. Carl McIntire. It operates from the Jarvis Street Baptist Church in Toronto, the focal point of the Baptist schism under Dr. T. T. Shields in 1927. It has an insignificant following, and only a few Baptist churches related to the Jarvis Street Church are affiliated with it. Nevertheless, its printed propaganda on the pages of The Gospel Witness reaches far beyond its limited constituency.

A new organization, the Evangelical Fellowship of Canada (EFC), was formed in 1964. In some respects it resembles the National Association of Evangelicals (in the U.S.A.), except that it is primarily a fellowship of individuals rather than a group of denominations. Members must endorse a doctrinal statement. Its numerical growth has been slow. Its fellowship is rather unique in that it includes not only members from the small denominations, traditionally classified as evangelical, but also members from the main-line Protestant churches (Anglican, Presbyterian, and United), some of whom regard it as no problem to be involved in the CCC at the same time. The EFC has received support from many individual Baptists.

Perhaps the most inclusive ecumenical gathering in Canada's history was the Canadian Congress on Evangelism held in Ottawa, August 24-28, 1970. Patterned after the Berlin and Minneapolis congresses, it involved delegates appointed by nearly all Protestant denominations. For Baptists it was the only gathering in several decades in which delegations from most, if not all, Baptist groups participated together.

RELATIONS WITH ROMAN CATHOLICS

Prior to Vatican Council II, Baptist attitudes to Roman Catholics were typical of most English-speaking Protestants in Canada. The fitting description of English and French Canada as "the two solitudes" could have been applied with equal justification to the Protestant and Catholic camps. Mutual ignorance led to suspicion; lack of personal contact to fear. The situation was further complicated by the identification of Protestantism with English Canada, and of Catholicism with French Canada.

The rapidly increasing numerical strength of the Roman Catholic Church in Canada and its repeated demands for additional privileges in a separate school system and in other areas called for watchful vigilance by Protestants. In 1945, the Inter-Church Committee on Protestant-Roman Catholic Relations (ICCPRCR) was organized in Toronto as an agency independent of the CCC. It had the support of all major Protestant denominations until 1971. The withdrawal of the Anglican Church precipitated its dissolution in 1972. The main task of ICCPRCR through the years has been to serve as a "watchdog" over Roman Catholic encroachments against Protestant rights and to act as a spokesman for Protestants. In recent years, in keeping with the warmer ecumenical climate, it redefined its purpose so as to include a more positive approach: "to suggest ways and means of working in good relations with Roman Catholics."[11]

Baptists supported ICCPRCR faithfully to the end. The BFC appointed its own Committee on Protestant-Roman Catholic Relationships in 1944. A Baptist study conference on Roman Catholicism was convened in Campbellton, New Brunswick, in May, 1960. It dealt with two major areas of concern: (1) Is the doctrine and piety of Roman Catholics such that they should be evangelized, or is evangelism among them mere proselytism? (2) What are the current areas of tension between Protestants and Roman Catholics in matters pertaining to religious liberty and human rights? With respect to the first question, the conference endorsed evangelism among Roman Catholics.[12]

In the years following Vatican II, Canadian Baptists have found it increasingly difficult to respond forthrightly and unequivocally to the dynamic waves of Roman Catholic ecumenism. Some ministers and lay people welcome the winds of change in the Roman Catholic Church as evidence of the work of God's Spirit. They fellowship and worship with Roman Catholics at joint services and conferences. Others have condemned such fraternizing as a betrayal of Baptist convictions. Many are showing a cautious "wait and see" attitude.

NEGOTIATIONS FOR CHURCH UNION

With the exception of the recent merger between the Reformed Baptists and Wesleyan Methodists in the Maritime area, Canadian Baptists have never been involved in official negotiations for church union with another (non-Baptist) body. Nevertheless, they have been confronted with the issue on at least four different occasions in this century.

In 1907, the Baptist Convention of Ontario and Quebec was invited by the United Committees of the Presbyterian, Methodist, and Congregational bodies to participate in a conference on the "Question of Union of Protestant Bodies in Canada." In a published *Reply*, the Baptists stated that "they did not admit that the organic union of all Christians is an essential condition of Christian unity, or even necessarily promotive of it."[13] The clear statement no doubt precluded further overtures to the Baptists during the negotiations leading to the formation of the United Church of Canada in 1925.

In 1943 the General Synod of the Anglican Church extended an invitation to other communions in Canada to join in the exploration of the subject of church unity. Only the United Church responded, and a joint committee of the two churches was formed in 1944. After two decades of preparatory talks, *The Principles of Union* between the two churches were approved in 1965 and 1966. Other Protestant churches were again invited to become full participants, or to send observers to the union negotiations. Comments on the *Principles* were also solicited from other church bodies. The Baptist Federation of Canada sent observers to the meetings and issued an official document, *A Baptist Response to the Principles of Union,* in 1970.[14] The Baptist *Response* expressed disagreement with the Anglican-United position on four major issues: the question of authority (Scripture, tradition, and the teaching office of the church); the concept of the church and church membership; the sacraments; and ministry. The document was drafted by Dr. Russell F. Aldwinckle, who had dealt more fully with the issues of baptism and church membership in his earlier book, *Of Water and the Spirit* (1964).[15]

In the early 1950s, Maritime Baptists met with representatives of the Disciples of Christ in a series of exploratory conversations which did not produce any decision.[16] In the mid-1960s, similar conversations were held between Baptists and Disciples in the Toronto-Hamilton area. A statement on theological beliefs and on areas of possible mutual cooperation was issued to the Baptist Convention of Ontario and Quebec in 1967.[17] The promising negotiations were ended rather abruptly soon afterward by the Disciples, who subsequently became full participants in the Anglican-United merger plan. The total Canadian constituency of the Disciples (including children and adherents) was reported by the 1961 census to be 19,512.

The most recent attempt in interchurch conversations involved a Baptist delegation appointed by the BFC and a Mennonite group selected by the Mennonite Central Committee (Canada). Two informal meetings have been held thus far, in Winnipeg (1970) and in Toronto (1972).

THE CONCEPT OF CHRISTIAN UNITY

The Canadian Baptists are sadly divided in their attitudes to cooperative Christianity. However, in spite of their disagreements over the extent of practical involvement in ecumenical relationships, they appear to be surprisingly unanimous in their understanding of Christian unity. Keeping in mind the risks implied in slogans, one may suggest the following summary of the Baptist consensus: Christian unity in free fellowship for the purpose of furtherance of the gospel? YES! Organic church union? NO!

If space permitted, one could compile several pages of quotations from Canadian Baptist writers, Convention resolutions, and other statements on the subject of unity.[18] The following excerpt from the Baptist *Response* (1970),[19] mentioned earlier, will illustrate the stance:

> We must express our regret that The Principles of Union seem to be moving in the direction of a more hierarchically organized and authoritarian church structure. We not only question the validity of this development on Scriptural grounds. We seriously doubt whether this "pattern of the church" is the one that is needed for the age in which we live. Freedom and flexibility would seem to be imperative needs of all church structures in the present. Nor do we believe that organic union either guarantees the power of the Spirit or necessarily results in an increase of Christian love. . . . We believe that institutional unity of all existing churches is a utopian dream which may never be realized.

THE CONFLICT BETWEEN SOCIAL AND THEOLOGICAL ECUMENICITY

The ecumenical relationships in Canada, as in other countries, have been and are being determined both by theological and nontheological factors.

In terms of "social ecumenicity" Canadian Baptists have gravitated, for several decades, toward the large Protestant denominations: Anglican, Presbyterian and United. We share with them a similar middle-class outlook and identical standards for the ministry. Family ties created by intermarriage usually point to the same denominational links [and social prestige]. . . .

Yet, at the same time, if we have any consciousness of our historical origins and theological convictions as Baptists, we know that in terms of "theological [ecclesiological] ecumenicity" our immediate ecumenical links ought to be sought elsewhere in the Christian family. Our closest spiritual brothers and cousins are not [members of] Episcopal and Presbyterian churches with their concepts of infant baptism, "mixed church membership" . . . and with their respective forms of church government, but rather [members of other] denominations . . . with [whom] we share a common understanding of the church as a fellowship of believers . . . constituted on a non-creedal and non-sacramental basis. But we must confess that in spite of such theological affinities, our practical contacts with these groups have been minimal.[20]

The problem of interchurch relationships has been made even more complex by theological issues other than the concepts of baptism and church membership. The authority of the Bible, its inspiration and interpretation, the power and the charismatic gifts of the Holy Spirit, the attitudes of Christians to social involvement and to political and economic questions, and many other burning issues of our day tend to divide Christians into groups and camps which often cut right across denominational loyalties. Christians in all church bodies appear to be making their individual choices regardless of their denominational affiliation.

THE ECLIPSE OF THE FREE CHURCH TRADITION IN CANADA AND THE BAPTIST ROLE IN THE BELIEVERS' CHURCH MOVEMENT

The gradual weakening of the Free church tradition in Canada has been discussed earlier in the context of the church union in 1925 and in the 1970s. If the present *Plan of Union*[21] is implemented in the proposed merger of the Anglican, Christian (Disciples) and United churches, there will be very little left of the Congregational and Methodist heritage in the new Church of Christ in Canada. Baptists will remain the only reminder of the Free church movement which once had been far stronger throughout Canada. Realizing the far-reaching changes taking place in the alignment of ecclesiastical forces in Canada at the present time, a growing number of Canadian Baptist leaders see a new dimension to ecumenical cooperation and a new leadership role for Baptists. Rev. Roy Bell of Vancouver, British Columbia, then president of the Baptist Union of Western Canada, stated in 1969:

> The choice that we have from a practical point of view is either to offer leadership of the Believers' Church Movement or to lose identity in the merger with the United and Anglican Churches. Our slogan cannot be isolation but must be cooperation.[22]

What is meant by the term "believers' church"? In the North American context, the term "free church" lacks the original English connotation of separation from a state church. Nonetheless, it can imply other dimensions of the Free-church tradition such as the principle of voluntaryism in membership (a gathered church) and a nonliturgical and noncreedal fellowship with central emphasis on individual freedom and responsibility.[23] The term "believers' church" suggests a gathered church of committed believers. It emphasizes regenerate church membership with its usual corollary of believer's baptism. In place of exaggerated modern religious individualism, so often confused with the Free-church tradition, the concept of the believers' church underscores "a covenanted and disciplined community, a fellowship of mutual correction and support."[24] It does not imply primacy of belief in the creedal sense, nor a self-righteous denial of true believers in other Christian communions.

Canadian Baptists (BFC) were well represented at the first Believers' Church Conference in Louisville, Kentucky, in 1967 and took part in the second conference in Chicago in 1970.[25]

The sense of urgent need for Baptist leadership in the Believers' Church Movement is stronger in the West than elsewhere in Canada because there are greater practical opportunities for cooperation with denominations in the Believers' Church tradition, such as the Mennonites and several other Baptist groups. At the present time, the movement is simply a necessary and healthy corrective to the somewhat lopsided ecumenicity to which Canadian Baptists subscribed in the past. Does not the very name "ecumenical" compel us to seek fellowship with the whole Body of Christ? That includes the denominations "to the left" of us as much as those "to the right" of us.

It is difficult to predict whether or not the movement will eventually evolve from its present stage of fraternal fellowship into some structural expression of unity (not necessarily union) such as a Canadian Federation of Free Churches. If it does, it might provide a needed counterbalance to the proposed Church of Christ in Canada.

CHAPTER 11

Caribbean*

Azariah McKenzie

Baptists are not famous for their relationships with other strands of Christian witness. There have grown up a myth of Baptist awkwardness with regard to ecumenical dialogue, a legend about their attitude toward church union discussions, and an astonishment when some Baptists actually do show a spirit of cooperation. Perhaps nowhere has this spirit of cooperation been more manifested than in the Caribbean, where Baptists have taken the lead in the establishment of theological education on a cooperative basis, have participated actively in many of the local councils of churches, and have provided leadership for many ecumenical ventures.

In order to understand this phenomenon, it is necessary to delve into the past. John Levo observed:

> Everybody's past is implicit in his present. This is true of races, nations and individuals. This is so true of the West Indies, that no one can be equipped for any approach to contemporary West Indian problems, who does not know something of that past.[1]

Just where and who are these people called West Indians or Caribbean communities? They stretch from the Bahama Islands in the North to Guyana on the South American mainland, from Honduras in the West to the Leeward and Windward chains in the East, involving in some cases more than a thousand miles of water between certain islands. Geographically they are a part of the Americas, but historically they have been linked to Europe and

121

Africa. So whether one is first struck by the outstanding degree of similarity or astonished by the diversity which obtains in their ethnic cultural mixture, their basic social configuration or the political, legal, educational, and religious institutions which they uphold, a brief examination will disclose that these are all the results of their common historical past, which was based in slavery, colonialism, feudalism, and foreign acculturation. The fact that the Caribbean communities share this common history makes it possible to consider them within one chapter.

This history must be borne in mind, since more than anything else it accounts for the dominance of certain religious groups in some territories and their sparsity, or in some cases complete absence, from others. It accounts for the fact, for example, that Cuba, Haiti, the Dominican Republic, Puerto Rico, Guadeloupe, and Martinique are predominantly Catholic, while Protestantism holds sway in all of the English-speaking islands. It explains the outstanding strength of the Episcopal Church in Barbados, as against Methodism in Antigua and the Baptists in Jamaica. It accounts, too, for what is unknown in many other territories of the region, the large congregations of Hindus and Moslems in Trinidad and Guyana.

Another important point to consider is that, whereas Canada or the United States of America consists, by and large, of homogeneous communities, located on the same general land mass where it is possible to cultivate something of a national consensus, the circumstances in the Caribbean are quite different. Here one finds a group of widely scattered islands with an ingrained tendency, born once again of historical circumstances, toward insularity and individualism. Each island has its own independent leadership. As in politics, so in religion, and one often responds to a given situation quite differently from the other. Whereas, therefore, it might well be possible to mobilize and express the collective judgment of a particular denomination toward a certain sociopolitical or socioreligious situation in North America, it would be very difficult to do the same thing in the Caribbean. In a sense it is an oversimplification, if not a misnomer, to talk in general terms of the "Caribbean Church" or of "Caribbean Baptists," as though the outlook and attitude of the different groups in the different island territories were characterized throughout by a common similarity. Even though they share much in common, there are significant differences.

BAPTISTS IN THE CARIBBEAN: AN HISTORICAL OVERVIEW

JAMAICA

Historically, Baptists in the Caribbean owe their existence to two main countries, the U.S.A. and England. The earliest pioneer was George Lisle, a freed Negro slave from Norfolk, Virginia. Single-handedly, without sponsorship or prospect of support from anyone, he came to Jamaica in 1783 and started an open-air evangelistic ministry in the heart of the capital city, in what was known as the Kingston Race Course, now George VI Memorial Park. The response was enthusiastic and progress phenomenal, despite the shortage of financial resources and trained leadership for the many congregations that were formed.

In 1814 an appeal was made to the Baptist Missionary Society in London for assistance. In response, the British Baptists sent in the same year their first representative, the Reverend John Rowe. This relationship has continued unbroken to the present day and more than anything else is responsible for what Baptists are in the entire region. For it was from Jamaica, through the auspices of its own Missionary Society, founded in 1842, that Baptist witness started in the following places: Haiti, 1843; Cuba, 1886; British Honduras, 1887; Costa Rica, 1888; Cayman Island, 1889; Bocas del Toro, 1894; and Nicaragua, 1904. Today, the Jamaica Baptist Union is an autonomous body with almost complete self-support. All of its eighty-three ministers are trained and 99 percent of them are native.

TRINIDAD

The history of the work in Trinidad bears close resemblance to that in Jamaica. In 1816, an American ex-slave, William Hamilton, who served in the British Marine Corps during the American Revolution, was later resettled together with his company of Negro loyalists in Trinidad. Unfortunately too little is known about him, but it is well attested that he established work in the southern part of Trinidad.

In 1843 George Cowen, a Britisher, who had been employed by the Mico Trust, became a Baptist and established a church in Port-of-Spain and Savannah Grande. In 1845 the Baptist Missionary Society sent out a Mr. Law, who by 1849 increased the membership to thiry-six, including some of the refugees from Madeira. The Port-of-Spain work grew and on March 26, 1854, St. John's Chapel was opened. Unfortunately, there was a dichotomy between the work in the North and that in the South, and although the Baptists probably knew of the existence of the work in both places, no substantial organization grew out of the situation. The legacy has been that, despite a century of Baptist Missionary Society presence in Trinidad, the work yet remains small and has become significant only recently with assistance from Jamaica, and still more recently, the advent of the Southern Baptist Convention.

BAHAMAS

In the Bahamas, the story is somewhat shrouded in the mists of uncertainty. It is maintained that Baptist witness was started there by one Prince Williams in the first half of the nineteenth century. It is quite probable that Williams was from the same group as Moses Baker, originating in New Amsterdam. For purposes of this study it is enough to observe that by 1833, when Jamaican Baptists took an interest through Joseph Burton and others, the numbers had already grown into many thousands.

Most of the work in other areas is less than ten years old with the exception of Guyana, where it is known that there were Baptists (in Demerara) as far back as 1824.

BAPTISTS AND CARIBBEAN HISTORY

In the Caribbean, emancipation and the growth toward political independence and nationhood are inseparable realities. The one was an indispensable predeterminant or *sine qua non* for the other. Emancipation resulted in a release of the human spirit and fostered that sense of worthwhileness which is always the driving force in man's search for independence and self-determination. And the story of the emancipation struggle and victory is in large measure the story of Baptist endeavor to be the church in the life of society. Names like William Knibb, Thomas Burchell, and James Phillippo have become immortalized, for while they were not the only ones to expose the barbarity and inhumanity of slavery, they certainly constituted the avante-garde in the campaign. It has been rightly said that no history of these islands would be complete without reference to the Baptists.

INTER-RELATIONSHIPS OF BAPTISTS AND CHRISTIANS OF OTHER COMMUNIONS

Broadly speaking, the Christian community in the Caribbean may be grouped into three main categories:

1. There is the mainstream, or older established churches, with a sense of historic continuity by the vast majority of their adherents. These include the Catholics (1492), Anglicans (1656), Moravians (1732), Lutherans (1743), Baptists (1783), Methodists (1787), Presbyterians (1824), Congregationalists (1827), etc.

2. The second stream is a paradox, since some are in the process of becoming mainstream while others are not. These include Seventh-Day Adventists, several brands of Pentecostalists, the Assemblies, Pilgrim Holiness, Open Bible, etc., and quasi-ecclesiastical organizations, such as the Salvation Army.

3. The third stream consists of the sects. These include various revivalist and nativistic groups and some cultic expressions which are basically more socioeconomic and sociopolitical than religious, to say the least Christian. Chief among them are the Rastafarian movement, Pocomania, Zionist, Kumina, and others of the "African connection," such as the Shango and Convince cults in Trinidad and Jamaica, respectively. These religious manifestations betray also syncretistic tendencies with other religions, e.g., Hinduism and Islam, which are present in the region.

It has been demonstrated, though not strongly, that Baptists owe their origins to the aid of other denominations. This was most certainly true in Jamaica, Trinidad, and Guyana. This relationship can be explained in that the Baptist conviction grew up in a world where the freedom of persons was separated from the freedom from sin. Within this situation, Baptists urged that there could be no dichotomy, that all life was free to be lived for God. This bond with those who fought for freedom in Whitehall and Westminster gave them a common cause with Methodists, Congregationalists, and Anglicans. There was also a common participation in Bible societies. In every island, the British and Foreign Bible Society was at work, and this common Book united Baptists with their brethren in Christ.

It was upon these bases, (a) the importance of the Bible as necessary to faith and doctrine, and (b) the proclamation of freedom from sin, which involved the freedom of the whole man, that Baptist cooperation rested.

It was cooperation but not in a uniform structure. This structure Baptists even among themselves found hard to sustain, but they recognized a diversity which did not give rise to competition, rivalry, and conflict.

THEOLOGICAL BASIS OF COOPERATION

Baptists in the Caribbean have always affirmed that the church is the Body of Christ.

> For just as the body is one and has many members, and all the members of the body, though many, are one body, so it is with Christ.... For the body does not consist of one member but of many.... But as it is, God arranged the organs in the body, each one of them, as he chose (1 Corinthians 12:12, 14, 18, RSV).

While it is clear that the concept has an individual and personal reference, it also has a communal and denominational application. The church is not *in toto* the denomination which we represent. It is a living reality of diversity in unity and unity in diversity.

Thus Baptists may not accept a principle of "compromise" or "accommodation" that would lead to the surrender of fundamental beliefs and practices for the sake of formal organizational unity either between denominations or even within the denomination. Unity is a matter of truth and as such is discovered as we pool our diversity in a common mission to demonstrate to the world that we are one "in Christ."

Therefore it would be wrong to approach another professed Christian with suspicion and mistrust. Nor should it be assumed that the practices of each denomination are solely Christian. We believe in graciousness and the responsibility to examine what others believe and to have them examine what we profess. Thus decisions to unite or disunite derive from the extent to which the revelation of God which we have in the Scriptures and through the enlightenment of the Holy Spirit is present in, and permeates the structure of, any particular branch of the church and is accepted as a cardinal doctrine of faith by its members.

It, of course, demands of us that as Baptists we reexamine ourselves in order to bring into "universal" or "catholic" focus the truths which we emphasize and whose trust God has given to us. We need to be critical of the historical molds of our faith, as handed to us by the missionaries, and also to find ways of closer cooperation with other denominations in order to do this task together.

AREAS OF COOPERATION

The major areas of cooperation in Jamaica, for example, have been those with an "outreach" character. There have been united theological training since 1910, joint evangelistic campaigns and worship as far back as records exist, a united effort to produce Sunday school lesson books, and cooperation in other areas of Christian education, mass communication, and social action.

Theological Education

Calabar Theological College was opened on October 6, 1843, with a two-fold purpose: *(a)* to send missionaries to Africa, and *(b)* to train men for ministry in Jamaica. During the ensuing decades its fortunes and location have changed. By 1858 it was teaching classical courses on the same pattern as London University and by 1865 had graduated men for Africa, the home ministry, and a few for the United States. At the turn of the century it had become quite a force in the land, having moved in 1869 to Kingston and having attached a high school and teacher training institution. At the very outset, the Jamaica Baptist Missionary Society had declared that high school aid should be interdenominational, with no creedal tests, since this was abhorrent to the principles of the "freedom of the Spirit." Whatever we might think of the dangers, it was remarkable that at such an early date our branch of the church was prepared to be "open." In due course the college opened its doors to Methodists, Congregationalists, Presbyterians, etc., and it is the alma mater of ministers to be found in most of the denominations throughout the region.

In 1957 joint teaching took on another form at Calabar, and by 1966 a United Theological College was established in close proximity to the University of the West Indies, founded by three existing denominational colleges and ten participating denominations. This college is now related to Codrington College in Barbados, St. John Vianney in Trinidad, and St. Michael's Roman Catholic Seminary in Kingston, in a teaching program for a B.A. degree.

Evangelism

Churches have found it easiest to unite in joint worship, and Baptists are no exception. In 1950 the Jamaica Crusade was held in which the Anglicans played a dominant role. In each island these united endeavors have occurred. There has also been the factor of renascent Eastern religions. In Guyana, for instance, this has stimulated many joint evangelistic endeavors. However, the question of intercommunion and significant dialogue in joint worship has not been pursued with much vigor. Yet, the high festivals of the church's year have always been times of sharing.

Christian Education

Under the auspices of the Caribbean Committee for Joint Christian Action (CCJCA), efforts have been made to develop on an ecumenical basis a Christian education program. Literature was written and produced in the region and had a wide circulation. But it did not affect the spirit of diversity in the denominations and at times fostered it because of the local treatment of biblical issues.

Mass Communication

In most islands a certain amount of time has been allotted to denominations, and the Baptists have had their share. In order to use it wisely, Caribbean Baptists have participated in training sessions promoted by the World Council of Churches and the Southern Baptist Convention, both of which have given training on an interdenominational basis. This participation has enabled Baptists to be a part of a total Christian onslaught on materialism and anti-Christian forces. At the same time it has afforded a means of communicating with the Christian community en masse.

BAPTISTS AND THE CONCILIAR MOVEMENT

Caribbean Baptists have been members of most national councils. In Guyana, Trinidad, and Jamaica, these councils are broadly based and include in their membership both Anglicans and Roman Catholics. This inclusiveness has meant that for some Baptists these are suspect. But despite this, many groups participate at the levels they are able to sustain, always maintaining the right of withdrawal. Even where Baptists as a denomination find it difficult to accept membership in such councils, individuals have nevertheless involved themselves, often with the encouragement of their pastors. Thus Baptists in the Caribbean, like elsewhere, have a paradoxical stance to the Conciliar Movement.

CONCLUSION

Caribbean Baptists, as a whole, may be classified among the old established churches of the region. As a "main stream" denomination, they possess an identity of their own, a distinctive historical stance and international relationship, built up over the centuries. Caribbean Baptists were represented in the parliamentary investigation on the ills of apprenticeship in 1837. They were among the first to evangelize Africa (1843). They were represented at almost all the international Evangelical conferences in the nineteenth century. When the Baptist World Alliance was formed in 1905, a Jamaican pastor was a founding member. In 1911, when the Alliance met again, the Caribbean had three officers, Robert Cleghorn of Belize, Philip Williams of Jamaica, and Murray Williams of Bahamas, as vice-presidents. It seems, therefore, that Caribbean Baptists have always been committed to an international and interdenominational stance over the centuries, and to do otherwise now would betray their ethos.

CHAPTER 12

Latin America

William R. Estep, Jr.

Evangelical mission endeavors in Latin America may be dated with the arrival of James Thomson, a Baptist lay preacher from Scotland, in Buenos Aires, Argentina, on October 6, 1818.[1] Some time later, on a Sunday, November 19, 1819, he conducted the first Protestant worship service in Argentina.[2] Even though Thomson was a Baptist, he established no churches. From the beginning, his work was interdenominational in character. He concentrated on a literacy program and Bible distribution. Using a system of education developed by Joseph Lancaster, an Englishman, Thomson established the first elementary school system in South America designed for the education of the masses. At first sent out by the English and Foreign School Society, he later became an agent of the British and Foreign Bible Society.

Thomson came to the South American continent at an opportune time. In fact, only two years earlier Argentina had won her independence from Spain. Taking advantage of the new era of freedom, he worked for two and one-half years in Argentina organizing his Lancastrian schools and Bible societies. Thomson continued his labors in Chile at the invitation of the Chilean government. Later he duplicated his earlier efforts in Peru, Colombia, and Mexico.

His work was made possible by the enthusiastic support of revolutionary leaders, among whom were San Martin of Argentina and Colonel James Fraser of Colombia.[3] In their initial stages

Thomson's endeavors received approval of the Roman Catholic hierarchies and the cooperation of numerous parish priests, some of whom assumed positions of leadership in both the schools and the Bible societies.

Unfortunately the support and cooperation which Thomson's initial efforts enjoyed did not last. "When Lucas Matthews, an English agent of the British and Foreign Bible Society, followed Thomson's trail in Colombia three years later, the climate was beginning to change. . . . Although he managed to sell some Bibles, the work became increasingly difficult as Roman Catholic opposition"[4] mounted. Matthews' efforts came to a sudden halt with his mysterious disappearance while en route to the coast from Bogota on the Magdalena River. His death is symbolic of evangelical beginnings in South America.

> It has been said that the work begun by Thomson received a warm welcome because "it purported to be educational, and met with death by priestly suffocation because it was evangelical."[5]

Before the doors began to slam shut on Thomson's work, he was able, as late as 1842, to circulate in Mexico an edition of the Bible without notes with the endorsement of Roman Catholic authorities.[6] Thus the seed was sown in a number of Latin American countries by Bible colporteurs for later evangelical work which began to appear even before 1846.

EARLY BAPTIST MISSION EFFORTS

A Baptist seaman, Philip Livingston of New York City, was on board a ship in 1844 which visited San Andrés, a Caribbean island belonging to Colombia. Here he distributed the Scriptures and preached the gospel. This experience caused him to dedicate his life to mission efforts in the islands. For this purpose he secured ordination to the ministry and some financial support from Leith Street Baptist Church in New York City. The following year he returned to San Andrés and Providence to continue the work he had started two years before. Livingston devoted the remainder of his life to establishing Baptist churches in the islands. When he died some fifty years later, he left behind a vigorous movement. Livingston's work was the earliest distinctive Baptist missionary effort in Latin America and one of the earliest evangelical works as well. However, the islanders were English-speaking and rather isolated from the Spanish-speaking mainland, so that the work did not become well known or widely influential.

Today numerous Baptist groups conduct some form of missionary work in Latin American countries. These include American Baptists, Canadian Baptists, Conservative Baptists, Mid-Missions (General Association of Regular Baptists), World Fellowship Baptists, and Southern Baptists as well as some independent and immigrant Baptist bodies. The oldest and most extensive work is that of the Southern Baptist Convention.

In 1880 Southern Baptists entered Mexico by assuming the financial responsibility for the support of John O. Westrup, who was a native of England but had lived in Mexico since early childhood. Westrup's service as a missionary of the Southern Baptist Convention was cut short by his death a few months later. The Foreign Mission Board was informed that "on the 18th of December, while on his way from Monterey to Musquiz, he was barbarously murdered and mutilated by a band of Indians and Mexicans."[7]

Undaunted, Southern Baptists continued the work so recently begun in Latin America and expanded their operations the next year (1881) to include Brazil. However, there were Baptists in Brazil before Southern Baptists came to stay. Following earlier efforts of Methodists, who soon abandoned the work, Presbyterians and Southern Baptists came to Brazil in 1858. No Baptist church was organized, however, until an immigrant group of Southerners established a church in Saõ Paulo in 1871. They sought the aid of the Foreign Mission Board in directing efforts toward the winning of Brazilians to Christ. Subsequently, Brazil was to become the most successful Latin American mission effort of Southern Baptists. Today, the total membership of all Baptist groups in Brazil numbers approximately 500,000.[8]

Baptist work in Argentina was inaugurated by a Swiss, Don Pablo Besson. Besson was formerly a Presbyterian who became a Baptist after a careful study of the baptismal teachings of the New Testament. Soon after joining the French Baptists, he migrated to Argentina, where he became pastor of a Baptist church made up of French immigrants in the province of Santa Fé. Besson later moved to Buenos Aires, where his influence as a Baptist minister and statesman in the fight for religious liberty was unsurpassed for almost a half a century.[9]

Before the turn of the century, German immigrants in Chile organized a Baptist church.[10] By 1907 a Chilean Baptist Union was formed with twelve churches and some five hundred members.

This organization was accomplished largely under the leadership of a Scotsman, W.D.T. MacDonald, a graduate of Spurgeon's College. He served for a time with the Christian and Missionary Alliance, but his Baptist convictions caused him to sever this relationship.

Before 1910 Baptists comprised an exceedingly small segment of the Evangelical movement in Latin America. All other countries in which Baptists are now found were entered after this date, and in all but Uruguay, the work was begun in 1941 or later.[11] Obviously Baptists were relatively slow in establishing churches and securing a following in Latin America. Baptist efforts were forced to wait on more favorable conditions than existed in the first half of the nineteenth century, as early failures indicate. Again, Baptists in Latin America received both their support and missionary personnel from North America.

At present, in no country do Baptists comprise a majority of the Protestant population in Latin America. Generally, they comprise a small segment of the Protestant minority in a country which is traditionally Roman Catholic. This minority status has some bearing, doubtless, upon how Baptists relate to the Roman Catholic majority and to fellow Evangelicals.

BAPTISTS AND ROMAN CATHOLICS TO 1958

Roman Catholicism claimed the allegiance of the vast majority of the peoples of Latin America on the eve of the Protestant missionary outreach. Latourette points out, "The region had been the scene of the largest scale missionary effort of that church in the preceding three centuries. To it more of its missionaries had gone than to all the rest of the world in that period."[12] Yet the results were disappointing if one were to judge in terms of the strength of the Catholic Church in Latin America.

> Latin America was still dependent upon a foreign priesthood to meet the needs of its Catholic constituency. Catholicism in Latin America was parasitic and a liability rather than an asset to the Roman Catholic Church as a whole.[13]

Latourette indicates some of the factors which have contributed to the lethargic and rather anemic condition of Catholicism in Latin America when he writes:

> Yet much of the conversion was superficial, and superstition and thinly veiled paganism survived. Many of the clergy were unworthy of their calling. Sometimes the home government used America as a dumping ground for priests who had caused trouble in Spain.[14]

The Church in colonial America was subservient to Spanish and Portuguese monarchs. It soon possessed enormous wealth. However, the Church's privileged position did not further the cause of Christ. To the contrary, Catholicism's moral and spiritual influence steadily declined, while anti-clericalism and skepticism mounted. The immorality of the clergy was scandalous and the ignorance of the masses appalling.[15]

The wars of independence brought trying times to the Roman Catholic Church in the new republics. Ties were broken with the mother country and severely strained with Rome. The Vatican delayed recognition of the sovereignty of the new countries as long as possible. In the meantime, Protestants began to project mission work in what had been considered Rome's exclusive vineyard. Their presence was often resented. And as the Roman Church claimed a privileged status in the various countries, discrimination, harassment, and even martyrdom became the price of Protestant advance.

The Roman Catholic opposition to the presence of the Evangelicals in Latin America has taken many forms. The various rather crude newspaper articles which attempted to link Protestants with bandits and Communists, "hate Protestant songs," mob violence, the burning of Protestant church and school buildings, the more subtle political maneuvering and economic discrimination are only suggestive of the myriad ways in which Rome has expressed her hostility toward the Protestant minority with varying degrees of intensity from time to time and from country to country.

Acts of violence against Protestants in Latin America reached a peak from 1948 to 1958 in Colombia. Buttressed by concordats with the Vatican, the Colombian government attempted to erect off-limit signs for Evangelicals in three-fourths of the country.[16]

In the face of the open hostility and acts of violence against Protestants, Colombian Baptists along with other Evangelicals reacted in a number of ways. They supported financially the work of the Evangelical Confederation of Colombia (CEDEC), while not formally joining the Federation. In this way they sought to publicize the plight of Colombian Evangelicals outside of Colombia. CEDEC also attempted to bring its grievances before Colombia's House of Representatives. In October, 1959, a memorial carrying the signatures of 14,000 Protestants and other Colombians and calling for a congressional investigation of religious persecution in Colombia was presented to Colombia's House of Representatives.

BAPTISTS AND CATHOLICS SINCE 1958

In the *Latin American Evangelist* of May–June, 1961, which carried an article about the era of persecution which Colombian Christians had suffered, the Colombian cardinal in Bogotá is quoted as admitting that some of his priests had acted "imprudently." As early as 1959, a prominent Roman Catholic priest, Ricardo Struve Haker, confessed in his book, *Inquisición, Tolerancia e Idea Ecuménica,* that Roman Catholics had been guilty of acts of violence against Protestants in Colombia.[17]

The significance of Father Haker's book lies in the fact that it was the first publication *(con licencia eclesiástica)* of the Roman Catholic Church in Colombia to call for a change of attitude on the part of the nation's Catholic constituency toward Protestants. That the change could hardly have been more drastic is evident when one compares Haker's book with that of his predecessor, Eduardo Ospina, vice-president of the Committee for Faith-Defense.[18]

Haker is no less a Roman Catholic than Ospina, but he calls for a different approach from that which prevailed in dealing with "las sectas heterodoxas que invadieron este continente" (the heretical sects which have invaded this continent).[19] Again, instead of attempting to explain away the acts of violence against the Protestants as Ospina does, Haker admits that some Catholics have reacted against what he terms "el proselitismo muchas veces impertinente e imprudente de las sectas (Proselytism by the sects, many times both impertinent and imprudent)," which appears to be an admission of the effectiveness of Protestant mission efforts. He offers in this work the new ecumenical approach to take the place of the former "posture of repression and ineffective tolerance."[20] Haker bases his appeal for a cessation of acts of hostility and the acceptance of the ecumenical approach upon three facts: (1) It will, in the long run, prove more effective; (2) it is the only authentic Christian approach; (3) it reflects the thinking of John XXIII and underlies the purpose of the forthcoming Vatican Council II.[21]

From 1958 the attitude and actions of the Roman Catholic Church began to change. The author was in Colombia for the first time in 1956, before the period of persecution *(violencia)* had come to an end. It is difficult to describe the tension, suspicion, and fear which characterized Baptists and other Evangelicals, missionaries and nationals alike, in those days. The third dictator of three in a series, Rojas Pinilla, was in power. Murder and death stalked the land. Attacks on Protestants were an everyday occurrence. Pinilla had the complete support of the Colombian hierarchy headed by the aging Cardinal Luque. Baptists had been spared much suffering and loss of life experienced by other denominations whose strength was in the rural areas. Nevertheless, in July of that year, the Baptist church building and parsonage in the village of Helvecia in the state of Tolima were burned to the ground. Even as late as 1960, mobs carried on a campaign of hate and violence at the instigation of local priests against the Evangelicals. Today, in spite of an occasional outburst of anti-Protestant feeling, there is no doubt that Roman Catholic policies toward Protestants in Latin America began to change with the ascendancy of John XXIII to the papal throne.

Colombian Christians rejoiced at the collapse of the corrupt anti-Protestant regime of Rojas Pinilla in 1958. Undoubtedly the fall of Pinilla and the death of Cardinal Luque, which came a short time later, had a liberating effect for Protestants as well as others. Yet the climate of suspicion, hate, and intolerance so characteristic of Roman Catholicism through four and one-half centuries in Latin America was undergoing a remarkable change, for which no one less than the pope himself was responsible.

As if to underline the sincerity inherent in the new approach, the Catholic Church began to project what was termed a "Holy Mission" for the enlightenment of the people in the doctrines of the church. One of the first such "services of reconciliation" was held in Cali, Colombia. A part of the Holy Mission included a joint service with Protestants, held in the Olympic gymnasium. A few hundred were expected. Eight thousand came. A priest, Father Florencio Alvarez, presided at the meeting. Some nine years before, this very priest had led a mob in stoning the Central Baptist Church of Bogota. Only two years before, he had attempted to halt the publication of the Colombian Baptist paper by intimidating the printer. He had also attempted to close the Baptist schools in Bogotá. But during the Holy Mission he called for cooperation between Catholics and Protestants against a common enemy, communism. The pastor of the First Baptist Church of Cali, Hugo Ruiz Roco, was one of three Evangelicals who spoke from the same platform as Alvarez upon this occasion. Clearly the period of persecution for Protestants in Latin America was coming to an end.

Baptists entered Latin America with a deep sense of mission. They did not consider themselves invaders of Christian territory already occupied by a sister communion. To the contrary, more often than not, they felt that Rome had completely failed in her efforts to make Christians out of nationals. Baptists tended to ignore what positive contributions Catholicism had made while magnifying the spiritual destitution that actually existed in the midst of so many religious trappings. Doubtless the anti-Catholic feelings often expressed by Baptist missionaries were not alleviated by the prestigious position enjoyed by the established church or the bitterness and violence with which their evangelistic efforts were often rejected. To pretend that the Baptist witness in Latin America was and is free of anti-Catholic sentiment is less than truthful.

A survey of the contemporary situation has revealed that Baptists have responded to Catholic-initiated contacts with a remarkable degree of openness and good faith. In Panamá, missionary L. D. Wood participated in a televised dialogue with the local Roman Catholic bishop and a Presbyterian missionary. In Venezuela Baptists are now permitted to conduct evangelistic services in the public parks without any opposition. Roy L. Lyon, missionary to Venezuela, reports an openness and eagerness on the part of local priests for fellowship and the exchange of ideas. A local Roman Catholic church is now using the Baptist hymnal in its services as a result of this new relationship. Recently, missionary John Thomas, who pioneered in opening Baptist work in Medellin, Colombia, was granted permission by city authorities to use the civic auditorium without charge. Several priests attended the services. This was in a city where Baptists a few years before had the utmost difficulty in securing an adequate place to meet due to the initial opposition of Roman Catholic authorities. In Peru, Bill Metheney, Baptist missionary, conducted a memorial service in honor of John F. Kennedy in a local Jesuit church, the oldest church in the city. The invitation came from a group of American Jesuit priests whose friendship Metheney had cultivated in Arequipa, Peru.

Charles W. Bryan, now field secretary for the Caribbean, Mexico, and Central America of the Foreign Mission Board of the Southern

Baptist Convention, feels that the spirit of openness is limited to a minority of relatively young priests. He believes that the bishops are more reluctant to engage in any meaningful dialogue or fellowship. He bases his opinion upon several years of observation and new episcopal directives that have appeared in the public news media in Mexico and Costa Rica, warning Catholics that the Ecumenical Movement does not mean that Catholics are free to attend Protestant worship services at will. Specifically Mexican Catholics were warned, in an article by Gloria Riestra appearing in *El Sol de México*, not to attend "the 'Crusade of the Americas' in which forty Baptist organizations are working among baptized Catholics as if we were a foreign mission field."[22] However, Bryan feels that Vatican Council II has given Latin Americans a new sense of freedom. They now have the papal blessing to relate to Protestants in a positive fashion—something they have wished to do for a long time. In his own personal relationship with Catholic businessmen, Bryan said, "We meet each other as equals before God in friendship and respect."[23] He relates one occasion upon which a local priest attended an ordination service for a Baptist minister.

Bill Coffman, missionary in the Dominican Republic, reports that with the fall of Dictator Trujillo restrictions against Protestants were removed. There is now complete freedom and an excellent relationship with the Roman Catholic Church.

Dr. Ben Welmaker, president of the International Baptist Seminary in Cali, Colombia, feels that the new stance can be traced to Pope John's emphasis upon the Bible and the necessity of Bible study on the part of all Catholic people. He reports that twenty-two Roman Catholic priests attended the last graduation exercises of the Baptist Seminary in Cali. An athletic program which consists mainly of soccer is now a cooperative enterprise between the Roman Catholic seminary in Cali and the Baptist seminary. Professor Don Orr directed the seminary choir in a concert at the Catholic seminary in May, 1969. Professor Alan P. Neely has been most active in carrying on theological dialogue with Roman Catholics in Colombia. The initiative was taken by the Roman Catholics who some four years ago stopped by the Baptist seminary in Cali for an informal visit. They were so impressed with the library that they asked the Baptists to help them reorganize their library along the same lines. This led not only to a complete reorganization of the Roman Catholic seminary library under the direction of Baptist missionaries but also to a continued relationship. Subsequently, upon two different occasions, Professor Neely has lectured at the Catholic seminary in Mantezales. When he asked his Catholic hosts what they wished him to lecture on, he was told, "Lecture on preaching the gospel of Jesus Christ."

Shortly after the last session of Vatican Council II, Brazilian Protestant leaders, including professors of the Baptist seminary in Recife, were invited to engage in an ecumenical conference at the local Roman Catholic seminary. Papers presented by the various participants were read before the entire student body of the seminary.[24] Subsequently, there have been indications that Baptists in Brazil are becoming more cautious in their relationship with the Roman Catholic Church.[25]

In Chile, the period of ecumenical dialogue with the Roman Catholics received its greatest stimulus with the publication of a book, *El Protestantismo en Chile* by a Roman Catholic priest, Ignacio Vergara. Vergara's work is objective, irenic, and ecumenical in tone. In his terminology and spirit, he follows the guidelines of Vatican Council II.[26] Professors from the Baptist seminary in Santiago engaged in a series of conferences with Vergara shortly after his book appeared in 1962. The meetings were friendly and evoked mutual respect. A Roman Catholic student delegation attended the dedication services of a Baptist student center in Concepción, Chile. When the Roman Catholic student center was opened some time later, the Baptist students were invited to attend the ceremony, which they did. In Valdivia, Baptist and Roman Catholic students inaugurated a program of joint Bible study in which missionary Bob Adams participated. At Antofagasta in the north of Chile, the Roman Catholic university offered the use of one of its classrooms as a meeting place for Baptist students. Some of the national Baptists have taken a very cautious attitude toward the current dialogue in progress between Baptists and Catholics. However, some Baptist missionaries, who were somewhat reluctant to engage in the conversations, have taken a more positive attitude since actually visiting in the home of a Roman Catholic bishop in Temuco.

Perhaps enough incidents relative to Baptist-Catholic relationships since 1958 have been cited to indicate a definite pattern. (1) Catholic-inspired acts of hostility have almost completely vanished. (2) Evidently a very earnest attempt to implement the ecumenical approach to Protestants is being made by certain Roman Catholic priests in every Latin American country. (3) The pattern is not altogether uniform. While some bishops seem reluctant to go along with the new approach, others are in the avant-garde of the new strategy. (4) Among Catholics in Latin America, there is a strong emphasis on Bible distribution and Bible study. (5) There seems to be a definite move to play down the role of the Virgin Mary in the life of the church and a corresponding attempt to magnify the place of preaching in worship.

The Baptist response to the new Catholic approach has been mixed. For the most part, Baptists have responded with an openness which has welcomed both dialogue and fellowship and has fostered a degree of cooperation as well. Some confusion is also apparent, since a certain amount of reorientation in Baptist mission strategy is in order. As one Colombian missionary put it, "The stones are easier to cope with than the new ecumenism." It is not too surprising that both suspicion and fear have appeared among Baptists in the wake of the first Catholic ecumenical decade (1958-1968).

BAPTISTS AND OTHER PROTESTANTS

The relationship of Baptists with other Protestants, with some exceptions, has been one marked by cordiality and mutual respect. Many factors account for this spirit. Protestants have always been a minority in Latin America. They have frequently used one another's hymnals, a common Bible translation, and Sunday school literature. In several countries, missionaries meet regularly in one another's homes for monthly fellowship meetings. Interdenominational evangelistic efforts have not been unusual.

When Baptists first entered some Latin American countries, they created some problems for themselves which had to be overcome. For example, when Southern Baptists entered Colombia in 1941, other denominations were using literature published by the Baptist Publishing House in El Paso, Texas. This soon ceased. Upon several occasions national ministers who were disgruntled with their own denominations became Baptists and found immediate opportunities for service and frequently better pay. At times Baptists also appeared to compete with other Evangelicals for members.

In recent years, Baptist fellowship and cooperation with other

Protestant groups have shown marked improvement. The language schools at San José, Costa Rica, and Campinas, Brazil, where Baptist missionary appointees study with missionaries of other denominations, comprise one factor accounting for the change. The cooperative evangelistic efforts of Billy Graham and the "Evangelism in Depth" campaigns sponsored by the Latin American Mission play a significant role in this development. Since Baptist seminaries accept students for the ministry from other Evangelical communions, the sense of unity is thereby enhanced among Evangelicals. In addition to these factors the basic conservative theological stance of Protestants in Latin America makes possible a genuine spirit of camaraderie.

Baptists, however, more frequently than not, stop short of joining any national confederations. The nature of their relationship with other Protestants is more a matter of spirit than of ecclesiastical structure. While there is a genuine sense of oneness in Christ, there is also a great reluctance to express this reality in ways other than in voluntary cooperative ventures of common concern.

Organizations related to the World Council of Churches have had little attraction for Latin American Baptists. Baptists were fairly well represented in the last Latin American Conference of Evangelicals meeting in Lima, Peru, in July, 1961. However, it is interesting to note that this conference was not organized along denominational lines. Thus Baptists could serve as representatives of their national delegations without representing in any official way their denomination. Therefore, Baptists were found among the delegates from Argentina, Mexico, Brazil, Bolivia, Chile, and Peru.[27]

BAPTISTS DEFINE THEIR POSITION

The older Baptist bodies in Latin America have begun to address themselves rather seriously to the challenge presented by the contemporary Ecumenical Movement. The Brazilian Baptist Convention rejected an invitation to join the Evangelical Confederation of Brazil (Confederação Evangélica do Brasil) in 1965.[28] Subsequently, the International Council of Christian Churches and Vatican Council II have compelled Brazilian Baptists to articulate their position relative to the Ecumenical Movement. This they did in 1968. In a forthright document entitled "Uma Decisão Sôbre Ecumenismo,"[29] Brazilian Baptists set themselves in opposition for the following reasons: It looks toward an artificial union contrary to the teachings of Christ; its teachings are not in accord with the New Testament; it attempts to form a super-church which eventually will return to Rome; it is dominated by persons whose thinking is not true to the Scriptures. "It is of no value to join in religious ceremonies with pastors and priests which leaves the impression that doctrinally we are the same and all religions are equally good."[30]

The position of Brazilian Baptists is then summarized in eight conclusions, as negative as the foregoing observations. However, the Convention affirmed its spiritual unity and identity with all believers "who recognize the exclusive sovereignty of Jesus Christ and the absolute validity of his Word."[31] The conclusions were full of warnings to pastors and young people about engaging in acts of worship, particularly the Mass, with Roman Catholics. The Convention admitted, however, that it could not command churches or pastors to follow its directives, but it could and would exercise supervision over the institutions of the Convention in this regard.[32]

Actually the Baptists of Brazil have entered into a number of cooperative arrangements with other Evangelicals in a variety of enterprises, such as the establishment and maintenance of hospitals, Bible societies, evangelistic campaigns, and a radio program, "Voz Evangélica." This pattern of cooperation seems fairly typical of Baptists in Latin America. Whereas there is an unwillingness to join ecumenical organizations, there is no hesitancy in cooperating in certain enterprises of mutual interest that pose no threat to the integrity of the Baptist witness.

Argentine Baptists in the same year (1968) took essentially the same position relative to the Ecumenical Movement as their Brazilian brethren. At the request of the Argentine Baptist Convention, Professor Justice Anderson of the seminary faculty prepared a pamphlet setting forth the historical development of the Ecumenical Movement. This pamphlet was distributed to all the churches. The Convention then at its annual meeting adopted a series of recommendations of a special commission on ecumenism.

The recommendations were presented under four headings: "I. Our Position; II. Toward Evangelical Ecumenical Organizations; III. Toward the Catholic Church; IV. Our Christian Attitude."[33] At the outset, Argentine Baptists declared their oneness in Christ with all those who through the Holy Spirit have been regenerated. They also affirmed their faith in the universal church composed of all the redeemed. They emphasized that Christian unity is expressed by love and fellowship with all those who are obedient to "our Lord Jesus Christ and his Word."[34]

Secondly, the Convention reaffirmed its position of non-affiliation with the Federation of Evangelical Churches and other ecumenical organizations. While the Convention refused to approve any official representatives of the Argentine Baptists, it did not bar the possibility of sending observers for the purpose "manifestar el compañerismo Cristiano y conocer más de cerca el movimiento ecumenico" (of manifesting Christian fellowship and of knowing more about the ecumenical movement).[35]

The third section dealing with the Roman Catholic ecumenism was wholly negative. Baptists voted not to participate in any religious ceremonies or ecumenical services. Since the Roman Church had not changed its doctrinal position on the Eucharist, the Virgin Mary, and the authority of the Church, it was believed there was no basis for fruitful dialogue.

The Convention voted in the fourth section to emphasize the preaching of the gospel as the only answer to a generation caught up in the crises of the twentieth century. They also voted to establish a standing Commission on Ecumenism for the purpose of compiling material on the subject and keeping the Convention informed in regard to ecumenical developments.[36]

At the 1969 annual assembly of the Argentine Evangelical Baptist Convention, the president of the Convention, Alfonso Olmedo, reiterated the stand taken by the Convention the previous year. In his presidential address he related how he had rejected all overtures from the Archbishop Coadjutor of the Roman Church to seek his participation in ecumenical services designed to encourage the "separated brethren" to return to Rome.[37]

CONCLUSION

Baptists entered Latin America with a deep sense of mission. From the earliest times their efforts have often been frustrated due to the opposition of the Roman Catholic Church. They have welcomed and responded favorably to the new ecumenical approach that has characterized Roman Catholic attitudes since 1958. It is clear that Baptists do not intend to permit Catholic ecumenism to compromise the Baptist witness. National leaders seem to feel more threatened from this source than do either the missionaries or the young people.

Baptists have also felt a kinship and sense of unity with other Evangelicals. This feeling has found overt expression in numerous acts of cooperation and fellowship. However, there has been a corresponding hesitancy to join any ecumenical organization that could possibly hinder their work, violate the autonomy of the local church, or compromise the integrity of their witness.

It seems incumbent upon Baptists in Latin America to continue to relate themselves positively to other Christians. While there is a certain amount of risk involved, are not the stakes worth the effort? Could this not be the very hour for Baptists to take the initiative in seeking creative ways in which to continue the dialogue? It would be tragic if, indeed, they hastily closed the door which Roman Catholics have so cautiously opened.

CHAPTER 13

South Asia

Mrs. Louise Paw

HISTORICAL BACKGROUND

South Asia, comprising India, Burma, Pakistan, Bangladesh, and Sri Lanka (Ceylon), has some of the strongest Baptist churches that were a result of the missionary movement of the West that began in the late eighteenth century and flourished through the nineteenth century and the first half of the twentieth century. The movement was helped to a great extent by the rise of colonial powers which gave protection and patronage to Western missions within their area of control. The decline of colonial power and the rise of nationalism with the resultant birth of new nations in this region after World War II saw a corresponding decline of foreign mission enterprise and the emergence of strong indigenous churches with well-trained and capable leadership. Thus, the presence of these churches today is in part the consequence of both the colonial period and the more recent rise of the new nations.

The Asian churches have reason to thank the churches of the West for bringing the gospel to them with all its liberating and transforming power, but with that gospel also came the divisiveness of the Western churches. In the midst of their struggle today to integrate the church into the life of their new nations, the Asian churches have the added burden of seeking a unity in the face of the colossal task of evangelism in a non-Christian region deeply rooted in ancient religions which are themselves rich in philosophy, culture, and tradition.

South Asia became a tempting field for mission with the gradual consolidation of the British Empire, which included India, Burma, and Ceylon. In response to the growing spirit of evangelism, mission agencies from the Western world set up work all over this region, working out a comity arrangement among themselves—Presbyterians, Methodists, Baptists, Lutherans, Anglicans, and a host of smaller groups. These denominations were again divided by the home bases from which they came. In retrospect one can only look upon this scramble a little philosophically and conclude that no one group could have achieved all that has been achieved and that the ugly image of a divided Christian church will gradually fade as strong indigenous churches emerge, richer for all the wealth of tradition and heritage drawn from Christendom around the world and woven into the fabric of their own culture and tradition.

COOPERATIVE WORK

From the early missionary era the major denominational mission agencies were not altogether unresponsive to the need of inter-mission relationships, and periodic conferences were held in which national leaders participated as their churches developed. In 1923 the National Christian Council of India, Burma, and Ceylon was organized, but after World War II Burma, Pakistan, and Ceylon formed their own Christian councils, of which Baptists of various backgrounds became members, providing leadership and support in many joint ventures. Some of these efforts resulted in outstanding institutions like Serampore Theological College near Calcutta; Andhra Christian Theological College at Rajamundry, now moving up to Hyderabad with an expanded program and support by the Samavesam of Telugu Baptists, the Convention of Baptist Churches of Northern Circars, Lutherans and the Church of South India; the Women's Christian College and St. Christopher's Training College in Madras; Vellore Christian Medical College and Hospital; and several colleges and schools throughout this region. A variety of projects coordinated and developed by the National Christian Council, especially the Institute for the Study of Religion and Society and the Henry Martyn School for Islamic Studies, have drawn both interest and support of many Baptist groups. The Southern Baptists, who have kept out of ecumenical structures, are beginning to show some interest and participation in a few joint projects which are now underway.

GROWTH OF THE UNION MOVEMENT

Continuing ferment of nationalism, closing of doors to foreign missions, the minority complex of Christian groups, decreasing financial support from abroad, and general poverty in this region are causing churches to close ranks. Another factor is the impatience and realistic approach of many educated laymen and youth who neither appreciate nor wish to be bothered with the theological arguments underlying the divisions of the church. More crucial than all these, in the words of U Kyaw Than, an Asian leader and a Baptist, "is the awakening of the national churches to a new sense of rendering our own obedience in Asia instead of expecting others to render it on our behalf. It is a new sense of responsibility to carry the cross."[1] To continue dependence on external help would only lead to the defeat of this purpose. Today Asian church leaders are very outspoken along this line, and the same voice is heard in all the young churches around the world. Many of the same forces and elements at work in the Asian scene have also been felt in other parts of the world where the older colonial power has declined and new national forces are rising.

Baptist churches in Asia, and particularly in this region, have been caught up with this new spirit and have responded with a willingness to seek out new ways of life and witness. One of these is the church union movement, which is gaining ground here more than in the West. Whereas in the past Baptists have been cautious regarding the union movement, today they show an increasing concern and participation in talks and negotiations as they explore how they may best fulfill their Christian task. Serious negotiations for church union began as far back as the early 1920s, and an All India Church Union Conference was held at Nagpur in 1931. As union talks progressed, it was clear that Baptists related to the British mission were more open and willing than other Baptists to find a working basis. Those related to American and Canadian missions were suspicious and afraid of too much concession to the Anglicans. They preferred to think of Christian unity in terms of cooperative work, advocating a cautious approach by a federation of churches rather than organic union. The churches of North India decided for a separate union. When the Church of South India was finally inaugurated in 1947, the British-related Baptists were not a part of it, presumably for theological reasons. However, their interest in union continued as they joined the talks for North India union.

SOUTH INDIA

To explore the possibility of a wider union, the Baptists of South India were invited along with the Lutherans to hold conversations with the Church of South India. An Inter-Church Group and a Joint Theological Commission were set up to carry on talks for union and to study the theological issues involved. Meetings were few and far between, and it was felt that the Baptists were half-hearted about them. They dropped out for a time and have since resumed with greater participation. In South India there are several federated churches dually aligned with Baptist and Lutheran bodies. Baptists and Mennonites are providing a joint ministry for the communities at dam construction sites. Rev. K. C. George, a Telugu Baptist, is the present chairman of the Andhra Christian Council, and this speaks well for the standing of Baptists in this area.

NORTH INDIA

As the negotiations for church union in North India proceeded, it became clear that it would be very difficult to find a workable basis that would include a wide range of Protestants separated by theology, language, culture, political realities, and geography— from West Pakistan across the subcontinent to Burma. So when Pakistan and Burma, now sovereign states, decided to drop out of negotiations and form their own committees, the situation was somewhat eased. Ceylon, which did not join the southern union, also decided for a separate one. Then the biggest breakaway came when North East India felt that there were too many factors that would make it impractical for them to be a part of the North India union, and these Christians set up their own regional committee. All these breakaway groups took out some very strong segments of Baptist churches from North India union plans, especially Burma and North East India. The British Baptists remained to continue their usual strong participation in and contribution to the talks which finally bore fruit in November, 1970, with the birth of the Church of North India.

NORTH EAST INDIA

Meanwhile, North East India with its own union plans has not yet achieved its goal. The situation here presents a completely different picture. This region is in many ways separated from the rest of India by geography, history, culture, and language. Its people, composed of several tribes, inhabit the mountains and valleys and are quite remote from the mainstream of Indian life. It has the highest percentage of Christians in India, and Baptists are in the majority. Their relationship and cooperation with Presbyterians and Anglicans is good, and comity arrangements work well among them. Church union talks are going on among the leaders of the Protestants, but the average Christian in the village has little idea what it is all about, or if he does, he feels no need for it. The negotiators are mostly Baptists, and they have no fear of being dominated by the Anglicans who are very much in the minority. A basis for church union has been worked out, and study is being made by all the groups, but nothing has yet come out of this, as conditions that make union urgent in other areas are not present here. There must exist some factors other than the theological which underlie resistance or indifference to church union. Dr. Fred S. Downs, an American Baptist, says: "Communalism . . . is one of the chief impediments to [India's] national development. The reluctance to lose this distinctive social identity within a larger church fellowship is . . . a more important factor in resistance to church union than are . . . denominational distinctives. . . ." But he also says: "If there is a growing interest in church union among Baptist leaders today, it is simply because this appears to be essential to the fulfillment of the mission of Christ in the Indian context."[2]

The recent centennial celebration of the Ao Naga Baptist Convention, including the visit of Evangelist Billy Graham, which drew over 50,000 Baptists to the town of Impur, seemed to point to a sense of pride and strength in being Baptists. It is our hope that plans for fresh evangelistic thrusts stemming from this historic occasion may not weaken Baptist resolve to seek for greater unity with other Christians.

BURMA

In Burma, church union has had a greater appeal to certain individuals rather than to the denominations in general. Cooperative work has been so strong through the Burma Christian Council that it seems redundant to speak of church union. The contention is that church union cannot be understood except in terms of concrete action and that union will eventually evolve when the spirit of unity finds expression in visible forms of action at all levels of church life. This hope seems to be borne out by some instances of local church actions between groups that have been traditionally and theologically poles apart. For the laymen theology has no great significance, and so it is hoped that, as the lay movement gets stronger, barriers will fade.

The Baptist position in Burma is overwhelmingly stronger than any other Protestant group, and the leadership of Baptists is accepted in very fine spirit in all cooperative efforts like the National Bible Society, the Christian Literature Society, audiovisual aids and the radio ministry, theological education, relief work, university student Christian program, YMCA and YWCA, and several other joint actions which also include the Roman Catholics. So the spirit in which this strong Baptist position is exercised for the total church witness will eventually decide the nature and extent of Christian unity in a land of strong Buddhist tradition. The negotiation committee keeps the discussion going, but there does not seem to be any sense of urgency for organic merger.

SRI LANKA

The Baptist Union of Sri Lanka (Ceylon) has a membership of only 1800, but, like the British Baptists to whom it is related, this Union is playing a prominent role in the church union negotiations of which Dr. W. Wickramasinghe, a Baptist, is chairman. He says:

> The primary task of the church is not to perpetuate denominationalism but to present Jesus Christ as Lord and Saviour. In a small country like Sri Lanka, with a major non-Christian religion as the inspiration of the culture and philosophy of our people, the divided church is a hindrance to the communication of the gospel. . . . At the theological level there is greater appreciation of our distinctive positions and a discovery of greater unity. Our doctrinal standpoints are not mutually exclusive. . . . The theological constraint that unity is the ultimate goal is our challenge.[3]

Rev. C. D. E. Premawardhana, another leading Baptist, speaks of "a deep sense of the irrelevance of denominational bias whose historical roots have no significance to our cultural context which is able to receive contradictory views more readily than western cultures are able to."[4] The facts that the negotiating committee has a Baptist for chairman and that they have all but achieved union, except for a technical hitch unrelated to the issues, speak to the strong Baptist leadership and the fine relationship between them and the other Christians in the land.

BANGLADESH

On March 1, 1973, indigenous leaders representing the major Baptist groups in Bangladesh met and decided to set up a planning committee to discuss the possibility of organizing a single Baptist union out of the three existing unions. A letter to this effect was sent to the three unions and the four Baptist missions[5] in Bangladesh. On the same day the group also met with representatives from the Anglicans, the Roman Catholics, and the National Church Council. A letter to the Council reporting on the meeting said:

> The members present felt very deeply the need to make sincere attempts towards the oneness of different churches in Bangladesh and a proposal was made and accepted that requests be sent to the Churches to discuss on the line of possible plans of church union in the near future.

The group specifically requested the Council to make attempts for wider cooperation between Protestants and Roman Catholics in Bangladesh in the following areas: social and economic programs, cooperatives, and medical and educational services. They requested the Roman Catholics to include the Protestants in their Directory. It is interesting to note that the Baptists of this region had in the past stood strongly against union and had spoken for federation as an alternative. This sudden turn for a unity that would embrace even the Roman Catholics can only be explained by the deep tragedy that the whole nation experienced in the recent civil war which erased all barriers and left only their humanity as a common bond.

CONCLUSION

There are many factors that exert their influence upon churches and color their attitudes and relationships with each other. For many Baptists, baptism, ordination, and autonomy of the local congregation are vital issues on which they cannot weaken their stand, while other Baptists are willing to make some concessions for the sake of unity. Nontheological factors, such as social, cultural, temporal, and personal matters, to our shame, decide much about our church relationships. The influence of the mission agencies and their personnel is a factor of no little importance. Though some have openly encouraged national churches along the path of greater unity with other Christians, some have held stands that perpetuate divisions. This stance is, however, breaking down at some points in the face of pressures and the growing self-determination of the national churches. The nature of Christian unity cannot be discovered for each region until denominations work together. "It is *not* easy," says Rev. Tracy Gipson of South India, "but it is delightful and eminently worthwhile, as we believe every attempt of Christians to work together and to grow in understanding is worthwhile."[6]

CHAPTER 14

East Asia

Princeton S. Hsu

MAINLAND CHINA

In 1836 the first Baptist missionary couple from the United States, Rev. and Mrs. J. Lewis Shuck, arrived in Macao. They moved to Hong Kong in the year 1842. In the same year, Rev. William Dean also came to work in Hong Kong. This was the beginning of Baptist mission work in China. Later, in 1875, the British Baptists sent their missionaries to China. In 1890 the Swedish Baptists opened their mission field in China. Baptist churches were formed in the provinces of Kwangtung, Kwangsi (these two provinces are also called South China), Kiangsu, Chekiang, Shantung, Shansi, Shensi, Honan, Anhwei, Szechwan, Sikang, and others. Church schools, church hospitals, orphanages, seminaries, publication work, colleges, and universities were also important projects of the Baptist work in China. In 1950 there were about six hundred Baptist churches and about eighty thousand Baptist church members in China. This was one-tenth of the total number of Protestant church members in China. Since the great change in politics following the takeover in 1949, Christian work in Mainland China has also greatly changed.

In Mainland China, all of the churches formed by British Baptists joined the Church of Christ in China. They also cooperated with other denominations in other projects, especially in schools, hospitals, and social work. The American Northern Baptists also had union work with other denominations in educational, medical, and social work. However, each church did not put aside its own Baptist beliefs. The British Baptists and the American Northern Baptists also became members of some general interdenominational organizations (i.e., China National Christian Council). The American Southern Baptist churches developed their own work and projects from the very beginning. They have never entered any interdenominational organization, though sometimes they have cooperated with other denominations in specific projects.

HONG KONG AND MACAO

In 1836 Rev. and Mrs. J. Lewis Shuck arrived in Macao, and in 1842 moved to Hong Kong. Following these, other missionaries of the American Southern and Northern Baptists arrived in Hong Kong. Macao is a Portugese colony and Hong Kong is a British colony. At that time, the population of these two cities was very small. The missionaries intended to enter Mainland China to preach the gospel of Christ through these two small commercial ports. This is the reason why from 1836 to 1950 Hong Kong and Macao did not play important roles in Baptist mission work in the larger area of Chinese influence. These were only small mission fields of the South China Baptist work.

After the takeover of Mainland China in the year 1949, Hong Kong became the main center for Baptist mission work to Chinese people. The population of Hong Kong has increased from several hundred thousand to four million. Baptist work has had a rapid growth. At present, there are more than seventy Baptist churches and chapels in Hong Kong (including all Baptist groups there). Macao has five Baptist churches and chapels. Hong Kong has twenty-two thousand Baptist church members, while Macao has about one thousand. There are also Baptist schools, a Baptist college, a hospital, and seminaries established in Hong Kong. Baptist work in Hong Kong is very prosperous. The percentage of Baptist church members in Hong Kong is about one-tenth of the total number of Protestant Christians in Hong Kong.

The American [Northern] Baptists in Hong Kong have tended more toward union work. The American Southern Baptist churches still work according to the traditional way of independence, characteristic of the South China (Kwangtung and Kwangsi) Baptist Association. They have their own ways of work and do not join with other denominations in organization. However, at times they do cooperate with other denominations.

For instance, some Baptist churches have entered the Hong Kong Association of Christian Churches. As to Baptist beliefs, all Baptist churches in Hong Kong and Macao have sustained their own viewpoint and have not changed. The majority of the Baptist churches in Hong Kong and Macao are connected with Southern Baptists.

TAIWAN

Before 1948 Taiwan had no Baptist work at all. During the Japanese reign, Presbyterians were the only Protestant denomination that had a firm foundation. In 1948 the American Southern Baptists began their work in Taiwan. After twenty-five years of work, there are 110 Baptist churches and chapels now connected with the Southern Baptists and about 10,000 Baptist church members in Taiwan.

Both the Conservative Baptists and the Baptist Bible Fellowship have established work in Taiwan. Their work is not yet as well established as that of Southern Baptists. They do not yet have many church members. At the present, a majority of the Baptist church members there belong to churches associated with Southern Baptists.

Baptist churches in Taiwan have worked freely and independently. They do not enter any interdenominational organization. However, they sometimes work with some other Christian denominations in a very friendly manner on projects which are of mutual interest.

In Taiwan, because the government emphasizes public education and medical work, the Baptist churches have not established their own high schools, colleges, or hospitals but have established a seminary. The Baptist work in Taiwan concentrates on spreading the gospel. This is a special characteristic of Taiwan Baptist work.

JAPAN

American Baptists (formerly Northern Baptists) were the first Baptists to undertake sustained work in Japan, although the first missionary, Jonathan Goble, a seaman, returned as a representative of the Free Baptists (U.S.A.) in 1860.

Southern Baptists in 1859 appointed their first missionaries, the Rohrers, but their ship was lost at sea. It was thirty years before the next missionaries were appointed in 1889. Other Baptists, such as the Baptist General Conference (U.S.A.), began work later, most of them in the period since World War II.

In prewar Japan the churches related to the Northern and the Southern Baptist Conventions were at best cool toward cooperation with other denominations. This was largely due to missionary influence. However, in the 1930s Dr. William Axling of the Northern Baptist Convention took an active part in ecumenical moves. Following the war he was instrumental, along with some of his Japanese colleagues, in keeping the Northern Baptist Convention-related churches affiliated with the United Church of Christ. It was not until after he had left Japan that several of these churches left the United Church and formed what is now called the Japan Baptist Union. There are, however, still a number of former Baptist churches (formerly related to the Northern Baptist Convention) within the United Church. They have, of course, lost their Baptist identity.

Churches related to the Southern Baptist Convention in general have reflected the conservatism of the Southern Baptist Convention. In 1941 these churches were forced into the United Church of Christ (Kyodan), along with most other denominations. In 1946 all of these churches still in existence following the war elected to withdraw from the United Church and formed the Japan Baptist Convention. In principle, however, these churches in the postwar years have maintained the attitude of cooperation with other denominations. For example, the Japan Baptist Convention has for many years been a member of the Japan Christian Council (National Christian Council of Japan), and a number of its pastors and laymen have served on committees of the Council.

The churches of the Japan Baptist Convention have participated in a number of interdenominational crusades, such as the Stanley Jones meetings, the Lacour Music campaigns, World Vision, etc. The leadership of the Japan Baptist Convention in the postwar period has been openly ecumenically minded, though insistent on the retention of their own principles of a free church. The cooperation and participation of the smaller Baptist groups have been minimal. In general the smaller groups reflect the conservatism and noncooperative stance of their supporters in the U.S.A.

There are now nineteen different Baptist groups working in Japan, including the Southern Baptist Convention, the American Baptist Churches in the U.S.A., the Baptist General Conference (U.S.A.), and such independent groups as that of Timothy Pietsch.

KOREA

In Korea, Baptist history is traceable from 1949 when certain remnants of the Church of Christ in Korea, founded by Malcolm C. Fenwick, became the Korea Baptist Convention. In 1950 the first Southern Baptist Convention missionaries entered Korea.

The Korea Baptist Convention and the Southern Baptist Mission (both nationals and missionaries) favor cordial Christian relations with other evangelical denominations and active participation in certain interdenominational projects which do not require compromise of Baptist beliefs. But they oppose membership in formal ecumenical organizations. The following activities seem to support this evaluation:

1. There is frequent interchange of speakers between denominations. Baptist ministers speak at revival services, conferences, and retreats of other denominations and ministers of other denominations are invited to lead similar services in Baptist churches, institutions, and conferences.
2. Baptists invited other denominations to participate in twenty city-wide evangelistic campaigns in 1970. Most evangelical churches responded positively by encouraging their members to attend these services, helping to provide special music and assisting in follow-up work. Baptists referred new converts to the church of their preference regardless of denominational affiliation.
3. Baptists often participate in Easter sunrise services and other interdenominational services of a special nature.
4. Generally, Baptist ministers hold membership in local interdenominational ministerial associations.
5. Baptists support the Korea Bible Society despite considerable dissatisfaction over the fact that the word used to translate "baptism" in the Korean Bible excludes the idea of immersion.
6. Baptists cooperate with several small denominations in filling a quota for military chaplains.
7. Baptist missionaries participate in nondenominational English language church services in Seoul and Taejon.

The Korea Bible Baptist Churches and the Baptist Bible Fellowship and their affiliated missionaries make no effort to cooperate with other denominations. The missionaries are sent out by local churches in America for the purpose of establishing local churches. They have no missionary organization and no national denominational organization.

National Baptists tend to avoid active participation in interdenominational activities because of inferiority feelings arising out of the small size of the Baptist denomination and the relatively low economic and social level of its members. Since Baptists are growing more rapidly than the larger denominations and are displaying marked upward social mobility, it seems likely that they will participate more actively in interdenominational projects in the future. However, there is no evidence of increased interest in membership in ecumenical organizations on the part of either nationals or missionaries as a whole.

The Korea Bible Baptist Churches and Baptist Bible Fellowship have a tendency to maintain the present attitude of noncooperation with other denominations.

There are 411 churches in the Korea Baptist Convention and 55 churches formed as Korea Bible Baptist Churches, making a total of 466 churches at the present. The number of members in these churches totals 21,000.

There are two Baptist missions at work in Korea, namely the Southern Baptist Mission and the Baptist Bible Fellowship.

PHILIPPINES

Baptist work was begun in 1900 in Jaro, Iloilo, by the Northern (later American) Baptist Convention.

Most of the Baptist groups have a good working relationship with all other Christian groups in the country. Most feel that they are fairly free to propagate the gospel wherever the Spirit leads. Most are fairly limited to a section of the country, although some overlap work is being done by other groups.

There is little effort by Baptists to share in cooperative work in the Philippines. It is not unusual, however, for one group to use the literature of another, especially Vacation Bible School materials. There is some overlapping of use of hymnals. No organization is established to bring the leaders together for discussion. Southern Baptists recognize the general area where American Baptists have been working and have not entered those regions.

Perhaps efforts should be made to bring the various Baptist groups into some kind of coordinating council. Action has been taken at Southern Baptist Mission meetings to promote this idea, but the response has been less than warm toward it. There is a feeling of independence on the part of each group. These groups are not related to each other in the home country, and there has been no need felt to relate to each other on the field. There are 722 Baptist churches with 59,869 members in the Philippines. There are seven Baptist mission groups in this country: American Baptists, Association of Baptists for World Evangelism, Baptist Bible Fellowship, Baptist General Conference, Conservative Baptists, General Baptists, and Southern Baptists.

THAILAND

Baptists began work in Thailand in 1832 when John Taylor Jones came from Burma. William Dean then came in 1834, and a church was organized in 1837, the Maitrichit Church, which has endured to this day as a very strong and active church. It is independent of foreign aid, but missionaries of the American Baptists cooperate with it, since it is for Swatow-speaking Chinese.

Southern Baptists began work in Thailand in 1949, and American Baptists returned a year later. In addition, there is the Philippine Association of Baptists for World Evangelism.

American Baptists have a more ecumenical approach than the other groups in that, although the Church of Christ in Thailand is primarily Presbyterian, the Twelfth District of this church is composed of Chinese Baptist churches. Southern Baptists have tended to shy away from formal alliances, to extend fellowship to other groups, and to cooperate at the functional level whenever possible, rather than participate at the organizational level.

Major groupings of churches have been formed in Thailand. The Church of Christ in Thailand embraces Presbyterians, Disciples, Marburgers, some Baptists (principally Chinese), and a few others. The other ecumenical group is called the Evangelical Fellowship of Thailand and includes the Christian and Missionary Alliance and Overseas Missionary Fellowship with a sprinkling of other very conservative groups. Churches resulting from the work of Southern Baptists have so far declined to join either of these bodies. But Baptists have formed the Thailand Baptist Council, which includes Karen, Lahu-Lisu, and Chinese Associations, and Thai Baptists are in the process of entering. Of course, some of these groups also have formal connections with the Church of Christ in Thailand.

MALAYSIA-SINGAPORE

Baptist work started in Malaysia-Singapore and churches were organized in 1937, although Baptist believers had been in this area as early as 1905.

Up to the present only one American Baptist missionary has taken any part in ecumenical work. He has been quite active, having served as an official of the local Council of Churches in Singapore. However, Baptists feel a strong kinship with other evangelical groups and join with them in support of evangelistic meetings, Billy Graham-sponsored projects, and the like. Baptist students also cooperate with like-minded Christians in Youth for Christ clubs and Inter-Varsity Christian Fellowship work.

Local Baptists show no signs of changing their basic attitude of determination to continue maintaining a strong distinctive Baptist witness, while at the same time contributing to and benefiting from evangelistic and evangelical campaigns and programs which appear to be likely to help the entire evangelical Christian community. Often this cooperation and participation is on an individual or informal level rather than being officially sanctioned by the Baptist churches as such.

OVERSEAS CHINESE BAPTISTS

There are 150 overseas Chinese Baptist churches all over the world with a total membership of 8,000. Over 95 percent of these churches follow the stand of the Hong Kong and Taiwan Baptist churches, which is nonorganizational cooperation with other denominations. Most of the overseas Chinese Baptists churches have a close relation with the Hong Kong Baptist churches.

INDONESIA

Southern Baptist work began rather late in Indonesia. The first Southern Baptist missionaries arrived there on Christmas Day, 1951. In the following year, the first Baptist church was formed in Bandung. There are some other Baptist missions also at work in Indonesia. They are the Conservative Baptist Mission in Kalimantan (Borneo), the Australia Baptist Mission in West Irian (West New Guinea), and the Fundamental Baptists from the U.S.A., who began work in West Java in 1972.

According to a report in May, 1972, there are 49 organized Baptist churches and 225 missions affiliated with the work begun by the Southern Baptist Mission with a total of 10,748 members. The Australian Baptists have between 8,000 and 10,000 members and the Conservative Baptists have about 2,000 members. The basic attitude of the Baptists toward other denominations has been fraternal with all efforts being made to live peaceably together without organizational unity. Up to the present time the Baptist churches related to the Southern Baptist Mission have felt that becoming a member of the National Council of Churches might limit their freedom to begin new work. Many churches have joint Christmas and Easter services with other denominations, including the Roman Catholics. The churches and the Mission cooperated with the National Council of Churches from 1969 to 1971 in an anthropological, sociological, methodological, and church survey. The Baptist churches related to the Southern Baptist Mission were the only churches that participated that were not members of the National Council of Churches. Relations were excellent and have helped open doors of communication. These same churches have also participated in conferences on theological education, programmed literature workshops, and a church growth seminar with members of the National Council and others not affiliated with them. However, the Baptist attitude tends to be toward more cooperation with other churches. It is rumored that the new Convention (called the Association of Baptist Churches in Indonesia) will seek closer ties with the National Council of Churches, but no positive steps have been taken as yet.

VIETNAM

The first Baptist missionary arrived in Vietnam in 1959, but work actually began in 1961. There are 25 Vietnamese-speaking Baptist churches related to the Southern Baptist Convention, which is the only Baptist mission at work in Vietnam. There is only one Chinese-speaking Baptist church in Saigon, formed in 1968 through the help of Hong Kong Baptist Churches United Association. The total number of Baptist church members is about 1,200.

Baptist churches have a good spirit of fellowship and coopera-tion. They have no connection or cooperation with certain interdenominational organizations, such as the National Chris-tian Council. They are moving toward cooperation in several areas in the future, especially lay training and publication. They have participated in several interdenominational workshops and rallies. The Chinese-speaking Baptist group joins in with the local workers' fellowship prayer meeting and also takes part in the evangelistic campaigns sponsored by the Christian and Missionary Alliance or other churches. In return, these denominations also join in and help with Baptist activities. They also exchange speakers in services and in conferences. In other words, they are working together in spreading the gospel. However, Baptist work in Vietnam is not yet well established. Now after the Vietnam War, there is plenty of work to do and help is needed very urgently.

GUAM

Baptist work began in 1922 when the General Baptists went to Guam. The first Guamanian pastor was Dr. Joaquin Sablan. In 1961 a small group of Christians began to meet for fellowship and prayer. They approached the Foreign Mission Board of the Southern Baptist Convention to send a missionary couple. At present, there are three organized Baptist churches on the island of Guam, related to the Southern Baptists, with about six hundred members. In addition to these three churches there are two new congregations, one on the island of Truk composed primarily of English-speaking people, and one on the island of Saipan. These two small congregations involve about sixty people.

There are three other Baptist missions also at work in Guam. They are the General Baptists, the Conservative Baptists, and the Independent Baptists. The General Baptists have been at work since about 1922. Conservative Baptists have been on Guam for some ten or twelve years, having offices on the west coast at present. They have one church and the possibility of a student outreach at the University of Guam. Independent Baptists have a small congregation on the island, but their work is primarily under the direction of a local Caucasian military-ordained pastor with no denominational or mission board connections anywhere.

All of the Baptist groups represented have a reasonably healthy attitude toward other denominations except those that are regarded as sects. They share in a monthly ministerial association. The General Baptists with their association of five churches are now participating in the Ministerial Association and its projects.

The denominations have shared for years in providing chaplains for the Guam Memorial Hospital. In this work currently Baptists are working together with twenty-five congregations averaging about one hundred members per congregation.

Cooperation in terms of joint institutions having legal involvements are not encouraged by any of the mission boards.[1]

CONCLUSIONS

The total number of Baptist church members in all of East Asia is approximately 272,171. This includes Japan (33,433), Korea (18,736), People's Republic of China (about 80,000 in 1950), Taiwan (12,175), Hong Kong (25,391), Macao (568), Philippines (59,869), South Vietnam (1,373), Thailand (7,054), Malaysia (4,144), Singapore (3,487), Indonesia (24,041), and Guam (1,900). During the past 150 years this area has contributed much to the cause of the Lord Jesus Christ.

The three strongest Baptist mission groups in East Asia have been the American Southern Baptists, the American Northern Baptists (now called the American Baptists), and the British Baptists. The largest mission field was Mainland China. Due to political changes, the present situation of Baptists in Mainland China is unknown to us and hence regrettably is not discussed here.

Generally speaking, the British Baptist missionaries have tended more toward cooperative work with other denominations in East Asia. There is a heavy emphasis on union work among them. The Southern Baptist missionaries and related national preachers and churches in East Asia insist on independent preaching. They do not pay attention to interdenominational organization. The Northern Baptist missionaries (American Baptists) and their churches in East Asia have an attitude somewhat between British Baptists and Southern Baptists. They join in quite a large number of union projects. However, the Baptist churches connected with the American Baptists do not give up Baptist beliefs. In recent years, Baptist churches in East Asia connected with the Southern Baptists have increased their cooperative work with other evangelical denominations. It must be understood clearly that cooperation is different from unification (or conformation), and these terms should not be confused. Working together does not necessarily mean joining together in a common organization.

Generally, the Baptist believers in East Asia have little enthusiasm for the extreme organizational expression of the Ecumenical Movement suggested now by the West. They are not interested in this movement. Perhaps there are some interested, but there are only a few of the leaders who have joined this movement individually. There are nine reasons why the East Asia Baptists are not interested in organizational ecumenism:

1. Baptist churches aim at being united in God, in the Spirit, and in the Bible. They do not think organizational unification or artificial unification is important.

2. Baptist churches are much more democratic. No one has the right to represent the group in attending ecumenical meetings or discussing the problem of unification of doctrine, unless all the church members agree.

3. All local Baptist churches are entirely independent. No leader and no organization in charge has the authority to order the churches to enter the interdenominational Ecumenical Movement.

4. Baptist believers like to refer everything to the Bible. If there is discussion on administrative or organizational ecumenism not in line with the Bible, they do not conscientiously agree, because each person's subjective opinion is always unstable.

5. From history the bad results which have come from certain ecumenical movements in the East may be learned. This is why Baptist believers are so careful in their attitude.

6. If we Baptists can do things within our own strength, why do we not do them ourselves? The main way to make our churches grow is to strengthen each local Baptist church. Basic groundwork is much more important than the superficial work done by the top level organizations.

7. In biology there are two laws: one is the law of unity and the other is the law of variation. Both of these laws are important. One cannot conclusively say that denominationalism is bad. Nationalism is bad but nationality has no wrong in itself. At the same time, denominationalism is bad but denominationality is not a mistake in itself.

8. The Bible asks disciples to unify (John 17:11) but also asks disciples to separate from doubtful groups (2 Corinthians 6:17; 1 John 4:1). Spiritual life has more value than mere organization with low standard compromise.

9. In the East there are many major religions. All major religious groups have denominations. To abolish sin is the right way toward unity in Christ. To abolish denominations is not the basic way to obtain Christian unity.

Generally, most of the Baptist churches n East Asia insist that Christians should cooperate in Christ, in the Bible, and in the

Spirit. They do not suggest being united in administration or in organization. This has been the strong attitude all the way through.

Among the East Asian peoples there are some special religious characteristics:

1. So many of the East Asian countries, such as China, Japan, Korea, and Vietnam have a long history of civilization and have several major religions. These religions have been existing side by side with each other for thousands of years without religious wars.

2. All major Eastern religions have their own denominations, and these denominations are not in rivalry with each other.

3. In most of the Eastern countries, racial and cultural prejudice is by no means strong.

4. The Eastern mind is much more synthetical than analytical. Many people tend to syncretism.

5. The first Protestant Christian missionaries to East Asia were Baptists. In many countries Baptists are the leading Christian denomination.

So religious conflicts, racial prejudice, and denominational hostility are more or less unknown to them. In Hong Kong, when some Baptists tried to define the meaning of reconciliation through Christ, they simply defined it as evangelism and church-membership training only. They do not think of it as racial reconciliation. They do not think of it as denominational reconciliation. They only feel that they must work diligently to bring the non-Christians to know Christ and to accept him as Savior. Their problems are thus different from those of other countries. As Baptists of the East Asia countries their most important involvement is evangelism and not ecumenical organization. They want to be very careful to remain true and faithful to the Bible. All Baptists in East Asia want to keep their Baptist distinctives.

Generally speaking, most of the East Asian Baptists do not feel that they ought to join the Roman Catholics in organization. National Christian Council projects do not have much attraction to most of them. Although Baptists in East Asia are not very compromising in doctrine and organization, they are cooperative in the larger Protestant family in matters of evangelism and philanthropy.

CHAPTER 15

Middle East

John David Hughey, Jr.

Christianity was born in the Middle East and was the predominant religion for several centuries, but it barely survived Islamic conquest and rule. The Coptic Church of Egypt, the Greek Orthodox Church, the Roman Catholic Church (and its Uniate branches, such as the Maronite Church in Lebanon), the Armenian Orthodox Church, and several smaller groups, such as the Assyrian (Nestorian) Church, are somewhat feeble reminders in the Middle East of past Christian strength and glory.

Protestantism was planted first in the area by Presbyterians, Congregationalists, and Anglicans. They tried to bring new life to the ancient churches but then accepted converts from these churches into their own. Most Protestants have come from the old Christian communities. In recent years conservative Christian groups, denominational and interdenominational, have been active in the Middle East.

Baptists are a tiny minority within the small Christian minority. They were late arrivals on the scene. Southern Baptists have borne the major responsibility in the area as far as Baptists are concerned. Their first missionaries arrived in Palestine in 1921. However, not until after World War II was very much attempted.

At the end of 1972 there were 472 Baptists in Lebanon, 210 in Jordan, 372 in Egypt, 28 in Gaza, and 241 in Israel. There is a little church of Spaniards in Melilla, a Spanish enclave on the coast of Morocco, and there are Baptist churches of Americans in Libya, Turkey, and Iran.

Since source materials and also his personal knowledge of the subject are quite limited, the author asked four Southern Baptist missionaries to prepare papers on areas they know especially well. Dwight L. Baker wrote on Israel, William O. Hern on Jordan and Egypt, J. Conrad Willmon on Lebanon, and George W. Braswell, Jr., on Iran. The author's indebtedness to them is gratefully acknowledged.

A MISSIONARY SITUATION

One of the distinctives of the Middle East is that, due to the small national constituency, missionaries still bear much of the responsibility for what Baptists do. Since the missionaries are Southern Baptists, except for those representing interdenominational faith missions and for those representing small church bodies such as Bible Baptists, the attitudes and policies of the Southern Baptist Foreign Mission Board are relevant.

The Southern Baptist Convention has not joined the World Council of Churches, the National Council of Churches, or any other such body. However, the Convention is on record as favoring spiritual unity among all followers of Christ and also cooperation with other Christians and churches. It does not limit Southern Baptist churches in their relationship to other churches or councils of churches.

The Foreign Mission Board of the Southern Baptist Convention respects the autonomy of Baptist churches and also that of national Baptist organizations around the world. It does not claim the authority to determine the relationship of overseas Baptist churches or conventions to other churches or interchurch organizations. However, it is understood that funds from the Foreign Mission Board are for the development of Baptist work.

Missionaries are sent out for Baptist work overseas. Their activities are varied, but an important goal of the whole missionary endeavor is the development of Baptist churches, not because others are not Christian but because Baptists have a special responsibility which can best be borne, at least for the present, if they maintain their own identity. Missionaries are permitted to become involved temporarily in non-Baptist projects. In recent years Presbyterians have shown their readiness for such cooperation in two places.

W. O. Hern was designated as the fraternal representative of Southern Baptists to Egyptian Baptists. Since in Egypt Southern

Baptists are a new missionary organization and therefore have no quota of missionaries, the Egyptian Evangelical Seminary (Presbyterian) agreed, with the support of the Egyptian Evangelical Church and the cooperating Presbyterian body in America, to invite him to join its faculty in addition to serving as counselor of Baptist pastors and churches. Unfortunately the government did not permit the arrangement, and Hern has had to live elsewhere and make periodic visits to Egypt as a tourist in order to maintain the relationship with Egyptian Baptists.

When the George Braswells went to Iran in 1968 to pioneer for Baptists, they were very cordially received by American Presbyterians, who have long had work there, and the Iranian Evangelical Church (which is Presbyterian). Braswell worked at Armaghan Institute, a university-ministry organization of the United Presbyterian Church, U.S.A., and thereby obtained a residence permit. He was introduced by Presbyterians to persons who made it possible for him to teach students in the Faculty of Muslim Theology of the University of Teheran. He established contacts with various Christian churches in Teheran, Isfahan, Shiraz, and Meshad. He wrote:

> The attitude toward other Christians in Iran by Baptist representatives has been one of deep appreciation of their historic Christian witness, of acceptance of them as Christian brothers and sisters in the discipleship of the Lord, of positive encouragement to them by word and deed to continue in the work and witness of Jesus Christ in Iran. The attitude has been one of openness to their ideas and postures in their varying traditions, of mutual cooperation in tasks either too large or too small for one group to undertake, of walking in the way together.

All of this has been quite acceptable to the Foreign Mission Board. However, Baptists need to have their own identity in Iran and to be free to determine what they will do, either alone or in cooperation with others. The organization of an English-language Baptist church in Teheran was a step in that direction. That Baptists are not isolating themselves from other Christians or are not rejected by them is indicated by the fact that Baptist services are being held in a new building belonging to a congregation (mainly Jewish) of the Iranian Evangelical Church.

What of Southern Baptist practices with regard to entering areas where there are other Christian groups? It is not the purpose of the Foreign Mission Board to develop Baptist work at the expense of other Christian churches. The Foreign Mission Board wants

Baptist witness and activities to strengthen the total Christian cause. It is true that it does not enter into comity agreements, because it does not necessarily believe that an area has been adequately evangelized because a few Christian churches are there. But it does usually confer with other Christians before entering an area and seeks to develop cooperative relationships with them. The executive secretary of the Foreign Mission Board once said, "We ought so to conduct ourselves wherever we go that all Christians will eventually be glad we are there."

EGYPT AND JORDAN

Baptist work in Egypt was started by an Egyptian who was converted, left the Coptic Orthodox Church, felt called to preach the gospel, studied in America, and there became a Baptist. Upon returning to Egypt he worked independently, but in 1955 his work was given support by the Southern Baptist Foreign Mission Board. In his effort to spread the Baptist witness in Egypt he employed workers from at least six different denominations, all of whom were baptized in local Baptist churches. These men have been quite ready to cooperate with Christians from all Evangelical denominations. It might be added that their varied backgrounds have hindered the development of unity among Baptists.

Egyptian Baptists, according to Hern, "by and large have a friendly, loving attitude toward Christians from most of the other evangelical denominations of Egypt." He adds:

> Presbyterian work was established by missionaries who were thoroughly evangelical. However, the practice of infant baptism has gradually developed a large number of "non-regenerate" church members. The Baptists are divided in their attitude toward Presbyterians. Many of the Baptists look upon all Presbyterian evangelicals as brethren in Christ and are careful to avoid proselytizing from their community. Other Baptists classify the Presbyterians to a degree with the members of the traditional Christian churches and seek to present their witness to them as the circumstances may allow.

The Egyptian government, following the old Turkish millet system of dividing the population according to religion, classifies the Evangelical denominations as a unit and deals with the Protestant Evangelical Council. All church groups having at least thirty units are entitled to one representative on the Council. Since there are only eleven Baptist churches in Egypt, they have had to share a seat on the Council with another denomination. However, in 1971 the smaller groups were required to "federalize" for the sake of representation on the Council. Baptists joined the Assemblies of God but are hoping to obtain independent representation.

Most Baptists in Egypt are converts from the Coptic Orthodox Church or from the Greek Orthodox Church. Hern says:

> Since the sacramental theology of the Coptic Church does not point the way to spiritual enlightenment, the Baptists of Egypt feel that the Coptic Christians are in need of the message of salvation. . . . Baptists are looked upon as heretics and proselytizers and are strongly opposed by the clergy of the traditional churches.

The first Baptist church in Jordan was made up of people coming from at least five denominations. Most Baptist pastors have come from other churches. Hern says that Baptists in Jordan "look upon other Evangelicals as brethren in Christ, and they respect their efforts in Christian service." Since in spite of their small numbers they have been able to obtain government recognition, they have not been forced into union with others. But they have joint retreats and conferences, and pastors often exchange pulpits.

Most Baptists in Jordan are converts from the Greek Orthodox or Roman Catholic Church. Relationships with these churches are not always cordial. However, Catholic priests and nuns are treated free of charge at the Baptist Hospital in Ajloun. The Roman Catholic bishop has usually been willing to use the influence of his office on behalf of Baptists and other Evangelicals. Hern concludes, "The scarcity of those who are even Christian in name in Jordan plus the pressure of a militant Islam has caused a development of friendship and unofficial cooperation."

LEBANON

In January, 1973, J. Conrad Willmon conducted a significant survey of Lebanese Baptist attitudes toward and relations with other religious bodies. A questionnaire in Arabic with twenty-three questions was submitted to one hundred Lebanese Baptists (one-fifth of the total). Seventy-three answered the questions in proper form.

With regard to previous religious affiliation, 32.9 percent said they came from other Evangelical groups, 28.8 percent from the Roman Catholic Church, 26 percent from the Greek Orthodox

Church, and 12.3 percent from the Maronite (Uniate) Church. None were converts from non-Christian religions.

When asked to list the most difficult religious group to cooperate with, the largest number indicated Islam, and this was followed by the Maronite Church. In a somewhat similar question a number of people indicated that cooperation is also difficult with the Baha'is, the Druzes, the Greek Orthodox, and the Roman Catholics. Most indicated little difficulty in cooperating with other Evangelicals.

Willmon describes as follows the responses to another question:

> Table 11 indicates that the majority felt "other evangelicals" were the only sect to be termed "very close" to the Bible, while Greek Orthodox, Roman Catholic, and Maronite Catholic (in that order) were termed "close." . . . The Armenian Orthodox Church was indicated as "average," Islam as "far," and Baha'i and Druze as "very far." . . . Baptists can cooperate with other religious sects only to the degree that their theology and religious practices are in harmony with those of Baptists.

A high percentage of respondents indicated a willingness and desire to participate in other Evangelical services. Less than half as many indicated interest in Greek Orthodox, Roman Catholic, and Maronite services. There was no interest in attending Armenian Orthodox, Muslim, Druze, or Baha'i worship.

One question was whether the respondent had ever met a representative of the other religious groups who revealed that he possessed true faith in God. There was an unqualified "yes" for other Evangelicals (94.5 percent), 45.2 percent for Greek Orthodox, 39.7 percent for Roman Catholics, and 28.8 percent for Maronites. It is interesting that 28.8 percent have met Druzes with genuine faith in God, and 37 percent have met Muslims whom they characterized as persons of faith.

The majority of those questioned indicated that they frequently invite other Evangelicals to their homes for dinner, or visit in their homes. A fairly high percentage indicated that they frequently or sometimes have non-Christians in their homes for dinner or visit in those homes. Willmon concludes: "Baptists tend to have very good social relations with the three large Christian groups in Lebanon; however, these relations are not carried over into the field of religion."

Willmon believes there are signs of a growing willingness to work with others. In a new program of Reconciliation through the Arts there is a high degree of cooperation and ecumenicity. A chorale group includes Baptists, Presbyterians, and Episcopalians, and two Muslims have applied for membership. The orchestra includes Christians of varied backgrounds, a Muslim, and a Jew. Baptists, Presbyterians, and Lutherans cooperate in broadcasting (with each group taking a segment of time) and in follow-up of the radio programs. Faculty members of the Arab Baptist Theological Seminary work with other Christians in the production of textbooks in Arabic. A group of Baptist ministers, laymen, and missionaries recently expressed a desire to "broaden the circle of fellowship" to include not only other Evangelicals but also members of the ancient Christian churches.

ISRAEL

Baptists in Israel have gone further in the development of relationships with other Christians than have Baptists of the Arab countries. Dwight Baker, whose ecumenical commitment probably even exceeds that of many of his colleagues in Israel, takes for granted Baptist cooperation with other Evangelicals and pleads for closer relationships with the ancient Christian churches.

Baker says that some Baptists in Israel have reached the conviction that they should seek closer relations with Eastern Christians. This conviction came

> after getting to know some of them personally; after coming to know of their deep commitment to Christ; after praying with them; after hearing them open their hearts and bare their faith; after receiving them as guests in their Baptist homes and being guests in their homes and relating as friends; and, above all, after experiencing the witness of God's Spirit that the Baptists and the Eastern Christians are sons and daughters of the same Father. These experiences of personal contact have been convincing beyond all argument that many indigenous Eastern Christians and their leaders are genuine Christians and that Baptists are the losers if they do not relate more closely with them as brothers and sisters in Christ.

In Israel, a Jewish state with a fairly large Muslim minority, there are about eighty thousand Christians of all denominations, including three thousand Evangelicals, of whom less than one-tenth are Baptists. The Baptist who goes to Israel usually seeks Christian fellowship first with fellow-Baptists, then with other Evangelicals, and finally with Christians of any denomination.

The United Christian Council in Israel, a nonaligned organization including churches, church groups, and missionary organizations, has enjoyed full support of Baptist missionaries and nationals in Israel and now has an Arab Baptist as its general secretary. In 1971 it agreed to a proposal by Dwight Baker that an ecumenical committee be established in order to strengthen relationships with Christian bodies that are not in the Council. The Baptist missionaries in Israel have set up an Inter-Community Study Committee which has similar functions.

Baptists have been involved with other Christians for several years in the Protestant Community Choir, which was organized by a Baptist missionary and is now directed by a Baptist who is a member of the Israel Philharmonic Orchestra. Handel's *Messiah* is presented annually in various places at Christmas, and other concerts are presented at Easter.

Baker, pleading for cooperation between the younger and older churches, says,

> Today a few Baptists are beginning to realize for the first time that they are the Johnny-come-latelys, the youngsters, the upstarts. These Baptists are at last becoming aware of the fact that there has *always* been a large repository of the Christian faith in the Middle East, nourished and kept alive by the Eastern churches. They have kept the faith in a sea of hostility for centuries and they have a long and, for the most part, an honorable tradition. The Eastern churches have occupied these lands, and while being whittled away at for centuries by their enemies, resulting in diminished numbers and strength, they have never abandoned the field nor surrendered to hostile forces. To the contrary, they have fought and won the battle for a continued Christian presence in these lands. . . .

It would be good for Evangelicals in the Middle East to stop referring disparagingly to members of the ancient churches as "nominal Christians." True believers in Christ should regard each other as Christian brothers and sisters, regardless of church affiliation. They all have a right and duty to offer the gospel of Christ to those who need it. Some Catholics and Orthodox will be converted, and some of these will become Baptists. However, the main missionary thrust in the Middle East should be in the direction of Jews, Muslims, and others who do not know Christ as Savior and Lord.

Several years ago in Baghdad two other Baptists and I asked a taxi driver whether he was a Muslim. He said, "No, I am a Christian," and he identified himself as a member of one of the ancient Christian churches. I said, "We are Baptists, but the most important thing is not which church we belong to but what relationship we have with Christ." He replied, "That is right. And I would die for Him."

We should thank God for persons like that.

CHAPTER 16

Australasia *

D. Mervyn Himbury

Australia and New Zealand are areas of Western culture, though geographically they are part of Southeast Asia. The pattern of ecclesiastical life there has been taken to a large extent from Britain, though both countries, and especially Australia, have been subject to American influence since the Second World War.

In neither land have Baptists been numerically strong or influential. Australian Baptists in 1972 numbered 48,621 out of a total population of about 13,000,000. New Zealand with a population of some 2,900,000 had at the same time 17,287 Baptists. Yet these two groups have little contact with each other, and there are considerable differences between them, particularly in their attitudes toward cooperation with other Christians.

COLONIAL BEGINNINGS

Australia was first colonized as a convict settlement in 1788, but there is no record of Baptist activity before April, 1831, when John McKaeg began preaching in the Rose and Crown Inn at Sydney. Shortly after this time the first baptisms were conducted in Woolloomooloo Bay. The first Baptist chapel was erected in 1836 as the result of the efforts of John Saunders, who had come two years earlier to New South Wales to minister to the Baptists.[1]

Baptists came to New Zealand at an even later date. It was in 1851 that Decimus Dolamore founded the church at Nelson. Like Saunders, he had come from Britain in response to an appeal for help in the colonies of the Antipodes.

177

In these early years the attitude of Baptists to other denominations was practically identical to that in Britain. They had little contact with Roman Catholics. They were afraid lest the Church of England would become established as the state church in the colonies on the analogy of the situation in the homeland, and they enjoyed the most cordial relationships with those who in Britain would have been regarded as the Free churches.

AUSTRALIA

A Wesleyan minister, R. Mansfield, led the deputation to the governor of New South Wales to seek a grant of land for the first Baptist building. He also gave the history of the cause at the opening of the chapel, when the service was led by W. P. Crook of the London Missionary Society and the sermon was preached by William Jarrett of Sydney's Independent church.[2]

The moral and spiritual condition of the colony made it essential for Christians to work together. In a letter dated June 16, 1837, John Saunders spoke of New South Wales as "a dangerous place for professors of the gospel." In the same letter he tells of the formation of a Baptist Home Missionary Society which was in correspondence with the Congregational Colonial Society Mission and of their efforts to meet the spiritual needs of Australia.[3] Further evidence of Christian cooperation is found in the account of the journey of William H. Carey to Victoria and Tasmania to raise funds for the new Baptist church at Parramatta, of which he was the pastor, and his report that he had received "the greatest kindness and liberality from Christians of all denominations...."[4]

Baptists played little part in the controversy over education which divided the churches and the nation in the mid-nineteenth century and which led to the establishment of a purely secular system of state education. They welcomed the Victorian Act of 1872, which laid down that such education should be "Free, Secular and Compulsory," but shortly afterward the denominational paper pleaded for all churches to come together, sink minor differences, and unite in a general scheme to improve the efficiency of the Sunday schools and provide good Christian education for the young.[5] To the present day, Baptists have cooperated fully in all states to provide voluntary instructors to take some religious instruction into state schools.

Until recent days Baptists were most vocal in their demands that no church schools should receive aid from the state. This opposition was based partly on their belief that church and state should be entirely separate and also was the result of the recognition that the Roman Catholics would benefit most from such aid. Baptists have only three schools, all of which are in Victoria, and when, in recent years, state aid became available to them, they hastened to accept it. State aid to church schools has now become established in the programs of all major political parties and has ceased to be an issue even among the Baptists.

Fear of the power of the Roman Catholic Church remains a major factor which prevents Australian Baptists from cooperating in ecumenical ventures. Catholics are a substantial minority in the community. They have represented about 30 percent of the population from the earliest days. Apart from theological differences certain other factors account for this fear. The Roman Catholic Church has been dominated by Irish priests and, during the First World War, because of the leadership of Archbishop Mannix, a great believer in Irish Home Rule, was regarded as anti-British and therefore disloyal.

The Catholic Church has also been greatly involved in Australian politics.[6] Its membership has included the least privileged section of the Australian working force. In the earlier days these were the Irish laborers. In more recent times it has been the migrants from Southern Europe. It was the Irish-Australian, Cardinal Moran, who did much to organize the Maritime Strike of 1890, which provided the context for the creation of the Australian Labour Party in 1891. It was also a Catholic-led movement which created conditions for the divison of that party in 1955 and the creation of the Democratic Labour Party. Thus, many Protestants have seen the Catholic Church as a political pressure group.

Baptists in Australia have worked happily with all Protestants and were members of all bodies designed to promote such cooperation until the formation of the World Council of Churches. The first theological students in both Victoria and New South Wales were trained in the colleges of the Methodists, Congregationalists, and Presbyterians.[7] The Australian Baptist Missionary Society was represented at Edinburgh in 1910, but they have not been members of the World Council of Churches, and there have been constant attempts, some of which have been successful, to extract Baptists from all ecumenical involvement.

Australian Baptists are members of six state unions which are constituents of the Baptist Union of Australia. While a decision in regard to membership in the World Council of Churches had to be made by the federal body, real determinative power resides in the state unions. It is these which determine relationships with other Christians in their own states, and it was within the states that the vital debates concerning membership of the World Council of Churches took place.

There was little excitement among Australian Baptists over the assembly in Amsterdam which brought the World Council of Churches into being. They were represented there by the Right Honorable Ernest Brown of England. Within the following year signs of future controversy became evident. Even early in 1949 many denominational leaders presumed that Australian Baptists would join the World Council. When the state unions met later that year, it was obvious that many were uncertain what attitude to take. The Tasmanian Union decided that Baptists ought to be members of the World Council until circumstances should compel them to leave. The New South Wales assembly referred the matter back to its Council so that both sides of the argument might be adequately presented. The Western Australian Union, however, voted against affiliation by what *The Australian Baptist* called "a surprisingly large majority."

At the triennial meeting of the Baptist Union of Australia in 1950 it was reported that Queensland, New South Wales, and Western Australia had voted against affiliation; Victoria and South Australia had voted in favor; and Tasmania had not made a final decision. The assembly therefore decided not to seek affiliation with the Australian branch of the World Council of Churches but to ask that the continuance of the privilege of sending observers to meetings of the World Council be sought.

This decision regarding observers was challenged at the assembly of 1953. The assembly decided that this was a matter for state unions and authorized its Executive to seek the opinions of the states and to act accordingly. Nothing was done.

The debate not only continued but became more heated. Many now wished Australian Baptists to withdraw from the national ecumenical body. At the assembly of the Baptist Union of Australia held at Perth the following resolution was therefore adopted:

> In view of the increasing desire being expressed in many States for a fuller participation by Baptists in conferences and work of the Christian Church in Australia, all State Unions be asked to re-examine earlier decisions regarding

affiliation with the Australian Council for the World Council of Churches and that another vote be taken at the 1962 Assembly.[8]

In January, 1961, the Executive Committee of the Baptist Union of Australia published a pamphlet entitled *Australian Baptists and the World Council of Churches.* This document presented both sides of the debate and carefully avoided either a conclusion or a solution to the denominational dilemma.

In 1962 at Melbourne the majority of the states resolved not to seek affiliation with the World Council and then resolved:

> That this Assembly, representing the Baptists of Australia, having resolved not to seek affiliation with the Australian Council of Churches (World Council of Churches) also resolved that, united, we will bend every endeavour and spare no effort in bringing people of Australia and the Mission Fields for which we have responsibility, the saving grace of Jesus Christ the Lord. At the same time we would assure our brethren in the Lord of other Denominations that we will happily continue to work with them in our joint task of spreading the Gospel and relieving the needy.[9]

This resolution had a double implication. While rejecting any move to create an institutional relationship with other denominations, it wished to leave open the opportunity for cooperation with other Christians which had been the tradition of the denomination. It is clear that Australian Baptists would have rejected membership with bodies like the International Council of Christian Churches even more overwhelmingly than the World Council of Churches.

There has been no attempt to alter the situation as defined by the 1962 assembly. Within individual states, however, the issue remains a live one. Each state union has had to define its own attitude to its local council of churches and to those other bodies like the National Missionary Council and the Australian Council of Christian Education which are affiliated with the Australian Council of Churches. The situation varies considerably among the states. Some, like Victoria, are fully involved in all interchurch bodies. The Queensland Union, on the other hand, resolved at its assembly in 1966 that neither the Union nor any of its committees might join any of the subsidiary committees or divisions of the Australian Council of Churches, though it does hold membership in certain interchurch bodies not affiliated with that council.

Many Australian Baptists reject membership in the World Council of Churches less because of distinctive Baptist principles than because they find their relationship with other Christians through Keswick-type movements. The extent of Baptist involvement in such conventions can be judged from the fact that 50 percent of Australian missionaries serving interdenominational missions are Baptists.[10] The student bodies of most of the Bible colleges are often dominated by Baptists. This type of undenominationalism probably represents one reason for the attitudes toward the Ecumenical Movement.

There has also been some reaction against the movement toward the reunion of the churches, begun by a Presbyterian proposal in 1912. In 1946, Presbyterians, Methodists, and Congregationalists combined to form a single church in the Northern Territory. Since 1957 there have been moves by these denominations to establish a uniting church throughout the rest of Australia. Such a church would represent considerable ecclesiastical power, especially as the Anglican Church has shown considerable interest in being associated with it. In 1912 it would have seemed that union between Baptists and Congregationalists would be a more promising scheme than the one which is about to be established.

NEW ZEALAND

In New Zealand, Baptist relationships with other denominations have always been cordial. Even in those settlements which had a distinctly ecclesiastical origin, such as Christchurch and Dunedin, Baptists found no difficulty in establishing churches or in cooperating with the other denominations. This harmony developed throughout the years, and when the New Zealand Council of Churches came into being on April 2, 1941, the Baptist Union was a foundation member and has been fully represented in all interchurch discussions arranged by the Council. The Union affiliated with the World Council of Churches in 1944 and in 1957 joined the East Asian Christian Conference.

Not all New Zealand Baptists were happy with such ecumenical involvements, and in 1949 questions were raised at the annual assembly of the Union concerning membership in the World Council of Churches. It was agreed in the following year to endorse the Union's membership in that body. The matter was raised again in 1964, and a report was prepared for the assembly to enable it to give adequate consideration to the matter. This report drew attention to three main issues:

1. Whether the World Council of Churches showed a tendency to become a super-church.

2. Whether Baptist principles were being compromised by membership in the World Council of Churches.

3. The relationship between the World Council of Churches and the Roman and Orthodox churches.

The majority report found no evidence that Baptists were yielding any of their basic principles by their membership in the World Council but rather were enabled better to serve the world and the gospel. A minority report took a different attitude, believing that out of the World Council would come a World Church with a liturgical and sacramental character. The assembly of the Union accepted the point of view of the majority report and by 229 votes to 65 resolved to continue in membership with the World Council but to review the position periodically.

While New Zealand Baptists are committed to ecumenicity, they have no part in the strong movement toward reunion which has been a feature of the life of the other major denominations. In 1964 the Council of the Union declared its belief that division among the denominations should not be maintained where it could be avoided but added that Baptists considered themselves unable to enter into negotiation for any scheme of church union which involved the acceptance of infant baptism.[11] This theme was developed by L. A. North, in a pamphlet published in 1967, when he concluded:

> We believe that where there is little of consequence that divides denominations on matters of faith and practice, they should enter into union as soon as possible. Where, however, the differences are deeply significant, union is impractical until such time as those differences are resolved in the light of further understanding.[12]

While New Zealand Baptists have cooperated fully with other Protestant churches, there has been a widespread reluctance to have dealings with the Roman Catholic Church. In May, 1966, Angus McLeod prepared a report for the Baptist Union Executive entitled *Baptists, the National Council of Churches, and the Roman Catholic Church.* This outlined the relationships that had existed between Baptists and the Roman Catholic Church and admitted that Baptists would not have joined the National Council of Churches if cooperation with Rome had been contemplated at that time. He then pointed out that Protestant-Catholic relationships had undergone radical changes between 1946 and 1960 and that the National Council of Churches was under pressure to seek a greater intimacy with the Roman communion.

In October, 1967, representatives of the National Council of Churches, including four Baptists, met with representatives of the Roman Church and proposed that a working group should be constituted. The Baptist Union submitted this proposal to the constituent churches, and 60 percent of them voted against it. A letter was then sent to the general secretary of the National Council of Churches indicating that the Union could not cooperate in this venture but adding that on the local level Baptist churches were free to cooperate with any churches and that many Baptist congregations were glad of the opportunities opening up for dialogue with Catholics, but that even these wished to see what would develop in their own localities before the denomination should commit itself on a national level.

Accounting for different attitudes which prevail toward ecumenical involvement in New Zealand as contrasted with Australia can lead to interesting speculation. Certainly historical factors are extremely important. The New Zealand nation has grown out of a different social structure from that which Australia knew, and there have been fewer tensions and less suspicion among differing sections of society. Baptists in New Zealand have, also, been members of one Union, which fact has allowed the growth of strong leadership from the center that has favored the Ecumenical Movement, while the division of Australian Baptists into state unions has hindered the growth of such leadership. It must then be noted that New Zealand has been less subject to American influence since the Second World War than Australia and has followed more closely the pattern of the British Baptists.

NEW GUINEA

On the mission field Australian and New Zealand Baptists have cooperated fully with other Christians. Both followed the British Baptists into the Indian subcontinent. A new development took place in 1948 when the New South Wales Baptist Union resolved to commence missionary work in New Guinea. This work was taken over by the Australian Baptist Missionary Society in 1951.

Missionary work began in New Guinea in the mid-nineteenth century with the work of French Catholics. In 1870 the London Missionary Society established stations on some of the islands off the coast and shortly afterward moved to the mainland. By the end of the century these missions had been joined by those of the Methodists and the Anglicans as well as other Catholic missions.

In 1908 the Seventh-Day Adventists began working near Port Moresby. A measure of cooperation between missions existed from 1890, when the Methodists, the Anglicans, and the London Missionary Society made a "gentleman's agreement" at the instigation of Sir William MacGregor, the commissioner. This defined their respective spheres of influence. Bitter sectarian rivalries did not disappear, however, as some missions were not content to accept any limitation of their activities.[13]

After the Second World War a great outburst of missionary activity took place in the country, and a number of societies, some denominational, very many undenominational and often of American origin, began to work there. The church has to confess that it has often added a religious element to a confusion which arose from a multiplicity of tribes and languages. Responsible Christians have therefore sought ways and means of cooperation, and Australian Baptists have been taking their full part.

There are now two ecumenical bodies in existence in Papua, New Guinea, to which Baptists belong and in which they exercise considerable influence.[14] It was largely as the result of work by a Baptist missionary that the Evangelical Alliance came into being in 1963 at a conference in Wewak. The Australian Baptist Missionary Society and the Australian Churches of Christ Overseas Mission were the only two denominational societies represented at this meeting. The other bodies involved were all inter-denominational. Membership in the Alliance is confined to churches, missions and fellowships that: "(a) recognise the Bible as the supreme and final authority in all matters of faith and practice, (b) insist on individual salvation through regeneration by faith in our Lord Jesus Christ." It was also agreed: "All members will undertake on acceptance, to refrain, in all fields of Alliance cooperation, from propagating doctrine peculiar to themselves." The Evangelical Alliance enables member bodies to cooperate in a variety of activities, including radio missions, translation, and education.

The Baptists also belong to the Melanesian Council of Churches, which was inaugurated at a meeting held at the Boroko Baptist Church in Port Moresby. The membership includes Anglican, Lutheran, Methodist, Baptist, and Salvation Army denominations and the Papua Ekklesia, which grew out of the work of the London Missionary Society. From the outset this Council has sought good relationships with a variety of bodies, including the Evangelical Alliance. It resolved also not to become affiliated with any interdenominational or ecumenical agencies. Thus there is no link between the Melanesian Council of Churches and the World Council of Churches, so that no wedge will be driven between the participating churches and between the Council and the Alliance.

In view of the fact that the Melanesian Council of Churches is not affiliated with any other body, it was able, without difficulty, to invite the Roman Catholic Church to join it, and in 1969 it corresponded with the Conference of Catholic Bishops asking whether their church would desire associate or full membership in the Council. The following year the bishops replied that they did not wish to seek membership at that stage. The situation changed rapidly in 1971. At a meeting of the Melanesian Council of Churches held at a Baptist mission station at Baiyer Valley, the Roman Catholic Church was received into membership. This event caused some disturbance among certain sections of Australian Baptists. However, the Australian Baptist Missionary Society has pointed out that a matter such as membership in a council of churches must be determined by the local indigenous Baptist church.

SUMMARY

New Zealand and Australian Baptists demonstrate a variety of attitudes toward other churches. Some are fearful of tendencies they believe to be in the Ecumenical Movement. Many will, in no circumstances, cooperate with the Roman Catholic Church; but all are anxious for some form of cooperation with other Christians, particularly in the tasks of evangelism and social service.

CHAPTER 17

Africa

Emanuel A. Dahunsi

NIGERIA

The Christian message was first proclaimed in the city of Ogbomoso in Western Nigeria in 1855 through Southern Baptist missionaries. A little later, the preachers of the Church Missionary Society followed. And so it has happened that from the first family that accepted Christianity in the city many are members of the Baptist church and some members of the Anglican church. A similar picture can be cited over and over again in most Nigerian towns. In one large compound will be found adherents not only of different Christian denominations but of different religious faiths. When members of the same extended family greet one another in their family compound on Sunday morning, then part to worship, some in Baptist churches, others in Anglican, Methodist, and other churches, then meet again in their family compounds, their attitude to one another can readily be imagined. We indicate here some of the most common features.

Members of a Baptist church do not hesitate to attend services in the churches of other denominations, especially Protestant denominations. Choir festivals; harvest thanksgiving services; dedication services of church building, equipment, and furniture; christening ceremonies of children; birthday anniversary services of friends and acquaintances; weddings; services on occasions of promotions and retirements of friends; graduation services; departures to and arrivals from foreign countries; funerals—these and many others are occasions when Baptists join other Christians in other churches for worship. No doctrinal or other differences will ever prevent a person from sharing in a special service with a relative or a friend in the church of his choice.

The only limitation in this respect is in the observance of the Lord's Supper. On some special occasions, for example, in an Anglican church, the celebration of the Lord's Supper is regarded as part of the service. Most Christian denominations restrict the participants in that part of the service to a select few usually regarded as "communicant members" of the celebrant's denomination. However, it should be noted that in many Baptist churches, the practice is to exclude non-Baptists from the Lord's Supper. There are some exceptions, of course; there are some Baptist churches which emphasize the fact that the observance is that of the *Lord's* Supper rather than that of the *church's* Supper.

In many towns in Nigeria, various denominations often join to arrange for revival services. In 1960, for example, when Dr. Billy Graham made his whirlwind tour of Africa, there were no denominational distinctions in the planning and attendance at the services throughout. Similar efforts take place from time to time in different places. One Anglican minister attended the Keswick Convention in England in 1912. When he returned to Lagos, he founded a similar convention in October of the same year. The joint annual services, sponsored by Anglicans, Methodists, Baptists, Presbyterians, and Salvation Army, have continued in Lagos until this day. During the week there is an exchange of pulpits in the churches of the sponsoring bodies.

In 1963 a veteran missionary of the Sudan Interior Mission inaugurated a revival campaign under the name "New Life for All." The movement has spread from Northern Nigeria to other parts of the country. Baptists join in such efforts without hesitation.

Annually, during the universal week of prayer held during the first week of the year, Baptists join others in the spirit of prayer to usher in the New Year.

Besides these regular involvements of a national character, there are in some places joint services, mostly open-air, on Good Friday, Easter morning, and at Christmas, involving the cooperation of many denominations. Baptists wholeheartedly join such services.

COOPERATION IN OTHER PARTS OF AFRICA

What has been said with particular reference to Nigeria is true in many other parts of Africa. With some slight variations we find a similar picture of Baptists cooperating with churches and persons of other denominations in several areas of Christian life.

Besides the points already indicated, we find that in many places there are regular meetings of the ministers of different denominations to foster their witness and deepen their fellowship with one another. Baptist ministers are not found wanting in their participation in such fellowships. Furthermore, in periods of national crises, it is often necessary for all Christian ministers to take concerted action in one form or another. Baptists usually join in such ad hoc efforts.

In many countries of Africa, there are Bible societies in which many Christian denominations cooperate to make the written Word of God available to every person in his own language at a price which he can afford. As of October, 1972, the United Bible Societies' list showed that some twenty-six countries of Africa have Bible societies.[1] Whatever else divides the multifarious Christian denominations, all agree on the place of the Bible in their life and witness. Hence the work of the Bible society has brought together a larger group of Christians than any other concern. Baptists actively cooperate with other Christians in the work of Bible societies. A unique feature of this cooperative effort not found in other areas is that the Roman Catholic Church has taken an active part in the work of the Bible societies. Strangely, some evangelical churches have refused to cooperate in Bible projects in which Catholics participate.

In many countries of Africa, the need to form one Christian council of Protestant churches in order to strengthen the witness of Christians has been felt.[2] Usually these councils define their aims and set up requirements for membership in such terms as to enhance the Christian message in their local situations. In Nigeria, for example, one condition that bars many groups is that, to qualify for membership, the church must uphold monogamy as the ideal of Christian marriage. Baptists actively participate in the work of such councils.

In April, 1963, the All-Africa Conference of Churches was inaugurated at Kampala, Uganda, "as a fellowship of consultation and cooperation within the wider fellowship of the universal Church." As of March, 1972, there were eighty-five member churches in the Conference. Of these, there are five Baptist groups, namely, those of Burundi, Cameroon, Nigeria, Rwanda, and Zaire.

The World Council of Churches has afforded to a few Baptist groups in Africa an opportunity for wider fellowship. As of October, 1972, there were about 240 member churches in some eighty-three countries in the World Council of Churches. Of these, there are forty-five member churches in twenty-one countries of Africa. The only Baptist groups are those of Cameroon and Nigeria.

It is probably fair to infer that, while Baptists in Africa readily cooperate with other Christian denominations in various ways, they do not embrace membership of international bodies with any measure of enthusiasm. The Nigerian Baptist Convention decided in 1969 to join both the All-Africa Conference of Churches and the World Council of Churches, after years of studying the question of membership, only after satisfying itself that its membership involved no more than its membership in the Baptist World Alliance.

Baptists in Africa, like Baptists in most other countries of the world, guard zealously the principle of autonomy of the local church. Consequently, they refrain from movements aimed at an organic union of churches. Probably one reason that most Baptist groups in Africa have not joined the All-Africa Conference of Churches and the World Council of Churches is the suspicion that these organizations ultimately aim at an organic union of their member churches. However, the present constitutions of these organizations make it clear that the affairs of each member church are not to be affected by any decision of the wider fellowship.

In most countries of Africa, Baptists retain their freedom to preach the gospel anywhere. They feel free to open a preaching station wherever they feel there is a need. No comity agreements are made with other denominations. Some denominations do enter into such agreements in the interest of the one witness, as they understand it. While it would appear that comity agreements are in line with the methods of the great apostle Paul, it is doubtful if the principle can be justifiably maintained in modern times in many places. What is of fundamental importance is that the efforts of various Christians in any one area should supplement one another rather than being antagonistic to one another.

CONCLUSION

There is one final point that is necessary to conclude this study. Sometimes Baptists in Africa speak as if they are the Christian group closest to the teachings of the New Testament. Many Baptists in other parts of the world speak in similar terms. The truth of the matter is that on some points Baptists are closer to the teachings of the New Testament. They share this honored position with some non-Baptists. However, on some other points, other denominations are closer to the teachings of the New Testament. This is a commonplace observation. No one Christian denomination can incorporate the richness and diversity of the church life as represented in the various writings of the New Testament. This indubitable fact has some important consequences. First, it makes a person hesitate to join efforts at organic union of churches which often lead to the loss of some distinctive contribution of some of the member churches to the richness of Christian life. However, one should not lose sight of the value of such efforts in breaking down barriers among Christian denominations. Secondly, a realization of this fact should make Baptists, as well as other Christians, more humble as all endeavor to grow in the grace and knowledge of the Lord Jesus Christ.[3]

EPILOGUE

James Leo Garrett, Jr.

The diversity among Baptist conventions (or unions), to say nothing of local congregations, in respect to their attitudes toward and relations with other Christians is so great that one may rightly ask whether any meaning can be derived from the preceding worldwide historical survey. Are there any patterns or trends that can be discerned? What do these suggest for the future? It is now fitting to pursue an answer to the question as to any patterns.

I

On the one side, there are some Baptist congregations and national bodies that practice a pronounced isolation or separatism in which they have very few meaningful contacts with non-Baptist Christians and denominations and often very few or no formal ties with their fellow Baptists, whether in their own nation or through the Baptist World Alliance. At least two distinct types of such Baptist conventions (or unions) can be identified: one whose isolation is due to beliefs predominant among the churches and members that comprise the convention (or union), and the other whose isolation is more traceable to the external pressures or the particular circumstances affecting the convention (or union).

One type espouses such isolation or separatism because of its persuasion, held in varying degrees to be sure, that other Baptists have become theologically heretical or religiously apostate, and thus isolation for the sake of truth is said to be necessary. Such an attitude is often then applied even more vigorously to non-Baptist

193

Christians. Instances of such attitudes include the Strict and Particular Baptists of England, who decry the abandonment of hyper-Calvinism by the churches affiliated with the Baptist Union of Great Britain and Ireland; the Baptist Union of Ireland, whose links even with the Baptist Union of Great Britain and Ireland for nearly a century have been nonexistent; the Primitive Baptists and Progressive Primitive Baptists (U.S.A.), who for a century and a half have rejected the missionary agencies and activities of the "Missionary" Baptists; the Free Will Baptists (U.S.A.), who advocate Arminianism over against the Calvinism, at least in earlier generations, of other Baptists; the Landmark Baptists (U.S.A.) in two separate, but similar, national associations, who, especially over against Southern Baptists, hold tenaciously to a Baptist "true church" separatism buttressed by the theory of Baptist historical continuity from the New Testament era advanced by James Robinson Graves and his co-laborers in the nineteenth century; the Fellowship of Evangelical Baptist Churches (Canada), that provides a fundamentalist protest against the Baptist Federation of Canada; and the Conservative Baptist Association (U.S.A.) and the General Association of Regular Baptist Churches (U.S.A.), together with the churches related to their overseas missionary work in such nations as Brazil, Japan, Korea, and the Philippines, that as avowed "evangelicals" protest against the alleged "liberalism" among the American Baptist Churches in the U.S.A. and in denominations that are members of the National Council of the Churches of Christ in the U.S.A. and of the World Council of Churches. Unlike most other Baptist bodies in this category, the Conservative Baptist Association does hold membership in the National Association of Evangelicals, and the General Association of Regular Baptists has had ties with the American Council of Christian Churches, founded by Carl McIntire.

The other type of Baptist isolation or separatism is due primarily to the persecution, ostracism, disenfranchisement, and/or harassment received by these Baptists at the hands of the civil state and/or at the instigation of established or "state" churches. The Council of Churches of the Evangelical Christians-Baptists (U.S.S.R.), also known as the *Initsiativniki*, though in a sense it constitutes a protest against the All-Union Council of Evangelical Christians-Baptists (U.S.S.R.), seemingly has few contacts with Baptists outside the U.S.S.R. or with other Christian bodies partly because of its tenuous relationship to the government of the U.S.S.R. The Baptist Union of Romania, still harassed by Romanian Orthodoxy and having few contacts with Lutherans and Reformed, is probably more isolated than would be true amid other circumstances.

II

On the other side, there are some Baptist congregations and unions (or councils) that have actually entered into a newly formed Protestant union church on a regional or national basis and others that have expressed a serious interest in participation in such a union church. The only clear example of Baptist entry into a united transconfessional Protestant structure is the Church of North India, formed in 1970, entry into which actually became a divisive issue among Baptists in North India and in which newly formed church a Baptist minister has become a bishop. But Baptists in South India and in Sri Lanka (formerly Ceylon) have participated in discussions that are designed to lead to united Protestant church formations in their respective areas. The reasons advanced for Baptist entry into an organic union of Protestants in South Asia seem to be chiefly two: the theological and ecclesiastical differences which have originated in Europe and North America have little significance today for Christians living in Asia, and the imperatives of the Christian mission in predominantly non-Christian nations call for a degree of unity not possible in denominational structures. Hence, for some Baptists in South Asia these considerations outweigh their continued denominational existence as Baptists.

III

But the majority of Baptist Christians, and this seems to be true on every continent, are opting for neither separatist isolation nor organic church union with other Protestant denominations. In so doing they are denying on the one hand the validity of an unnecessary isolation or self-contained independency and are affirming on the other hand that there still exists a *raison d'être* for Baptist Christians. This overwhelming majority of Baptists favors and practices some kind of cooperation with non-Baptist Christians as well as close relations with their fellow Baptists, though this cooperation varies greatly and may be found to different degrees, in different channels or modes, and with differing groups of non-Baptist Christians. Implicit in such cooperation is the recognition of the validity of the Christian faith and discipleship of those with whom they cooperate, though differences of doctrine, church order, and/or obedience are not denied. At least five distinct types of contemporary Baptist cooperation with other Christians may be identified.

First, some cooperation is limited to interdenominational functional cooperation, i.e., for specific *ad hoc* projects, with the permanent structured relations being usually limited to local, national, or world Baptist bodies. Projects may include Bible translation and distribution, evangelistic campaigns, radio and television production, Christian literature, and the like. The Southern Baptist Convention (U.S.A.) practices this type of cooperation. Having declined to become a member of the Federal Council of Churches, the National Council of Churches, and the World Council of Churches, this Convention supports the American Bible Society and various evangelistic campaigns such as those of Billy Graham and Key '73 and has in recent years had dialogues with Roman Catholics. A similar form of cooperation, though in some instances less in degree, characterizes the North American Baptist General Conference (U.S.A.), the General Association of General Baptists (U.S.A.), and the Atlantic and Western Canada Conventions (Canada). The Baptist unions (or conventions) in Norway, Yugoslavia, Spain, and Portugal engage in some forms of cooperation, and the Union of Baptist Churches in the Netherlands, since its conciliar withdrawals, may be so classified. Most of the Baptist conventions in Latin America participate in some cooperative activity with other Evangelical denominations but without membership in national Evangelical confederations. The same pattern characterizes the Baptist conventions of Hong Kong–Macao, Taiwan, Korea, Malaysia–Singapore, Indonesia, Vietnam, Guam, and the Southern Baptist-oriented churches of Thailand. The Australian Baptists, especially in New South Wales, Queensland, and Western Australia, are active in non-conciliar cooperation. The Baptist conventions of East and Central Africa may be classified similarly, and the small Baptist communities in the Arab nations are in fellowship with other Protestants. The Baptist situation in Bangladesh, now in transition, is difficult to categorize.

Secondly, some Baptists cooperate with other Protestant

Christians at least partly through continental or national councils of churches, but not through the World Council of Churches, usually with a stance clearly in opposition to organic church union. The Baptist unions of Scotland, Sweden, West Germany, East Germany, Switzerland, Czechoslovakia, Poland, France, and Italy are members of such councils or confederations. The Baptist unions in the Caribbean are participants in insular councils. The Baptist Convention of Ontario and Quebec (Canada) belongs to this category, though a segment of its membership has desired affiliation with the World Council of Churches. The Baptist General Conference (U.S.A.), though inclined to more separatism, does belong to the National Association of Evangelicals. The Council of Baptist Churches in North East India and the American Baptist-oriented churches in Thailand are fully involved in Christian councils. Both the Japan Baptist Union and the Japan Baptist Convention are members of the Japan Christian Council. Baptist unions in Burundi, Rwanda, and Zaire belong to the All-Africa Conference of Churches. In Israel, Baptists belong to the United Christian Council, and in Papua New Guinea, Baptists belong to the Evangelical Alliance, and Baptists and Roman Catholics as well as other Protestants jointly share in the nonaligned Melanesian Council of Churches. Virtually all Baptist bodies in this category are members of the Baptist World Alliance.

Thirdly, some Baptist churches belong to "denominational" unions which themselves consist of both Baptist and non-Baptist churches. Such is the situation of Baptists in the U.S.S.R. and in the Federal Republic of Germany (West Germany). In the U.S.S.R. the All-Union Council of Evangelical Christians-Baptists consists of congregations of Baptists, Evangelical Christians, Pentecostals, and Mennonite Brethren. In West Germany the Bund Evangelisch-Freikirchlicher Gemeinden includes Pentecostals and Plymouth Brethren as well as Baptists. Within such unions the distinctive beliefs of each confession are respected, and each confession is fully represented in the union itself.

Fourthly, some Baptist conventions (or unions) are members of the World Council of Churches as well as national or continental councils or conferences and have avowed the continuation of the denominational identity. The Baptist unions of Denmark and Hungary are European examples of this pattern. The Nat' Baptist Convention, U.S.A., Inc., the National Baptist Conv of America, and the Progressive National Baptist Conven'

(U.S.A.) are members of the World Council of Churches, and the Seventh Day Baptist General Conference (U.S.A.) has a consistent record of ecumenical participation. The Baptist Union of New Zealand, the Burma Baptist Convention, the Nigerian Baptist Convention, and the Baptist Union of Cameroon are similarly member bodies in the World Council of Churches.

Fifthly, some Baptist conventions (or unions) are fully involved in ecumenical conciliar participation from the local level to the national and the World Council of Churches level, while participating fully also in continental Baptist fellowships and the Baptist World Alliance, with at least a considerable segment of their membership being interested in interdenominational mergers or a new united Protestant church on a nationwide scale. Such is the situation of the Baptist Union of Great Britain and Ireland, though the "conservative evangelicals" within the union represent a contrary trend. The American Baptist Churches in the U.S.A. have entered into an "associated relationship" with the Progressive National Baptist Convention, Inc. (1970), and with the Church of the Brethren (1973). Although there are in their ranks some who have desired full participation in the Consultation on Church Union (U.S.A.), the denomination maintains only an "observer-consultant" relationship to this merger effort. The Baptists in South India and in Sri Lanka are continuing discussions regarding possible entry into the Church of South India and into a projected Church of Sri Lanka.

IV

In summary it may be noted that, while some Baptist bodies are in separatism, isolation, or alienation from other Christians and indeed from other Baptists and while other Baptists have with conviction entered into a new organic union of Protestant churches, the majority of Baptists today engage in some form of cooperation with non-Baptist Christians, whether *ad hoc* functional, national conciliar, umbrella denominational union, world conciliar with continued denominational identity, or pan-conciliar with some advocacy of mergers and/or organic union.

V

While the various chapters of this present volume have made it possible to identify these various patterns of Baptist relationships or non-relationships with other Christians, there yet needs to be much investigation of the factors, sociological, cultural, and economic as well as theological, ecclesiological, and missiological, that have shaped the attitudes and relationships of Baptists on the various continents, in the different nations, and within the distinctive conventions (or unions).

To such studies of the factors that have shaped Baptists should be added the continuing quest for patterns and degrees of Christian unity and/or union by Christian leaders of many denominations. An important example of the latter has been the Concepts of Unity and Models of Union Consultation sponsored by the Faith and Order Commission of the World Council of Churches in Salamanca, Spain, in 1973.

Such probings of possible modes of Christian unity and/or union today need always to be infused by continuing studies of the Old and the New Testaments regarding the people of God and by important lessons from the post-biblical history of Christianity.

Moreover, Baptists ought to consider carefully the worldwide needs of the last quarter of the twentieth century and the changing situation of Christians within that era as they make decisions about future relationships of Baptists with other Christians.

It is increasingly evident that Baptists now respond most readily to cooperation with other Christians in evangelistic and missionary proclamation. Baptist responses to transdenominational cooperation in teaching and training within the church and in diaconal ministries and Christian social action outside the church are fewer. Furthermore, Baptist interest in structural church union is modest, if existent at all.

Such differences seem to be relatable to J. K. Zeman's application of the Troeltschian, and essentially European, distinction between "church" and "sect." Zeman has suggested that "the tension between the church and [the] sect patterns of Christianity," if and when "properly understood and held in creative tension" by the Baptists, "may yet prove to be the most important Baptist contribution to the life of the whole Church of Jesus Christ in an ecumenical age."

Earnest and constructive efforts are needed to remove the ignorance, misunderstanding, and mistrust of Baptists concerning their fellow Baptists of other conventions and unions and to foster a genuine understanding and appreciation of such other Baptist bodies. Such a strengthening of Christian fellowship within the

Baptist family would then serve to make more viable and effective Baptist cooperative relationships with non-Baptist Christians.

Hopefully the concern of Baptists for both the churchly and the sectarian patterns in Christianity may help Christians to avoid both unbrotherly alienation and isolation and oppressive and decadent ecclesiasticism and contribute to that unity for mission for which Jesus Christ prayed and which Christians have sought.

NOTES

CHAPTER I

[1] On Anabaptism in England and its possible relationship to developments in England, see I. B. Horst, *The Radical Brethren: Anabaptism and the English Reformation to 1558* (Nieuwkoop: B. de Graaf, 1972) and B. R. White, *The English Separatist Tradition: From the Marian Martyrs to the Pilgrim Fathers* (London: Oxford University Press, 1971). For the seventeenth-century correspondence between the English and Dutch, see Benjamin Evans, *The Early English Baptists* (London: J. Heaton and Son, 1862, 1864), vol. 1, pp. 208f.; vol. 2, pp. 20f.; and Champlin Burrage, *The Early English Dissenters in the Light of Recent Research, 1550-1641* (Cambridge: University Press, 1912), vol. 2, pp. 172-260. For an outline of contacts from the seventeenth century to the present day, see E. A. Payne, "Contacts Between Mennonites and Baptists," *Foundations*, vol. 4 (January, 1961); pp. 39-55, and also E. A. Payne, *Free Churchmen Unrepentant and Repentant and Other Essays* (London: Carey Kingsgate Press Ltd., 1965), pp. 75-92.

[2] For Bunyan, see George Offor's edition of his works. On the general question of relationships, see E. A. Payne, *The Fellowship of Believers: Baptist Thought and Practice Yesterday and Today*, enl. ed. (London: Carey Kingsgate Press, 1952), and *Free Churchmen Unrepentant and Repentant and Other Essays*, pp. 93-104. The early approaches of the Three Denominations to the throne are recounted in the standard Baptist histories of Crosby and Ivimey. See also Bernard L. Manning, *The Protestant Dissenting Deputies*, ed. Ormerod Greenwood (Cambridge: University Press, 1952). On the struggle of Nonconformists for civil rights in nineteenth-century England, see William H. Mackintosh, *Disestablishment and Liberation* (London: Epworth Press, 1972).

[3] See E. A. Payne, "The Development of Nonconformist Theological Education in the Nineteenth Century with Special Reference to Regent's Park College," in E. A. Payne, ed., *Studies in History and Religion: Presented to Dr. H. Wheeler Robinson, M.A., on His Seventieth Birthday* (London: Lutterworth Press, 1942), pp. 229-253, and Robert Edward Cooper, *From Stepney to St. Giles': The Story of Regent's Park College, 1810-1960* (London: Carey Kingsgate Press, 1960).

[4] See J. H. Shakespeare, *The Churches at the Cross-roads: A Study in Church Unity* (London: Williams and Norgate, 1918). For a "Letter on Re-union" adopted by the Baptist Union in 1889, the Declaratory Statement of Common Faith and Practice of the Federal Council, the Baptist Reply to the Lambeth Appeal (1926), and a report, "Church Relations in England," adopted by the Baptist Union Council in 1953, see E. A. Payne, *The Baptist Union: A Short History* (London: Carey Kingsgate Press, 1959), Appendices VII, VIII, IX, and XI. In general see E. K. H. Jordan, *Free Church Unity: History of the Free Church Council Movement, 1896-1941* (London: Lutterworth Press, 1956) and E. A. Payne, *The Free Churches: Today's Challenges* (London: Free Church Federal Council, 1972).

[5] See F. Townley Lord, *Achievement: A Short History of the Baptist Missionary Society, 1792-1942* (London: Carey Press, 1941) and W. G. Wickramasinghe, "Church Union: A Call to Obedience," *The Baptist Quarterly*, vol. 22 (July, 1967), pp. 166-175.

[6] See Ruth Rouse and Stephen Charles Neill, eds., *A History of the Ecumenical Movement, 1517-1948* (Philadelphia: The Westminster Press, 1954; vol. 2, 1948-1968, ed. Harold E. Fey, 1970) and E. A. Payne, *Free Churchmen Unrepentant and Repentant and Other Essays*, pp. 120-141.

[7] See E. A. Payne, *Thirty Years of the British Council of Churches, 1942-1972* (London: British Council of Churches, 1972). For the recommendations of the Nottingham Conference, see the official report, *Unity Begins at Home* (London: SCM Press, 1964) and *Baptists and Unity* (London: Baptist Union of Great Britain and Ireland, 1967). Appendices I and II. On the Birmingham Conference, see David

Edwards. *The British Churches Turn to the Future* (London: SCM Press, 1973).

[8] See *Towards Union: A Suggested Scheme for Church Union in Wales* (Cardiff: Joint Committee of the Four Denominations, 1963); *Supplementary Report on Baptism* (Cardiff: Joint Committee of the Four Denominations, 1963); *The Call to Covenant* (Aberystwyth: Council of Churches for Wales, 1966); and *Covenanting in Wales* (Carnarvon: Council of Churches for Wales, 1968). See also *Christian Unity* (Glasgow: Baptist Union of Scotland, 1967).

[9] See *Ecumenism Examined* (Belfast: Baptist Union of Ireland, 1966).

[10] See L. G. Champion, *Baptists and Unity* (London: A. R. Mowbray & Co., 1962); E. Roberts-Thomson, *With Hands Outstretched: Baptists and the Ecumenical Movement* (London: Marshall, Morgan & Scott, 1962); Alec Gilmore, ed., *The Pattern of the Church: A Baptist View* (London: Lutterworth Press, 1963); *Liberty in the Lord: Comments on Trends in Baptist Thought Today* (London: Baptist Revival Fellowship, 1964); G. R. Beasley-Murray, *Reflections on the Ecumenical Movement* (London: Baptist Union of Great Britain and Ireland, 1965); Alec Gilmore, *Baptism and Christian Unity* (Valley Forge, Pa.: Judson Press, 1966); E. A. Payne, *Some Recent Happenings in the Roman Church* (London: Baptist Union of Great Britain and Ireland, 1966); *Baptist and Unity* (London: Baptist Union of Great Britain and Ireland, 1967); *Baptists and Unity Reviewed* (London: Baptist Union of Great Britain and Ireland, 1969); *Baptists for Unity*, foreword by Paul Rowntree Clifford (Coventry, 1968); and David S. Russell, *Baptists and Some Contemporary Issues* (London: Baptist Union of Great Britain and Ireland, 1968).

[11] See Percy W. Evans, Henry Townsend, William Robinson et al., *Infant Baptism Today* (London: Carey Kingsgate Press; Birmingham: Berean Press, 1948); and E. Roberts-Thomson, *Baptists and Disciples of Christ* (London: Carey Kingsgate Press Ltd., 1951).

CHAPTER 2

[1] See Johann Gerhard Oncken, *Licht und Recht: Eine Sammlung von Predigten und Reden gehalten von J. G. Oncken* (Cassel: J. G. Oncken Nachfolger, 1901); Theodor Dupree, *Ein Bahnbrecher für biblische Wahrheiten; Leben und Wirken von J. G. Oncken, dem Gründer der deutschen Baptisten-Gemeinden* Kassel: Verlag und Druck vom Verlagshaus der deutschen Baptisten, 1900); John Hunt Cooke, *Johann Gerhard Oncken: His Life and Work* (London: S. W. Partridge and Co., 1908); Hans Luckey, *Johann Gerhard Oncken und die Anfänge des deutschen Baptismus* (Kassel: J. G. Oncken Nachfolger, 1934, 1958).

[2] From a letter to the author written by Knud Wümplemann in 1970.·

[3] From a letter to the author in 1972.

CHAPTER 3

[1] The following materials in English and in German concerning the Baptists and Evangelical Christians in the Soviet Union have for the most part been taken from a bibliography prepared by Professor Albert W. Wardin, Jr., of Belmont College, Nashville, Tennessee: Robert Sloan Latimer, *With Christ in Russia* (London: Hodder and Stoughton, 1910): J. H. Rushbrooke, ed., *The Baptist Movement in the Continent of Europe* (London: Carey Press and Kingsgate Press, 1915), pp. 69-87; J. H. Rushbrooke, *The Baptist Movement in the Continent of Europe* (London: Kingsgate Press, 1923), pp. 107-143; J. H. Rushbrooke, *Some Chapters of European Baptist History* (London: Kingsgate Press, 1929), pp. 36-103; N. I. Saloff-Astakhoff, *Christianity in Russia* (New York: Loizeaux Brothers, 1941), pp. 83-149; J. H. Rushbrooke, *Baptists in the U. S. S. R.* (Nashville: Broadman Press, 1943); Louie D. Newton, *An American Churchman in the Soviet Union* (New York: American Russian Institute, 1946); John David Hughey, Jr., "Baptists in Soviet Russia,"

Review of Religion, vol. 12 (1947-1948), pp. 193-203; Serge Bolshakoff, *Russian Nonconformity* (Philadelphia: The Westminster Press, 1950), pp. 111-129; Fürstin Sophie Lieven, *Eine Saat die reiche Fruchte brachte* (Basel: Brunnen-Verlag, 1952); Irwin Barnes, *Truth Is Immortal: The Story of Baptists in Europe* (London: Kingsgate Press, 1955), pp. 52-61; Alexander Karev, "The Union of Evangelical Christians-Baptists in the U.S.S.R. and Its Work," *Fraternal* (October, 1955), pp. 39-44; Günter Wirth, ed., *Evangelische Christen in der Sowjetunion* (Berlin: Union Verlag, 1955); Waldemar Gutsche, *Westliche Quellen des russischen Stundismus*, 2nd. ed. (Kassel: J. G. Oncken Verlag, 1957); John David Hughey, Jr., "Baptists in Communist Russia," *Congregational Quarterly*, vol. 35 (1957), pp. 153-161; Michael Klimenko, "Anfänge des Baptismus in Südrussland [Ukraine] nach offiziellen Dokumenten," Th.D. dissertation, Friedrich-Alexander-Universität, Erlangen, 1957; Waldemar Gutsche, *Religion und Evangelium in Sowjetrussland zwischen zwei Weltkriegen, 1917-1944* (Kassel: J. G. Oncken Verlag, 1959); V. Carney Hargroves, "The Russian Baptists: A Brief History and an Appraisal," *Foundations*, vol. 2 (1959), pp. 250-257; Rudolf Donat, *Das wachsende Werk* (Kassel: J. G. Oncken Verlag, 1960), pp. 129-189, 376-379; Walter Kolarz, *Religion in the Soviet Union* (New York: St. Martin's Press, 1961), pp. 283-321; Andrew Quarles Blane, "The Relations Between the Russian Protestant Sects and the State, 1900-1921," Ph.D. dissertation, Duke University, Durham, N.C., 1964; J. C. Pollock, *The Faith of the Russian Evangelicals* (New York: McGraw-Hill Book Company, 1964); J. C. Pollock, "In Soviet Central Asia," *Churchman*, vol. 78 (1964), pp. 211-216; Michael Bourdeaux, *Opium of the People: The Christian Religion in the U.S.S.R.* (Indianapolis: Bobbs-Merrill Company, 1966), pp. 151-172; All-Union Council of Evangelical Christians-Baptists, *Conference* (Moscow, 1966); *The Baptist World*, vol. 14 (February, 1967); William C. Fletcher and Anthony J. Strover, eds., *Religion and the Search for New Ideals in the USSR* (New York: Frederick A. Praeger, 1967), pp. 62-82; Michael Bourdeaux and Peter Reddaway, "Soviet Baptists Today," *Survey*, no. 66 (January, 1968), pp. 48-66; Michael Bourdeaux, *Religious Ferment in Russia* (London: Macmillan; New York: St. Martin's Press, 1968); All-Union Council of Evangelical Christians-Baptists, *Congress* (Moscow, 1969); Michael Bourdeaux et al, *Religious Minorities in the Soviet Union, 1960-70* (London: Minority Rights Group, 1970); Edmund Heier, *Religious Schism in the Russian Aristocracy, 1860-1900: Radstockism and Pashkovism* (The Hague: Martinus Nijhoff, 1970); James Leo Garrett, Jr., "All-Union Council of Evangelical Christians-Baptists and Council of Churches of the Evangelical Christians and Baptists," *Encyclopedia of Southern Baptists* (Nashville: Broadman Press, 1971), vol. 3, pp. 1563f.; Michael Bourdeaux, *Faith on Trial in Russia* (New York: Harper & Row, Publishers, 1971); Michael Bourdeaux and Albert Boiter, *Baptists in the Soviet Union, 1960-1971: The History of the Schism and Its After-Effects* (New York: Radio Liberty Committee, 1972); Rosemary Harris and Xenia Howard-Johnston, eds., *Christian Prisoners in Russia* (Wheaton, Ill.: Tyndale House Publishers, 1972); Paul D. Steeves, "The Experience of the Russian Baptists, 1922 to 1929" (M.A. Thesis, University of Kansas, 1972); and Robert D. Linder, ed., *God and Caesar: Case Studies in the Relationship Between Christianity and the State* (Longview, Texas: Conference on Faith and History, 1971).—Editor.

[2] During the 1960s, "a separation occurred within the fellowship of Baptists and Evangelical Christians. Following stricter enforcement of government measures against religious bodies and augmented by the Evangelical Free Christians and the Pure Baptists, neither of whom had entered the union of 1944, and by other groups, a group protesting the policies of the AUCECB emerged in 1961 under the leadership of Alexei F. Prokofiev and Gennadi K. Kryuchkov. Called *Prokofievtsy* ("Prokofievites") and *Initsiativniki* ("Initiative-Group" or "Action-Group"), the group became the Council of Churches of the Evangelical Christians and Baptists (CCECB) in 1965. Its protest against the AUCECB was threefold: too great conformity to governmental control (especially in registration), too centralized and unrepresentative church polity (especially the 10-member council and the senior presbyters), and too little aggressive evangelization. National congresses called by the AUCECB in 1963 and 1966 adopted constitutional changes designed to meet

objections raised by the *Initsiativniki,* and some of the latter reunited with the AUCECB at its 1969 congress. (Garrett, *op. cit.,* p. 1564.)

CHAPTER 4

[1] This use of the word "brethren" should not be confused with the nineteenth-century English group founded by J. N. Darby, known under several names, and commonly called Plymouth Brethren in the English-speaking world.

[2] If ecumenism is defined as "drawing nearer to Christ," then one could say that all Baptists in Eastern Europe are determined to be ecumenical!

[3] Generally speaking, in all of Europe those churches which practice believer s baptism are continuously under pressure from churches practicing infant baptism and are accused of "sheep stealing," etc. The fact that the "sheep" was an atheist and nonbeliever is irrelevant.

[4] For further information on the Baptist and Protestant ecumenical situation in Yugoslavia, see Horak's article, "Protestantism and Ecumenism," in Zlatko Frid, ed., *Religions in Yugoslavia* (Zagreb: Binoza Press, 1971), pp. 132-139.

CHAPTER 5

[1] The French paper *(Croire et Servir)* and the Italian magazine *(Il Messaggero Evangelico)* have been examined relative to the period 1954-1968. The Portuguese paper *(Semeador Baptista)* was used only for the years 1964-1969. The Spanish magazine was available only for the years 1950-1955 *(El Eco de la Verdad),* 1956-1957 *(Entre Nosotro),* 1959-1960, 1962 *(Es Tu Dio),* April, 1965, February-April, 1966 *(El Eco).*

[2] Mr. J. P. Dassonville, a student at the Rüschlikon Seminary, has been interviewed for French Baptists, and Rev. C. Santin, pastor among Spanish migrants in Switzerland, for Spanish Baptists. To both the author expresses his gratitude. Facts on Italian Baptists are his own.

[3] *Bilan du Monde* 1964, Encyclopédie Catholique du Monde Chrétien (Louvain: Casterman, vol. 1, 1964), pp. 480-481. For Protestants the traditional figures have been given.

[4] Dr. E. Willard, cf. G. Rousseau, *Histoire des Eglises Baptistes* (Paris: Société de Publications Baptistes, 1951), p. 119.

[5] Robert G. Torbet, *A History of the Baptists* (Valley Forge: Judson Press, 1973), p. 170.

[6] *La France Protestante,* Annuaire publié sour les auspices de la Fédération Protestante de France (Paris: 1955), pp. 294-295.

[7] J. D. Franks, *European Baptists Today* (Rüschlikon: Baublatt ÅG, 1952), p. 34.

[8] *The European Baptist,* April, 1965, pp. 6-7.

[9] Cf. S. Corda, *Baptist Beginnings in Italy* (Rüschlikon, 1964), unpublished B.D. treatise. For more recent history, see P. Sanfilippo, *L'Italia Battista* (Rome: Unione Cristiana Evangelica Battista d'Italia, 1959).

[10] These figures are probably overstated. See discussion and new estimate in J. Estruch, *Los Protestantes Españoles* (Barcelona: Editorial Nova Terra, 1968), pp. 38-40.

[11] J. D. Hughey, *Historia de los Bautistas en España,* p. 13.

[12] *Ibid.,* p. 61.

[13] Franks, *op. cit.,* p. 67.

[14] Hughey, *op. cit.,* p. 58.

[15] Franks, *op. cit.,* p. 68.

[16] 4,600 members according to the official report of the Baptist World Alliance Congress of 1965 [J. Nordenhaug, ed., *The Truth That Makes Men Free* (Nashville: Broadman Press, 1966), p. 561], which includes, however, Baptists not affiliated with the Spanish Union. For the year 1961, Estruch gives an estimate between 3,472 and 4,060 (p. 39).

[17] E. Rüdén and G. R. Lahrson, *An Outline of Baptist Life on the European Continent* (1963), [a paper prepared by the European Baptist Federation Commission on Bible Study and Membership Training and the American Baptist Foreign Mission Society, mimeographed], p. 94.

[18] E. Moreira, *The Significance of Portugal* (London: World Dominion Press, 1933), p. 44.

[19] *Ibid.*

[20] Rüdén and Lahrson, *op. cit.,* p. 93.

[21] P. Spanu, "Notizie dal Portogallo," *Mess. Evangelico,* January, 1959, pp. 49-51.

[22] Rüdén and Lahrson, *op. cit.,* p. 95.

[23] Cf. *Croire et Servir,* December, 1966, pp. 1, 3. The same view was stated by the president of the Baptist Union at the Convention of 1967 (mimeographed report of A. Thobois to the Convention in Antony, May 3-4, 1967, pp. 9-10).

[24] Full report in *Il Testimonio,* November, 1920.

[25] J. D. Hughey, *Religious Freedom in Spain* (London: Carey Kingsgate Press, 1955), p. 114.

[26] *Croire et Servir,* June, 1964, p. 4.

[27] On the friendly attitude of Baptists toward the believers' churches and on their readiness to cooperate with them for evangelistic campaigns, cf. particularly the following numbers of *Croire et Servir,* December, 1954, p. 2; February, 1955, p. 2; June, 1955, p. 4; February, 1956, p. 3; July, 1956, p. 4; December, 1960, p. 4; November, 1962, p. 4.

[28] *The European Baptist,* vol. 3, no. 1, p. 13.

[29] As early as 1952 the Baptist pastors of Sicily were organizing meetings with other Protestants, particularly with Waldensians and Methodists *(Mess. Evangelico,* December, 1952, pp. 362-363). Also the resolution to participate in the Second National Congress of Evangelical Churches was taken almost unanimously (cf. *Mess. Evangelico,* November, 1963, pp. 321-322).

[30] See, for instance, J. A. Marques, "Unificaçao," *Semeador Baptista,* March, 1965, p. 2.

[31] See report in *Mess. Evangelico,* August–September, 1968, p. 246.

[32] *El Eco,* March–April, 1966, pp. 32-33. See also the favorable comment of the editorial in the same number.

[33] The Italian Baptist magazine, *Il Messaggero Evangelico,* is a typical example: over against the four longer articles on Christian unity which appeared during the period 1953-1959 there are the fourteen articles published in the period 1960-1968. We might recall also that at the Convention of 1960, for the first time in their history, Italian Baptists appointed a Commission for the Study of Ecumenical Relations (cf. *Mess. Evangelico,* June–July, 1962, p. 186, n. 2). Christian unity was also one of the main topics at the French Baptist Convention of 1961 (cf. *Croire et Servir,* May, 1961, p. 3).

[34] The statements that follow are based on an examination of several articles published in the official Baptist magazines in France, Italy, Spain, and Portugal during the 1960s and on the assumption that they reflect widespread opinions of Baptists at that time in each country.

[35] The passage on Gamaliel (Acts 5:33-39) is actually quoted, for instance, in J. Lacue, "Por la unidad Cristiana," *El Eco,* March, 1962, pp. 5-7.

CHAPTER 6

[1] *Annual of Northern Baptist Convention* for 1919, pp. 229-230.

[2] *Yearbook of the American Baptist Convention, 1967-1968* (Valley Forge, Pa.: Judson Press, 1968), p. 548.

CHAPTER 7

[1] Editorial, *Western Recorder,* vol. 64 (December 26, 1889), p. 4.

[2] *Proceedings . . . of the Southern Baptist Convention . . .*, 1890 (Atlanta, Ga.: Franklin Printing House, 1890), p. 22. (Records of the conventions will be referred to as *Annual, S.B.C.*, with the appropriate year.)

[3] Editorial, *Western Recorder*, vol. 65 (December 4, 1890), p. 4.

[4] *Ibid.*, vol. 67 (October 6, 1892), p. 4.

[5] "Proceedings of the General Christian Missionary Convention—Forty-Fifth Anniversary," *The Missionary Intelligencer*, vol. 7, no. 10 (October, 1894), p. 346.

[6] Quoted by Eaton in an editorial, *Western Recorder*, vol. 69 (November 15, 1894), p. 4.

[7] *Annual, S.B.C.*, 1912, p. 14.

[8] "Christian Union, A Deliverance by the Baptist General Convention of Texas," quoted by James B. Gambrell, *Baptists and Their Business* (Nashville: Sunday School Board, Southern Baptist Convention, 1919), p. 140.

[9] *Ibid.*, pp. 149, 150.

[10] *Annual, S.B.C.*, 1914, p. 73.

[11] *Ibid.*, pp. 74-76.

[12] *Ibid.*, pp. 77f.

[13] William R. Estep, *Baptists and Christian Unity* (Nashville: Broadman Press, 1966), p. 153.

[14] *Ibid.*

[15] E. Roberts-Thomson, *With Hands Outstretched: Baptists and the Ecumenical Movement* (London: Marshall, Morgan and Scott, 1962), p. 97.

[16] *Annual, S.B.C.*, 1915, p. 17.

[17] *Annual, S.B.C.*, 1916, pp. 42-44.

[18] *Annual, S.B.C.*, 1918, p. 137.

[19] James B. Gambrell, "The Union Movement and Baptist Fundamentals," *Southwestern Journal of Theology*, vol. 3 [Old Series] (January, 1919), p. 39.

[20] *Ibid.*, p. 43.

[21] J. S. Rogers et al., "A Symposium by Southern State Secretaries on the Union Movement," *Southwestern Journal of Theology*, vol. 3 [Old Series] (January, 1919), p. 23.

[22] *Annual, S.B.C.*, 1919, pp. 19-23.

[23] Gambrell, *Baptists and Their Business*, pp. 95f.

[24] *Annual, S.B.C.*, 1919, pp. 111-113.

[25] Edgar Y. Mullins et al., "Fraternal Address of Southern Baptists to Those of 'Like Precious Faith with Us' Scattered Abroad, Beloved in the Lord," *Baptist Standard*, vol. 32 (February 26, 1920), p. 24.

[26] J. B. Gambrell, "Two Notable Conventions," *Baptist Standard*, vol. 31 (May 29, 1919), p. 5.

[27] William L. Lumpkin, *Baptist Confessions of Faith* (Valley Forge: Judson Press, 1959), p. 397.

[28] *Annual, S.B.C.*, 1937, pp. 79f.

[29] *Annual, S.B.C.*, 1940, p. 99.

[30] *Annual, S.B.C.*, 1948, p. 58.

[31] *Annual, S.B.C.*, 1949, p. 53.

[32] *Annual, S.B.C.*, 1950, p. 37.

[33] *Annual, S.B.C.*, 1951, p. 36.

[34] *Annual, S.B.C.*, 1953, p. 51.

[35] Wayne Dehoney, "Issues and Imperatives," *Annual, S.B.C.*, 1965, p. 95.

[36] See James Leo Garrett, Jr., ed., *The Concept of the Believers' Church: Addresses from the 1967 Louisville Conference* (Scottdale, Pa.: Herald Press, 1970).

[37] James Leo Garrett, Jr., *Baptists and Roman Catholicism* (Nashville: Broadman Press, 1965), p. 45.

[38] A Jewish-Baptist Scholars' Conference was held at Southern Baptist Theological Seminary, August 18-20, 1969, under the sponsorship of the Home Mission Board's Department of Work Related to Nonevangelicals and the Interreligious Affairs Department of the American Jewish Committee. Southeastern Baptist Theological Seminary at Wake Forest, North Carolina, joined the American Jewish Committee's Interreligious Affairs Department in sponsoring

at the seminary a Jewish-Christian colloquium on "Civil Religion in America," October 30–November 1, 1972.

[39] Phrases taken from the writings of critics of the Southern Baptist movement.

[40] Walter D. Wagoner, "Thoughts for Protestants to Be Static By," *The Christian Century*, vol. 86 (February 19, 1969), p. 249.

[41] Southern Baptists would agree with much that is said on this subject in a recent book by an official of the National Council of Churches. See Dean M. Kelley, *Why Conservative Churches Are Growing: A Study in Sociology of Religion* (New York: Harper & Row, Publishers, 1972).

[42] *Annual, S.B.C.*, 1914, p. 77.

CHAPTER 8

[1] Carter G. Woodson, *The History of the Negro Church*, 2nd ed. (Washington, D.C.: The Associated Publishers, 1945), p. 1.

[2] Edward A. Freeman, *The Epoch of Negro Baptists and the Foreign Mission Board, National Baptist Convention, U.S.A., Inc.* (Kansas City, Kansas: Central Seminary Press, 1953), p. 8.

[3] Woodson, *op. cit.*, pp. 6-7.

[4] Miles Mark Fisher, *Crisis*, vol. 45 (July, 1938), p. 220.

[5] Melville J. Herskovits, *Social History of the Negro: A Handbook on Social Psychology* (Worcester, Mass.: Clark University Press, 1935), p. 256.

[6] Freeman, *op. cit.* p. 19.

[7] *Ibid.*, p. 23.

[8] Walter H. Brooks, *The Silver Bluff Church: A History of Negro Baptist Churches in America* (Washington, D.C.: Press of R. L. Pendleton, 1910), pp. 5-17.

[9] Woodson, *op.cit.*, pp. 76-78.

[10] Freeman, *op. cit.*, p. 61.

[11] Lewis G. Jordan, *Negro Baptist History, U.S.A.* (Nashville: The Sunday School Publishing Board of the National Baptist Convention, 1930), p. 83.

[12] Freeman, *op. cit.*, pp. 70-73.

[13] *Ibid.*, pp. 75-76.

[14] *Ibid.*, p. 77.

[15] *Ibid.*, pp. 81-83.

[16] *Ibid.*, pp. 87-88.

[17] Jordan, *op. cit.*, p. 142, as quoted by Freeman, *op. cit.*, p. 88.

[18] Minutes of the National Baptist Convention, U.S.A., Inc., 1952, 1956, 1957, 1962.

[19] Woodson, *op. cit.*, p. 5.

[20] *Ibid.*, pp. 21-22.

CHAPTER 9

[1] Assistance has been received from the following: Baptist General Conference— Donald E. Anderson, editor, and Virgil A. Olson, historian; General Association of General Baptists—Ollie Latch, historian; North American Baptist General Conference—Reinhold J. Kerstan, editor; Seventh Day Baptist General Conference—Albert N. Rogers, historian; American Baptist Association—I. K. Cross, promotional director; Conservative Baptist Association of America—Bruce L. Shelley, historian; General Association of Regular Baptist Churches—Joseph M. Stowell, national representative; National Association of Free Will Baptists— Rufus Coffey, executive secretary; Primitive Baptists and Progressive Primitive Baptists—W. H. Cayce, editor. When the names of these men are cited hereafter, reference is being made to correspondence received from them.

[2] Robert A. Frykholm, "The Mission of the Conference," in *The 1960's in the Ministry of the Baptist General Conference,* ed. Donald E. Anderson (Evanston, Ill.: Harvest Publications, 1971), pp. 369-370.

[3] For further information see A. D. Williams, *Benoni Stinson and the General Baptists* (Owensville, Ind.: General Baptist Press, c. 1880); D. B. Montgomery,

History of the General Baptists (Owensville: General Baptist Press, c. 1890); Ollie Latch, *History of the General Baptists*, rev. ed. (Poplar Bluff, Mo.: General Baptist Press, 1972).

[4] For further information see O. E. Krueger, *In God's Hand* (Forest Park, Ill.: Roger Williams Press, 1958); Martin L. Leuschner, "North American Baptist General Conference" in *Baptist Advance*, ed. D. C. Woolley (Nashville: Broadman Press, 1964), pp. 227-250; Reinhold J. Kerstan, "Historical Factors in the Formation of the Ethnically Oriented North American Baptist General Conference "(Unpublished Ph.D. Dissertation, Northwestern University, 1971).

[5] For further information see A. N. Rogers et al., "Seventh Day Baptist General Conference," in *Baptist Advance*, ed. D. C. Woolley (Nashville, Tenn.: Broadman Press, 1964); pp. 251-260; Russel J. Thomsen, *Seventh-Day Baptists: Their Legacy to Adventists* (Mountain View, Calif.: Pacific Press Publishing Association, 1971); and Albert N. Rogers, *Seventh Day Baptists in Europe and America, Vol. 3, 1900-1955* (Plainfield, N.J.: Seventh Day Baptists Publishing House, 1972).

[6] Robert G. Torbet, *A History of the Baptists*, 3rd edition (Valley Forge: Judson Press, 1973), p. 54.

[7] For further information see I. K. Cross, *Who Are We?* (Texarkana: Baptist Sunday School Committee of the American Baptist Association, n.d.); Robert G. Torbet, "Landmarkism," in *Baptist Concepts of the Church*, ed. Winthrop S. Hudson (Valley Forge: Judson Press, 1959), pp. 170-195; William Wright Barnes, *The Southern Baptist Convention, 1845-1953* (Nashville: Broadman Press, 1954), pp. 98-119.

[8] For further information see Louis Gasper, *The Fundamentalist Movement* (The Hague: Mouton and Co., 1963); Bruce L. Shelley, *A History of Conservative Baptists* (Wheaton, Ill.: Conservative Baptist Press, 1971); and fifteen policy statements published under series title *Literature Item* (Des Plaines, Ill.: General Association of Regular Baptist Churches, n.d.). The name of the Northern Baptist Convention was changed in 1950 to American Baptist Convention and in 1972 to American Baptist Churches in the U.S.A.

[9] The Association of Baptists for World Evangelism, Inc., had been organized in 1928.

[10] For further information see Damon C. Dodd, *The Free Will Baptist Story* (Nashville: National Association of Free Will Baptists, 1956).

[11] See Norman A. Baxter, *History of the Freewill Baptists: A Study in New England Separatism* (Rochester, N. Y.: American Baptist Historical Society, 1957).

[12] For further information see Julietta Haynes, "A History of the Primitive Baptists" (Unpublished Ph.D. Dissertation, University of Texas, 1959).

CHAPTER 10

*The full text of this study appeared in *Foundations*, vol. 15 (July-September, 1972), pp. 211-240. The text which follows has been abbreviated and revised. Printed by permission of the American Baptist Historical Society.

[1] A critical up-to-date history of Baptists in Canada is yet to be written. For concise information, consult the following literature. Gaylord P. Albaugh, "Themes for Research in Canadian Baptist History," *Foundations*, vol. 6 (January, 1963), pp. 42-56; G. Gerald Harrop, "Canadian Baptists in Their North American Context," *Foundations*, vol. 4 (July, 1961), pp. 216-224 and "The Canadian Baptists—An Historical Sketch," *Southwestern Journal of Theology*, vol. 6, no. 2 (April, 1964), pp. 26-37; Stuart Ivison, "Is There a Canadian Baptist Tradition?" in John Webster Grant, ed., *The Churches and the Canadian Experience* (Toronto, 1963), pp. 53-68; Leslie K. Tarr, *This Dominion—His Dominion* (Willowdale, Ontario, 1968); Davis C. Woolley, ed., *Baptist Advance* (Nashville, Tenn.: Broadman Press, 1964), pp. 131-185.

[2] Robert G. Torbet, *Ecumenism: Free Church Dilemma* (Valley Forge: Judson Press, 1968), p. 67.

[3] Cf. the article by Calvin Redekop, "The Sect Cycle in Perspective," *Mennonite Quarterly Review*, vol. 36 (1962), pp. 155-161 and the sociological study of class tensions among Ontario Baptists by Mary B. R. Hill, "From Sect to Denomination in the Baptist Church in Canada" (Ph.D.dissertation, State University of New York at Buffalo, 1971), available from University Microfilms.

[4] No study of Canadian Baptist attitudes to and involvement in ecumenism has been published thus far. In the preparation of this chapter, we have examined the official minutes of the BFC Council and Assembly (1944-1970), minutes and resolutions printed in the recent *Year Books* of the three Baptist conventions, and a few articles in the three main denominational papers, *The Atlantic Baptist*, *The Canadian Baptist*, and *The Evangelical Baptist*. Other source materials remain to be researched.

[5] *The Baptist Position* (Toronto, 1947); *Protestantism—A Baptist Interpretation*, ed. F. W. Waters (Toronto, 1958) and *Things Most Surely Believed: A Baptist View*, ed. R. F. Aldwinckle (Toronto, 1965, mimeographed).

[6] J. Murray Armstrong, *Baptist Principles* (Saint John, N.B., n.d., about 1966) and Harold L. Mitton, *Facing . . . the New World* (Saint John, N.B., n.d., about 1968).

[7] Charles A. Tipp, "Objections to Unity," in the symposium *One Church, Two Nations?* ed. Philip LeBlanc, O.P., and Arnold Edinborough (Don Mills, Ont.: Longmans, 1968), pp. 54-68.

[8] Atlantic Convention *Year Book*, 1971, p. 24a and pp. 8-10.

[9] *BFC Minutes*, 1947, pp. 6-7 and 1958, p. 27.

[10] Ontario-Quebec Convention *Year Book*, 1965-1966, pp. C 15 and C 26; 1967-1968, p. 12; 1968-1969, pp. 58-61 and 167f.; 1969-1970, p. 78; 1970-1971, pp. 82, 157, and 223.

[11] Reported in the *BFC Minutes*, 1962, pp. 83-84.

[12] See the report in *The Canadian Baptist*, June 1, 1960.

[13] See the full text of the *Reply* in the Ontario-Quebec Convention *Year Book*, 1907, pp. 223-225.

[14] *BFC Report Volume*, 1967-1970, pp. 116-123. Reprints available from the BFC office, Box 1298, Brantford, Ontario.

[15] Published by and available from the BFC office.

[16] Maritime Convention *Year Book*, 1951, p. 181.

[17] Ontario-Quebec Convention *Year Book*, 1966-1967, pp. 135f.

[18] See examples quoted in *Foundations*, vol. 15 (July-September, 1972), pp. 233f.

[19] *BFC Report Volume*, 1967-1970 (Winnipeg Assembly, 1970), pp. 94-101.

[20] J. K. Zeman, "Pathways to Better Evangelism" (address at the BFC Assembly, Ottawa, 1967), printed in *BFC Minutes*, 1967, p. 54.

[21] The more general *Principles of Union* (1965) were followed by the more specific *Plan of Union—First Draft* (1971). A revised text of the *Plan of Union* and the proposed By-Laws were approved in 1972 for presentation to the three churches. Copies are available from the General Commission on Church Union, 85 St. Clair Ave. East, Toronto, Ontario M4T 1M8.

[22] Roy Bell, "Our Church Situation Today," *The Canadian Baptist*, August 1, 1969.

[23] Cf. the discussion of the Free-church concept by Torbet, *op. cit.*, pp. 14-48 and by Donald F. Durnbaugh, *The Believers' Church* (New York: The Macmillan Company, 1968), pp. 4-8.

[24] Durnbaugh, *op. cit.*, p. 33.

[25] See James Leo Garrett, ed., *The Concept of the Believers' Church: Addresses from the 1967 Louisville Conference* (Scottdale, Pa.: Herald Press, 1970) and reports on the second conference in the *Chicago Theological Seminary Register*, vol. 60, no. 6 (September, 1970).

CHAPTER 11

*This chapter is adapted from an article published in *Foundations*, vol. 17 (January–March, 1974), pp. 51-57, and is used with permission of the American Baptist Historical Society.

[1] John Levo, *Black and White in the West Indies* (London; S.P.C.K., 1930), p. 11.

CHAPTER 12

[1] Juan G. Varetto, *Diego Thomson* (Buenos Aires: Imprenta Evangélica, 1918), p. 5.

[2] Roberto Cecil Moore, *Los Evangélicos en Marcha en América Latina* (El Paso: Casa Bautista de Publicaciones, 1960), p. 23.

[3] Francisco Ordoñez, *Historia del Cristianismo Evangélico en Colombia* (Tipografia Union, n.d.), p. 16.

[4] W. R. Estep, Jr., *Colombia: Land of Conflict and Promise* (Nashville: Convention Press, 1968), p. 30.

[5] *Ibid.*, p. 31.

[6] Kenneth Scott Latourette, *The Nineteenth Century Outside Europe*, vol. 3, "Christianity in a Revolutionary Age: A History of Christianity in the Nineteenth and Twentieth Centuries" (New York: Harper & Row, Publishers, 1961), p. 301.

[7] Cited by Francis Marquis Dubose, "A History of Southern Baptist Missions in Latin America" (Th.D. dissertation, Southwestern Baptist Theological Seminary, 1961), p. 27.

[8] H. Wakelin Coxill and Kenneth Grubb, eds., *World Christian Handbook: 1968* (London: Lutterworth Press, 1968), p. 134. In the 1968 edition, Baptists in Brazil numbered 468,000.

[9] Dubose, *op. cit.*, p. 134.

[10] *Ibid.*, p. 163.

[11] *Ibid.*, pp. 176ff.

[12] Latourette, *op. cit.*, p. 284.

[13] *Ibid.*, p. 285.

[14] *Ibid.*, p. 287.

[15] See W. R. Estep, Jr., "Church and Culture in Latin America," *Southwestern Journal of Theology*, vol. 4 (April, 1962), pp. 40, 41. Also, see Salvador de Madariaga, *The Rise of the Spanish American Empire* (New York: The Macmillan Company, 1947), p. 144.

[16] *Bulletin of the Evangelical Confederation of Colombia*, November 7, 1959. See Gabriel Muñoz Uribe, *La Libertad Religiosa: ¿Hacia Donde Vamos?* (Bogota: Talleres Gráficos San Jorge, 1955), and William C. Easton, *Colombian Conflict* (London: Christian Literature Crusade, 1954). For an understanding of the relationship between Baptists and Roman Catholics as well as with other Evangelicals in Argentina, see Santiago Canclini, *Los Evangélicos en el Tiempo de Peron* (Buenos Aires: Editorial Mundo Hispano, 1972).

[17] Estep, *Colombia . . .*, p. 66.

[18] Compare Ricardo Struve Haker, *Inquisicion, Tolerancia e Idea Ecuménica* (Bogota: Centro Mariano Nacional de Colombia, 1959), with Eduardo Ospina, *The Protestant Denominations in Colombia* (Bogotá: National Press, 1954). The Spanish title of Ospina's work is *Las Sectas Protestantes en Colombia*.

[19] Haker, *op. cit.*, p. 3.

[20] *Ibid.*

[21] *Ibid.*, p. 4.

[22] Gloria Riestra, "Ecumenismo Catolico y Compañas de Iglesias Disidentes," *El Sol de Mexico*, May 7, 1969.

[23] A personal interview with Rev. Charles Bryan, June 12, 1969.

[24] Professor Travis Berry of the North Brazil Baptist Theological Seminary was one of those attending the meeting.

[25] "Uma Decisao Sôbre Ecumenismo," *O Jornal Batista*, vol. 68 (March 10, 1968), p. 3.

[26] Ignacio Vergara, *El Protestantismo en Chile*, 3rd ed. (Santiago: Editorial del Pacífico, S.A., 1962), p. 8.

[27] Justo C. Anderson, *El Movimiento Ecumenico* (Buenos Aires: La Junta Directiva de la Convención Evangélica Bautista, 1968), p. 10. In 1949 the Priméra Conferencia Evangelica Latinoamericana had only 56 delegates from 15 countries and 18 denominations in attendance. In 1961 there were 130 delegates of 28 nations from 48 denominations, according to Anderson.

[28] A personal letter to the writer from J. Reis Pereira, director of *O Jornal Batista*, the official paper of the Brazilian Baptist Convention. Pereira writes: "O ecumenismo protestante era representado no Brasil pela Confederação Evangélica do Brasil, órgão subsisiario do Concilio Mundial de Igrejas. Os Batistas, embora confidados, recusaram-se a entrar para a Confederação tendo sido a decisao tomada na Convencao Batista Brasileira, reunida em 1965. Agora a Confederacao Evangélica esta em crise. O grupo fundamentalista de McIntire tambem nao conta com o apoio dos batistas. As tentativas de aproximacão dos católicas, após o Concélio Vaticano II, também tem sido repelidas." [Protestant ecumenism was represented in Brazil by the Evangelical Confederation of Brazil, and auxiliary of the World Council of Churches. The Baptists, although invited, refused to enter the Confederation. This decision dates from the 1965 meeting of the Brazilian Baptist Convention. At this time, the Evangelical Confederation is in a crisis. Neither does the McIntire fundamentalist faction count on the support or approval of the Baptists. The overtures of the Roman Catholics, since Vatican Council II, have also been rejected. At least, this is the case at present.]

[29] *O Jornal Batista*, vol. 68 (March 10, 1968), p. 3.

[30] *Ibid.*

[31] *Ibid.*, p. 2.

[32] *Ibid.*, Article 7.

[33] *Informe de la Junta Directiva y Recomendación sobre la actitud a asumir frente a los Movimientos Ecuménicos Protestantes y Catolicos.*

[34] *Ibid.*, p. 1.

[35] *Ibid.*, p. 2.

[36] *Ibid.*, p. 3.

[37] Alfonso Olmedo, "Presidential Address," La Comision. "La Comision de Ecumenismo del Consejo Doctrinal de la Arquidiocesis de Buenos Aires nos invitó a participar en los actos de la SEMANA DE ORACION PARA LA UNIDAD CRISTIANA que clausuraron con un servicio de Oración Ecuménica en la catedral porteña, servicio en el cual-se nos decía en la invitacion-EL ARZOBISPO COADJUTOR DESEABA VIVAMENTE NUESTRA PRESENCIA, pidiéndosenos observaciones y sugestiones para una celebracion verdaderamente comun . . . CON SINCERA CORTECIA agradecemos la invitación declarando se nos hacia UN DEBER DE CONCIENCIA declinar aceptarla POR ESTIMAR QUE NO SE DABAN LAS CONDICIONES DOCTRINALES ACORDES CON NUESTRO PENSAMIENTO CRISTIANO, EVANGELICO y BAUTISTA, que justificarian, o haria verdaderamente provechosa nuestra participacion, SIN QUE ELLO SIGNIFICARA E ESTAR A JENOS a la esperanza de la llegada de un día en que DIOS haga posible.la unidad de sus hijos bajo 'SOLO UN SEÑOR, una fe, un bautismo, un Dios y Padre de todos' (version catolica de Efesios 4:5)."

Translation of footnote 37 reads: The Commission on Ecumenism of the Doctrinal Council of the Archdiocese of Buenos Aires invited us to participate in the functions of the Week of Prayer for Christian Unity which closed with a service of ecumenical prayer in the Metropolitan Cathedral. The archbishop expressed his earnest desire for our presence in this service. He also asked for our comments and suggestions for a truly cooperative celebration. With sincere expression of gratitude, we courteously declined to accept the invitation, declaring that conscience would not permit its acceptance since doctrinal conditions, according to our way of thinking as Christians, Evangelicals, and Baptists, would not permit our participation. However, this situation does not keep us from sharing in the hope that some day

God would make possible the unity of his children under "only one Lord, one faith, one baptism, one God and Father of us all" (Catholic version of Ephesians 4:5).

CHAPTER 13

[1] Letter of U Kyaw Than to author, February 6, 1973.

[2] "Church Union in Context," *The American Baptist*, vol. 170 (October, 1972), p. 35.

[3] Letter of W. Wickramasinghe to author, March 5, 1973.

[4] Letter of C. D. E. Premawardhana to author, February 11, 1973.

[5] The Garo Baptist Union (Australian Baptist Mission), the Baptist Union of Pakistan (Baptist Missionary Society, Great Britain), and the East Pakistan Baptist Union (Australian Baptist Missionary Society, New Zealand Baptist Missionary Society, Southern Baptist Convention).

[6] Tracy Gipson, Letter no. 17 (Christmas, 1972).

CHAPTER 14

[1] The author is indebted to the following Baptist leaders for reports which have formed the basis for much of the preceding interpretation of Baptists in East Asia: George H. Hays, Japan; Albert W. Gammage, Jr., Korea; Grover F. Tyner, Jr., Philippines; Frances Hudgins, Thailand; Bill Clark Thomas, Malaysia-Singapore; Avery Willis, Jr., Indonesia; Ronald Merrell, Vietnam; and Louis E. McCall, Guam.

CHAPTER 16

*This chapter is adapted from an article published in *Foundations*, vol. 17 (January–March, 1974), pp. 36-50, and is used with permission of the American Baptist Historical Society.

[1] Alan C. Prior, *Some Fell on Good Ground: A History of the Beginnings and Development of the Baptist Church in New South Wales, Australia, 1831-1965* (Sydney: Baptist Union of New South Wales, 1966), pp. 19ff.

[2] *The Baptist Magazine*, vol. 29 (1837), p. 210.

[3] *Ibid.*, vol. 30 (1838), pp. 25f.

[4] *Ibid.*, vol. 44 (1852), p. 285.

[5] *The Victorian Freeman*, vol. 2 (October, 1878), p. 162.

[6] Johannis J. Mol, *Religion in Australia: A Sociological Investigation* (Melbourne: Nelson, 1971), pp. 151f.

[7] B. S. Brown, *Members One of Another: The Story of a Century of Baptist Fellowship and Service in the State of Victoria, Australia* (Melbourne: Baptist Union of Victoria, 1962), p. 122.

[8] Minutes of the Baptist Union of Australia, September 4, 1959. The name of the Australian Council for the World Council of Churches was changed in 1960 to the Australian Council of Churches.

[9] Minutes of the Baptist Union of Australia, September 6, 1962.

[10] *The Australian Baptist*, vol. 60 (May 24, 1972), p. 1.

[11] *The New Zealand Baptist*, vol. 80 (August, 1964), p. 201.

[12] L. A. North, *The Baptist Churches of New Zealand, the Ecumenical Movement and Church Union* (Baptist Union of New Zealand, 1967).

[13] R. J. Lacey, "Missions," *Encyclopaedia of Papua and New Guinea*, ed. Peter Ryan (Melbourne: University Press, 1972), vol. 2, p. 774.

[14] The writer is indebted to Rev. A. Cupit of the Australian Baptist Missionary Society, who is making a special study of Christian cooperation in New Guinea, for allowing him to see the documents relating to these bodies.

CHAPTER 17

[1] These are Algeria, Angola, Burundi, Rwanda, Cameroon, Gabon, Central African Republic, Egypt, Ethiopia, Ghana, Ivory Coast, Kenya, Liberia, Malagasy Republic, Malawi, Mauritius, Mozambique, Nigeria, Rhodesia, Sierra Leone, South Africa, Sudan, Tanzania, Uganda, Zaire, and Zambia.

² Such Councils exist, for example, in Botswana, Burundi, Ghana, Malawi, Nigeria, Rhodesia, Rwanda, Sierra Leone, South Africa, Sudan, Zaire, and Zambia. (The list is not exhaustive.)
³ See Charles Pelham Groves, *The Planting of Christianity in Africa*, 4 vols. (London: Lutterworth Press, 1948-58); J. Herbert Kane, *A Global View of Christian Missions from Pentecost to the Present* (Grand Rapids: Baker Book House, 1971); Kenneth Scott Latourette, *A History of the Expansion of Christianity*, 7 vols. (New York, London: Harper & Row, Publishers, 1937-1945); *World Council of Churches: List of Member Churches, October, 1972* (Geneva); "All-Africa Conference of Churches: Member Bodies" (mimeographed); also, correspondence with H. Cornell Goerner, Richmond, Virginia; N. R. Richardson, Monrovia, Liberia; and Solomon N. Gwei, Bambili-Bamenda, Cameroon.

Index

215